Solutions

Teacher Planning Book

M A T H S

7C

David Baker

Paul Hogan

Simon Longman

Graham Macphail

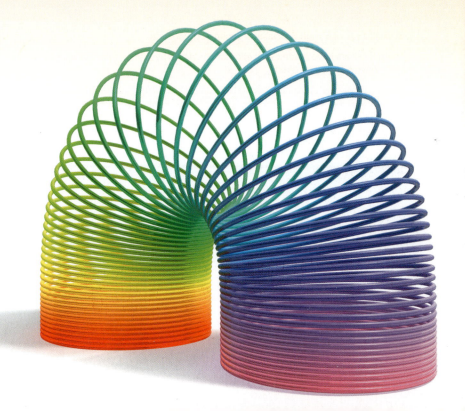

Text © David Baker, Paul Hogan, Simon Longman and Graham Macphail

Original illustrations © Nelson Thornes Ltd 2005

The right of David Baker, Paul Hogan, Simon Longman and Graham Macphail to be identified as authors of this work has been asserted by them in accordance with the Copyright, Designs and Patents Act 1988.

Published in 2005 by:
Nelson Thornes Ltd
Delta Place
27 Bath Road
CHELTENHAM
GL53 7TH
United Kingdom

05 06 07 08 09 / 10 9 8 7 6 5 4 3 2 1

A catalogue record of this book is available from the British Library

ISBN 07487 9327 5

Page make-up by Tech-Set Ltd

Printed and bound in Croatia by Zrinski

Acknowledgements

The authors and publishers wish to thank the following for their contribution:

Starters and plenary notes – Steven Lomax and Matthew Nixon
Notes to support Maths Interact – Peter Sherran
Andrew Brown
Rob Eastaway
Maureen Hayes
Barbara Job
Paul Metcalf
Adrian Parkinson
Louise Petheram
Bryn Roberts
Sue Thompson

Thank you to the following schools

Anthony Gell School
Park House School
Tewkesbury School
St Wilfrid's C of E High School and Technology College

The publishers have made every effort to contact copyright holders but apologise if any have been overlooked.

Contents

Introduction

Solutions provides a totally integrated blend of resources to support fully and deliver the Framework for Teaching Mathematics and the Medium Term Plans and the National Curriculum.

A course overview

Solutions comprises the following extensive resources.

The Year 7 Support (S), Core (C) and Extension (E) Books have been written in parallel.

There is greater differentiation in Years 8 and 9.

Solutions components in Year 7

Pupil Books – an overview

There are four books per year. Support (S), Core (C) and Extension (E) follow the programmes contained in the Medium Term Plans. Target (T) is aimed at the lower ability levels and is in line with *Targeting Level 4* of the Key Stage 3 initiative. Each Unit (or chapter) is broken down into, on average, four sections. Each section covers a particular mathematical area of the Medium Term Plans. Each section is divided into colour-coded topics and is designed to provide around one and a half hours of work. This ensures you have everything you need to cover the Framework.

By the end of Key Stage 3, the four books in Year 9 will cover these SATs tier levels:

Target	3–5
Support	4–6
Core	5–7
Extension	6–8

Features of the Pupil Books

Unit opening page

Each Pupil Book has 18 **Units** or chapters.

The Unit opening page lists the sections in the Unit.

This shows you what the pupils have done before …

… and what they will do.

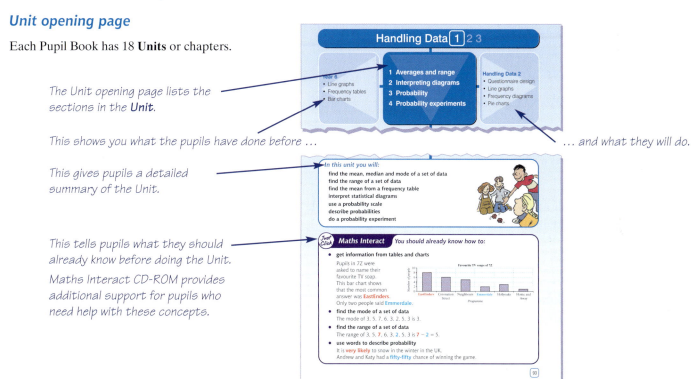

This gives pupils a detailed summary of the Unit.

This tells pupils what they should already know before doing the Unit.

Maths Interact CD-ROM provides additional support for pupils who need help with these concepts.

Start of section page

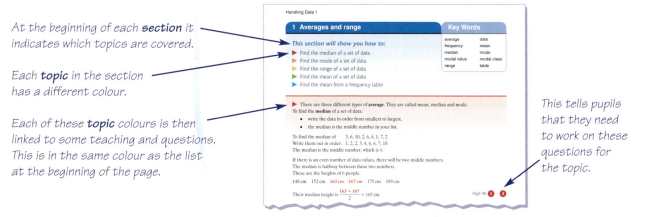

*At the beginning of each **section** it indicates which topics are covered.*

*Each **topic** in the section has a different colour.*

*Each of these **topic** colours is then linked to some teaching and questions. This is in the same colour as the list at the beginning of the page.*

This tells pupils that they need to work on these questions for the topic.

Introduction

Unit questions

Near the end of the Unit are extra practice questions. These are coloured blue. They cover material from the whole Unit.

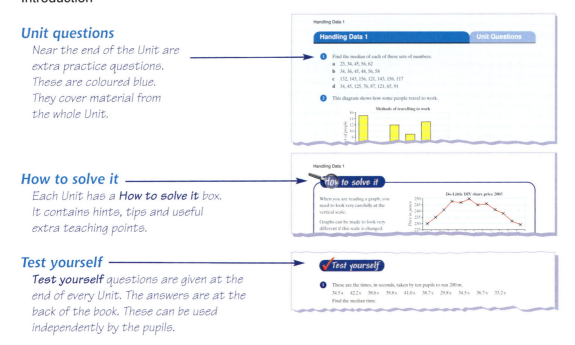

How to solve it

Each Unit has a **How to solve it** box. It contains hints, tips and useful extra teaching points.

Test yourself

Test yourself questions are given at the end of every Unit. The answers are at the back of the book. These can be used independently by the pupils.

Icons and symbols

 This indicates a **SAT question**.

 This indicates a **Welsh SAT question**.

 This indicates a more challenging question!

 This is where a pupil should use a calculator …

and this is where they shouldn't!

 This indicates where extra electronic support is available on the Maths Interact CD-ROM.

Developing thinking skills using the Amazing Maths pages

There are three sets of *Amazing Maths* pages in each of the Pupil Books – one for each term's work, in line with the Medium Term Plans.

They provide stimulating games, investigations, open-ended challenges and opportunities for research. Further examples appear on our website (www.nelsonthornes.com/mathsolutions).

As well as providing different ways in which you can explore maths, these pages could also form part of the development of thinking skills (see also www.teachernet.gov.uk, for example, for more detail about developing thinking skills in maths). They are designed so that pupils are encouraged to think mathematically about everyday things. They will allow you to explore work visually, verbally and symbolically, and encourage interpersonal skills by setting the activities as group projects.

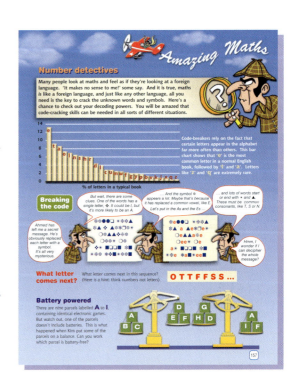

Teacher Planning Books

There is one full colour Teacher Planning Book to fully support each of the Pupil Books. They have the following features:

Unit opening page

This opening page mirrors that in the Pupil Book. Framework objectives to be covered and a Unit overview are provided.

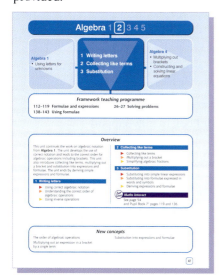

Section page

This page is designed to show you at a glance all that you need for teaching a section of work.

Starters and Plenaries
Suggested Starters and Plenaries are given here.

Resources box
*This contains lists of all the resources you will find on the **Teacher Resource CD-ROM.** These include Worksheets, Homework Sheets and Starter and Plenary resources to fully support your teaching.*

Maths Interact
These provide notes about animations on the Maths Interact CD-ROM that support activities in the Pupil Book.

Key words box
These are from the Vocabulary checklist in the Framework.

Homework
This contains references to Unit questions in the Pupil Book that can be used for homework.

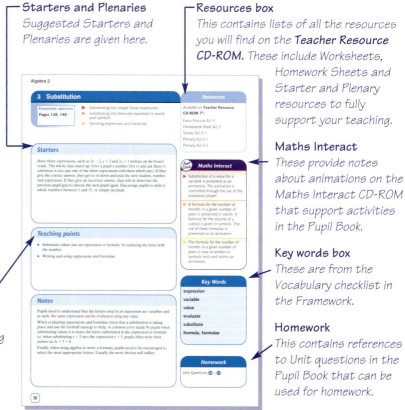

Teaching points box
This provides a quick summary of the teaching points for the section.

Answers page

Answers are provided at the end of the Unit. They are fully colour coded.

Maths Interact page

This gives detailed guidance on using the Maths Interact electronic resources for the Unit.

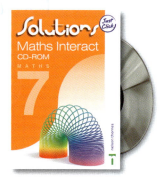

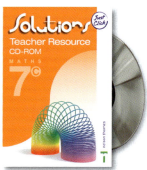

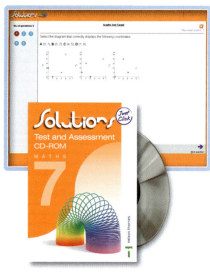

Maths Interact CD-ROM

There is one Maths Interact CD-ROM fully linked to the Support, Core and Extension Books. It covers three key areas:

1 Prior knowledge: activities that are designed for individual or whole-class work that revise knowledge and understanding listed on the Unit opening page of the Pupil Books.

2 Teaching concepts: explanations in the Pupil Books are animated to provide interactive support for teaching.

3 Summary knowledge: ICT activities that build from the work in the unit.

In addition, this resource contains:

● A Resource Finder
● A Favourites section.

Teacher Resource CD-ROM

There is one Teacher Resource CD-ROM per book to fully support teaching and learning. This contains:

● Worksheets to support work in the Pupil Book; these are listed in the Teacher Planning Book
● Extra Practice worksheets to extend and / or support each section of each Unit of the Pupil Book
● Homework Sheets for each section of each Unit of the book
● Starter activities for each section
● Plenary activities for each section
● A fully editable scheme of work
● Appropriate mathematical Resource Sheets.

Test and Assessment Online

This Online Test and Assessment Service allows you to access and manage assessments according to your needs. The online service is supported by a single CD-ROM that contains a bank of printable tests. This Service provides three main question types:

1 Pre-tests: these Online tests are linked to the objectives provided on each of the Unit opening pages. They assess baseline knowledge. They are fully interactive and allow you to see how ready a pupil is to begin a topic or whether further support is needed. They are then marked online.

2 Post-tests: these Online tests can be used once a Unit has been completed. They provide summative assessment. They will allow you to assess how well a pupil has performed after doing the work, and plan for their future learning.

3 Question Bank: this provides you with an extensive range of questions from which you can create tests according to your needs. Questions are National Curriculum levelled and are designed to be used as standard paper-based assessments.

This resource enables you to produce reports to track pupil performance.

Workbooks

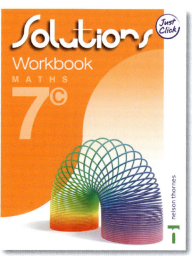

There are four Workbooks for each year. They can be used to consolidate work in class or for homework. Each section contains a summary of the concepts in the Pupil Books and provides a range of practice questions. These are designed for pupils to write on.

Algebra 1 2 3 4 5

Year 6
- Counting forward and backward in equal steps from any starting number
- Filling in missing numbers in sequences

1 **Sequences**
2 **Sequences from patterns**
3 **Function machines**
4 **Algebraic notation**

Algebra 2
- Algebraic operations

Algebra 3
- nth terms of sequences

Framework teaching programme

112–113	Formulae and identities	160–163	Functions and mappings
144–159	Generate and describe sequences	32–35	Solving problems

Overview

This unit builds on the work on number sequences from Years 5 and 6. Pupils use the correct terminology for sequences and common sequences are covered in detail. Sequences from practical contexts are also covered. The unit goes on to look at an introduction to functions and algebraic notation.

1 Sequences
- ▶ Generating and describing simple sequences
- ▶ Using term-to-term and position-to-term rules to generate sequences

2 Sequences from patterns
- ▶ Generating sequences from patterns
- ▶ Describing general patterns in sequences

3 Function machines
- ▶ Drawing and using function machines
- ▶ Finding the function given the input and output values
- ▶ Simple mapping diagrams
- ▶ Using inverse operations

4 Algebraic notation
- ▶ Using letters to stand for variables
- ▶ Using correct algebraic notation

Just Click Maths Interact
See page 10
and Pupil Book 7^c pages 1 and 24.

New concepts

Position-to-term rules for generating sequences
Functions and function machines

Algebraic notation

1 Sequences

FRAMEWORK OBJECTIVES
Pages 144, 146, 148

▶ Generating and describing simple sequences
▶ Using term-to-term and position-to-term rules to generate sequences

Resources

Available on **Teacher Resource CD-ROM 7ᶜ:**

Extra Practice A1-1
Homework Sheet A1-1
Starter A1-1-1
Plenary A1-1-1

Plenaries

- Check vocabulary: e.g. Is 91, 85, 79, 73, 67, … **ascending** or **descending**?
- Check misconceptions: The rule for 4, 7, 10, 13, … is **not** term number + 3.

Key Words

sequence

term

consecutive

rule, relationship

continue

generate, predict

increase, decrease

finite, infinite

ascending

descending

Teaching points

- The correct terminology for sequences.
- Sequence diagrams for even, odd numbers, multiples of a given integer, square and triangular numbers.
- Term-to-term rules for generating sequences.
- Position-to-term rules for generating sequences.

Notes

It takes a long time to answer questions that require particular terms that are not near the beginning of the sequence as all terms have to be generated up to and including the one required. Using position-to-term rules is more difficult but it enables any term to be generated without having to work out all the terms of the sequence up to that term.

nth term notation is not introduced at this stage but is left for **Algebra 3** once algebraic notation has been properly introduced later in this unit and in **Algebra 2**.

Question ❼ requires pupils to describe the various sequences given and the idea of the question is to generate discussion about the types of sequence and to allow pupils to see that there are sequences of numbers which do not follow a pattern but which still have meaning.

In the orange topic, term-to-term sequence generation is straightforward while position-to-term rules will require discussion and careful explanation.

Question ⓭ asks pupils to recognise the even and odd numbers from the position-to-term expressions.

Homework

Unit Questions ❶ – ❹

2 Sequences from patterns

FRAMEWORK OBJECTIVES
Pages 32, 34

▶ Using letters to stand for variables
▶ Using correct algebraic notation

Resources

Available on **Teacher Resource CD-ROM 7ᶜ:**

Extra Practice A1-2
Homework Sheet A1-2
Starter A1-2-1
Plenary A1-2-1

Starters

Ensure that pupils understand the idea of **systematic** pattern growth by drawing examples on the board (or OHT) and discussing. Give examples of right and wrong possibilities, such as:

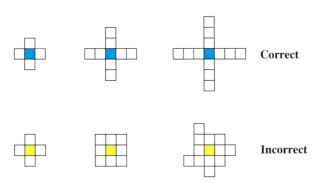

Correct

Incorrect

Key Words

sequence

rule

term

predict

Teaching points

- Generating number sequences from patterns.
- Using term-to-term and position-to-term rules to find terms of a sequence.
- Checking if particular numbers can be terms in a sequence.
- Predicting and checking terms of the sequence.
- Making general statements about the terms of a sequence.

Notes

Questions ❸ and ❻ require pupils to invent their own matchstick patterns and letter patterns and investigate the associated sequences. Encourage pupils to follow the structure of the other questions.

Pupils are not required to discover the position-to-term rules for themselves at this stage as this is covered in **Algebra 3**, together with the use of algebraic notation to describe the position-to-term rules. You could start to show the pupils how to find the rules if you wish.

Homework

Unit Questions ❺

3 Function machines

FRAMEWORK OBJECTIVES

Pages 160, 162

▶ Drawing and using function machines
▶ Finding the function given the input and output values
▶ Simple mapping diagrams
▶ Using inverse operations

Resources

Available on **Teacher Resource CD-ROM 7ᶜ:**

Worksheet A1-3-1 ❶ – ❹
Worksheet A1-3-2 ❻ and ❼
Worksheet A1-3-3 ❿ – ⓬
Worksheet A1-3-4 ❻ – ❽
Extra Practice A1-3
Homework Sheet A1-3
Starter A1-3-1
Plenary A1-3-1

Starters

One pupil stands at the front of the class with a whiteboard. This pupil is a function machine, and a rule, such as '+4' is on their board. Other pupils pass through the function machine. They call out their input number and output number as they pass through.

Maths Interact

▶ On the first screen, the rule for a single stage function machine may be defined using one of the operations +, − or ×. Input values of 4, 7 and 11 are then used to generate the output values.

The second screen works in the same way but with a two stage function machine.

▶ The same input values 4, 7 and 11 are used with a single stage function machine. The output values are displayed and the object is to determine the rule for the function.

Teaching points

● The construction and use of function machines.
● Writing the function being used in words.
● Writing the function being used as a mapping in words.
● How to draw simple mapping diagrams.
● Using inverse operations to work backwards through a function machine.

Key Words

function machine

input

output

function

mapping

inverse

Notes

Use the Worksheets for less able pupils at this level to avoid them having to copy the diagrams.

The use of algebraic functions and mappings is not introduced at this stage as this is left for **Algebra 3** and **Algebra 5**.

Inverse function machines are not introduced at this stage but you may wish to extend the work in the yellow topic to ask pupils to draw the inverse function machines and reverse the arrows on the diagrams to work out the original input values.

Homework

Unit Questions –

4 Algebraic notation

Resources

Available on **Teacher Resource CD-ROM 7^c:**

Worksheet A1-4-1 **8**, **9** and **11**

Extra practice A1-4

Homework Sheet A1-4

Starter A1-4-1

Plenary A1-4-1

FRAMEWORK OBJECTIVES

Page 112

▶ Generating sequences from patterns
▶ Describing general patterns in sequences

Plenaries

Check misconceptions: $n^2 \neq 2n$
$(n + 2) \times 4 \neq n + 2 \times 4$

Key Words

symbol

unknown

expression

variable

equation

equals (=)

brackets

Teaching points

- The use of symbols to represent unknowns.
- In an expression the unknown can take any value and therefore the expression can take any value.
- When an expression has a given value you obtain an equation and the unknown will now have a fixed value. (At this level the unknown has one value in any equation but equations can of course have more than one solution.)
- The meaning of algebraic expressions involving the 4 rules.
- Correct algebraic notation for products, quotients and squares.
- The use of brackets is correct in the orange topic. However, BODMAS is not properly covered until **Number 3**. **Algebra 2** also introduces the concept of the order of operations.

Notes

Use the Worksheet to allow pupils to fill in the tables in the later questions rather than copying the tables.

Because BODMAS has not been covered explicitly at this stage you can omit questions **5 h** and **7** if you wish and return to this after **Number 3**. You can also leave the SATs questions at this stage if you wish and return to these after further work on algebraic simplification.

Homework

Unit Questions **9** – **11**

1 Sequences

1   **a**   (1) 12   (2) Infinite   (3) Ascending
    b   (1) 8   (2) Finite   (3) Ascending
    c   (1) 27   (2) Infinite   (3) Descending
    d   (1) 8   (2) Finite   (3) Ascending
    e   (1) 100   (2) Finite   (3) Descending
    f   (1) 65   (2) Infinite   (3) Descending

2   **a**   23, 27, 31   **d** $^-9, ^-12, ^-15$
    b   27, 30, 33   **e**   0, 3, 6
    c   5, 3, 1   **f**   14, 3, $^-8$

3   **a**   The **infinite** sequence 2, 4, 6, 8, … is the sequence of even numbers. The first **term** is 2 and the sequence increases in **equal** steps.
    b   The sequence 7, 12, 17, 22, 27 is a **finite** sequence. The terms 12, 17 and 22 are **consecutive** terms.
    c   The sequence 1, 4, 9, 16, 25 is a **finite** sequence. It is the sequence of square numbers. The first square number is 1 and the sequence increases in **unequal** steps.

4   **a**   Even numbers   **d**   Multiples of 3
    b   Odd numbers   **e**   Multiples of 7
    c   Prime numbers   **f**   Square numbers

5   **a**   14, **21**, 28, 35, **42**, 49, **56**
    b   25, 20, **15**, **10**, 5, 0, **$^-$5**
    c   0, 0.5, **1.0**, 1.5, 2, **2.5**, **3**
    d $^-$2.5, $^-$2.8, $^-$3.1, **$^-$3.4**, **$^-$3.7**, $^-$4, $^-$4.3
    e   1, 2, **4**, 8, 16, **32**, 64
    f   160, **80**, 40, 20, 10, **5**, **2.5**

6   **a**   (1)
        1   3   5   7   9
       (2)
        11   13
       (3) Odd numbers

    b   (1)
        3   6   9   12   15
       (2)
        18   21
       (3) Multiples of 3

    c   (1)
        1   4   9   16   25
       (2)
        36   49
       (3) Square numbers

d   (1)
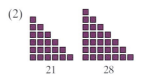
        1   3   6   10   15
       (2)
        21   28
       (3) Triangular numbers

7   All answers depend on pupil's own information.
    a   Probably numbers starting from 1, which will continue to the last house in the given road.
    b   Probably no pattern beyond wet or dry and cannot predict how sequence continues.
    c   Random sequence of numbers, cannot be predicted.
    d   Increasing or decreasing sequence depending on time of year, can be predicted.

8   **a**   (1) 14   (2) Add 3
    b   (1) 6   (2) Subtract 3
    c   (1) 1   (2) Multiply by 3
    d   (1) 400   (2) Divide by 2
    e   (1) 46   (2) Subtract 10
    f   (1) 324   (2) Divide by 3

9   **a**   12, 15, 18, 21, 24
    b   50, 62, 74, 86, 98
    c   24, 21, 18, 15, 12
    d $^-35, ^-30, ^-25, ^-20, ^-15$

10   **a**   31
    b $^-35$
    c   42.5

11   **a**   51
    b   65
    c   48
    d   100
    e   101
    f   149

12   **a**   5, 6, 7, 8, 9
    b $^-12, ^-11, ^-10, ^-9, ^-8$
    c   7, 9, 11, 13, 15
    d   4, 7, 10, 13, 16
    e   0.5, 2.5, 4.5, 6.5, 8.5
    f   1, 0, $^-1, ^-2, ^-3$

13   **a**   Even numbers
    b   Odd numbers

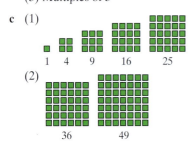

2 Sequences from patterns

1 a

b

pattern 4
4 squares
16 matchsticks

pattern 5
5 squares
20 matchsticks

c 4, 8, 12, 16, 20

d Increase by 4 matchsticks each time

e **Numbers of matchsticks = 4 × pattern number**

f 40

2 a

b

pattern 4
4 rhombuses   13 matchsticks

pattern 5
5 rhombuses 16 matchsticks

c 4, 7, 10, 13, 16

d Increases by 3 each time

e Add 3 each time until you have 10 terms

f 151

g No, as 62 − 1 is not divisible by 3. This is in between the 20th and 21st patterns.

3 Project question

4 a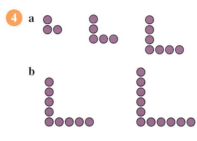

b

pattern 4   pattern 5
9 counters   11 counters

c 3, 5, 7, 9, 11

d Increases by 2 each time

e Add a counter to each end of the pattern

f 81

g No, as 80 − 1 = 79. This is not exactly divisible by 2.

5 a

b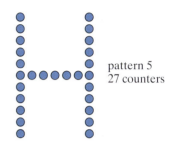

pattern 4
22 counters

pattern 5
27 counters

c 7, 12, 17, 22, 27

d Each pattern increases by 5 counters each time.

e A counter is added to every one of the 4 ends and the middle of the H.

f 202

g Yes, it is the 108th pattern: 542 − 2 = 540, 540 ÷ 5 = 108

6 Project question
Open-ended letters work best.
Good letters:
A, C, E, F, H, I, J, K, L, M, N, S, T, U, V, W, X, Y, Z

7 a 4   **b** 24   **c** 36   **d** 10

3 Function machines

1 a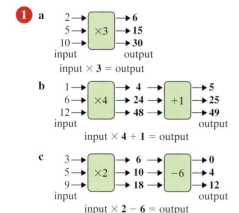

2 a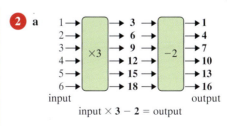

input × 3 − 2 = output

b

Input	1	2	3	4	5	6
Output	1	4	7	10	13	16

3 **a**

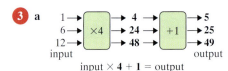

input × **4** + **1** = output

b

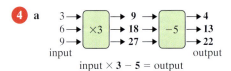

(input + **1**) × **4** = output

c Order is very important as the results will be different if the order is changed.

4 **a**

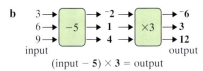

input × **3** − **5** = output

b

3 → [−5] → ⁻2 → [×3] → ⁻6
6 → → 1 → → 3
9 → → 4 → → 12
input output

(input − **5**) × **3** = output

c Order is important as the results will be different if the order is changed.

5 **a** Pupils will probably answer that you always get different answers when you reverse the order of the pair of functions.

b Any pair of inverse functions such as add 3 and subtract 3, multiply by 4 and divide by 4, square and square root etc. or a repeated self inverse function such as **output** = 10 − **input**. The only pairs including a mixture of multiplications, divisions, additions and subtractions which give the same answers when reversed must include multiply or divide by 1 or add or subtract 0. This therefore will change the above answer to part **a**.

6 **a** Add 5   **c** Multiply by 7
   b Subtract 2   **d** Divide by 3

7 **a**

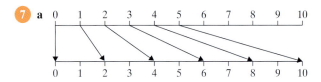

b

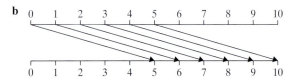

c

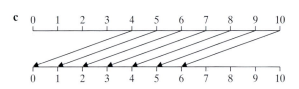

8

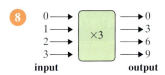

9 Game

10 **a**

7 → [+5] → 12
11 → → 16
21 → → 26
input output

e

1 → [×2] → 2
3 → → 6
10.5 → → 21
input output

b

4 → [×3] → 12
6 → → 18
17 → → 51
input output

f

2 → [×4] → 8
6 → → 24
10 → → 40
input output

c

8 → [−6] → 2
6 → → 0
29 → → 23
input output

g

6 → [÷2] → 3
15 → → 7.5
42 → → 21
input output

d

1 → [+7] → 8
8 → → 15
26 → → 33
input output

h

5 → [÷5] → 1
20 → → 4
50 → → 10
input output

11 **a**

2 → [×4] → 8 → [+3] → 11
0 → → 0 → → 3
6 → → 24 → → 27
input output

b

3 → [×5] → 15 → [−2] → 13
7 → → 35 → → 33
11 → → 55 → → 53
input output

c

6 → [×3] → 18 → [−1] → 17
12 → → 36 → → 35
20 → → 60 → → 59
input output

d

1 → [×2] → 2 → [÷2] → 1
2 → → 4 → → 2
3 → → 6 → → 3
input output

12 **a**

1 → [×2] → 2 → [+4] → 6
2 → → 4 → → 8
3 → → 6 → → 10
input output

b

1 → [×4] → 4 → [−1] → 3
5 → → 20 → → 19
7 → → 28 → → 27
input output

c

4 → [+2] → 6 → [÷2] → 3
8 → → 10 → → 5
10 → → 12 → → 6
input output

d

15 → [÷5] → 3 → [−1] → 2
35 → → 7 → → 6
60 → → 12 → → 11
input output

4 Algebraic notation
Answers

1
a 13 c 3 e 27 g 5
b 6 d 15 f 3 h 4

2
a $2l$ d $c + t$ g $\dfrac{p}{4}$
b $4m$ e $b + f$ h $D - 10$
c $6h$ f $30 - e$

3
a 13 c 3 e 5 g 3
b 15 d 10 f 2 h 2

4
a
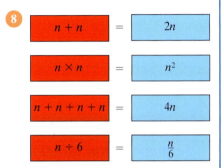

▼	■
1	14
2	13
3	12
4	11
5	10
6	9
7	8
8	7
9	6
10	5
11	4
12	3
13	2
14	1

b

a	b
1	16
2	8
4	4
8	2
16	1

5
a $p + 7$ e $2g + 1$
b $x - 15$ f z^2
c $4r$ g $\left(\dfrac{a}{2}\right)b$ or $\dfrac{ab}{2}$
d $\dfrac{y}{6}$ h $3(n + 4)$

6
a $3p$ d $2z$
b $4x$ e $4a$
c $5g$ f $6b$

7
a $2n$ is 2 times n.
  $n + 2$ is add 2 to n.
b $2n$ is 2 times n.
  n^2 is n times n.
c $2(n + 3)$ is add 3 to n then multiply by 2.
  $2n + 3$ means multiply n by 2 and then add 3.
d $2n^2$ means multiply n by n and then multiply the answer by 2.
  $(2n)^2$ means multiply n by 2 and then square the answer.

8

$n + n$	$=$	$2n$
$n \times n$	$=$	n^2
$n + n + n + n$	$=$	$4n$
$n \div 6$	$=$	$\dfrac{n}{6}$

9
a Barry is **one year younger than Tina**.
  Carol is **twice as old as Tina**.
b Ann $n + 4$, Barry n, Carol $2n + 1$

10
a $a + 2$, $4a$
b $b - 2$, $4(b - 2)$
c $\dfrac{c}{4} + 2$

11
a

Pattern number	Number of blue tiles	Number of red tiles
5	6	10
16	17	32

b

Pattern number	Number of blue tiles	Number of red tiles
n	$n + 1$	$2n$

c $n + 1 + 2n = 3n + 1$

Unit Questions: **Algebra 1**
Answers

1
a 24, 29, 34 c 21, 17, 13 e ⁻18, ⁻20, ⁻22
b 20, 23, 26 d ⁻13, ⁻18, ⁻23 f 0, 6, 12

2
a 23, **25**, 27, 29, **31**, 33, **35**
b 42, 36, **30**, **24**, 18, 12, **6**
c 3, 3.5, **4**, 4.5, 5, **5.5**, 6
d ⁻2, ⁻2.5, ⁻3, **⁻3.5**, ⁻**4**, ⁻4.5, ⁻5
e 2, 4, **8**, 16, 32, **64**, 128
f 240, **120**, 60, 30, **15**, 7.5

3
a 23 b 64 c 23.5

4
a (1) 5, 6, 7, 8, 9 (2) 54
b (1) 4, 6, 8, 10, 12 (2) 102
c (1) 4, 7, 10, 13, 16 (2) 151
d (1) 49, 48, 47, 46, 45 (2) 0

5
a
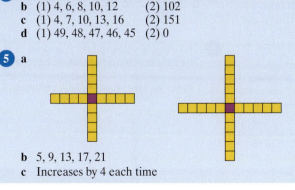

b 5, 9, 13, 17, 21
c Increases by 4 each time

d For each term one tile is added to each arm of the star.
e 161
f No. 82 − 1 = 81. 81 cannot be divided by 4

6
a
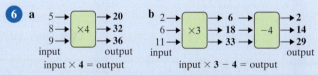
input × 4 = output

b input × 3 − 4 = output

7
a
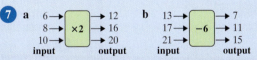

8
a
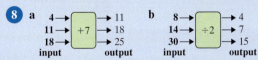

9
a 16 b 14 c 6 d 12 e 3 f 4

10
a $k + 5$ c $5y$ e h^2
b $p - 3$ d $2m + 3$ f $3w$

11
a $n - 4$ c $3n + 4$ e $\dfrac{n}{2} + 3$
b $3n$ d $5n - 2$

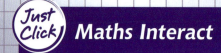

Maths Interact

Pupil Book page 1

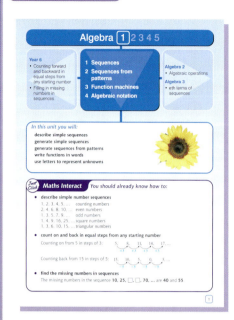

Pupils should already know how to:

- **describe simple number sequences**

  The names of the standard number sequences are listed. Click a sequence name to select and display information about the sequence.

- **count on and back in equal steps from any starting number**

  A sequence is defined by giving its starting number and a term to term rule. Enter the missing values.

- **find the missing numbers in sequences**

  Part of a sequence is shown and the object is to use this information to complete the missing terms.

Pupil Book page 24

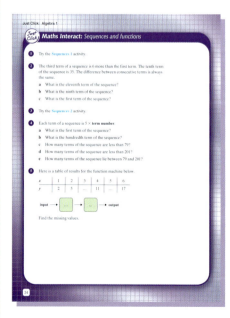

Sequences and functions

Maths Interact summary

1. Part of a sequence is shown and the object is to use this information to complete the missing terms.

2. Information about a sequence is presented in words. The object is to calculate the value of specific terms.

3. Enter a value to complete a rule for the terms of a sequence. You can then see the first thirty terms displayed ten at a time when Next is clicked.

4. A rule is given for a sequence which defines each term by its position. Calculations are needed to find specific terms and the number of terms in a given range.

5. A table of results is shown for a function machine with some missing values. The object is to use this information to complete the table and then to fill in the function machine.

Pupil Book answers

1. Refer to the *Maths Interact* activity.

2. **a** 38   **c** 8
   b 32

3. Refer to the *Maths Interact* activity.

4. **a** 5   **c** 15   **e** 25
   b 500   **d** 40

5. The missing *y* values are: 8 and 14
   The function machine should be:

   $$\text{input} \rightarrow \boxed{\times 3} \rightarrow 3n \rightarrow \boxed{-1} \rightarrow \text{output}$$

Number ①2345

Year 6

- Place value
- Ordering and rounding
- Properties of numbers
- Fractions and decimals
- Mental calculation strategies

1 **Place value**
2 **Negative numbers**
3 **Calculations**
4 **Adding and subtracting**

Number 3

- Estimates and approximation
- Multiplying and dividing
- Units of measurement

Framework teaching programme

36–41	Place value	102–105	Calculations
48–51	Integers	108–109	Calculator methods
88–91	Calculations	2–11	Solving problems

Overview

This unit develops the work that pupils saw in Year 6. The unit deals with place value, the ordering of decimals, positive and negative integers, the rapid recall of number facts and making and justifying estimates. The unit links to the work on rounding and relationships between units in **Number 3**, which is revisited in **Number 5**. There is a recap of column procedures and how a calculator display is interpreted in different contexts involving decimals and money.

1 Place value

- ▶ Decimal notation
- ▶ Multiplying and dividing by 10, 100, 1000
- ▶ Ordering decimals
- ▶ Comparing measurements

2 Integers

- ▶ Ordering integers
- ▶ Adding and subtracting positive and negative integers

3 Calculations

- ▶ Number facts
- ▶ Estimates and approximations

4 Adding and subtracting

- ▶ Standard column procedures
- ▶ Calculator skills

Just Click **Maths Interact**

See page 20
and Pupil Book 7^c pages 25 and 46.

New concepts

Adding and subtracting negative numbers   The square root of perfect squares

1 Place value

FRAMEWORK OBJECTIVES
Pages 36, 38, 40

▶ Decimal notation
▶ Multiplying and dividing by 10, 100, 1000
▶ Ordering decimals
▶ Comparing measurements

Resources

Available on **Teacher Resource CD-ROM 7ᶜ:**

Extra Practice N1-1
Homework Sheet N1-1
Starter N1-1-1
Plenary N1-1-1
Plenary N1-1-2

Starters

Pupils draw 4 boxes □□.□□. Roll a dice or use a random integer number generator and ask the pupils to place the number in one of their boxes. The pupil with the largest number after four goes is the winner. Change the rules so that the smallest number wins.

Plenaries

- Check misconceptions: 3.3 < 3.31. Encourage pupils to think of 3.3 as 3.30 in these situations.
- Check vocabulary: Column headings after thousandths, ten thousandths, hundred thousandths, not straight to millionths.

Teaching points

- Interchanging fractions and decimals between words and figures.
- Multiplying and dividing by 10, 100 or 1000.
- Comparing and ordering decimal numbers.
- Comparing measurements by changing into the same unit.

Key Words

tenth
hundredth
thousandth
decimal number
mixed number
increase, decrease
digit
compare
convert
order

Notes

All pupils should be confident recognising hundreds, tens, units, tenths and hundredths before proceeding.

In question ❶ d some pupils may ignore the zero, giving the answer seven tenths. A second opportunity involving thousandths is given in question ❶ e. If pupils cannot recognise the values of the red digits, use the opening page *Maths Interact* to revisit prior work on tenths and hundredths.

Question ❷ uses a zero as a place value holder when writing decimal numbers. Some pupils may find this easier if they write the number as a fraction first, then change it into a decimal.

Question ❻ consolidates interchanging between words, fractions and decimals.

Question ❼ requires a good appreciation of zero as a place value holder. Watch out for pupils adding a zero when multiplying by ten. Use a table to demonstrate the effect of moving to the left for multiplying and the right for dividing.

For question ⑬ pupils must appreciate that numbers with one decimal place can be larger or smaller than those with several decimal places, depending upon the value of the digit in the tenths column. Emphasise, when ordering decimals, it can help to write out the list first lining up the decimal point, then write the numbers in order.

Question ⑰ requires pupils to change measurements into the same unit first, before comparing them. A good approach is to change the larger unit into the smaller one as this uses multiplying which is easier than dividing.

Question ⑳ requires pupils to change $\frac{3}{4}$ into a decimal.

Homework

Unit Questions ❶ – ❺

2 Negative numbers

FRAMEWORK OBJECTIVES
Pages 48, 50

▶ Ordering integers
▶ Adding and subtracting positive and negative integers

Resources

Available on **Teacher Resource CD-ROM 7ᶜ:**

Worksheet N1-2-1 ❶ and ❸
Worksheet N1-2-2 ❼ and ❿
Extra Practice N1-2
Homework Sheet N1-2
Starter N1-2-1
Plenary N1-2-1

Plenaries

Check vocabulary: ⁻4 is read as 'negative 4'. 'Minus 4' refers to the operation 'subtract 4' and should not be used. '4' is read as 'positive 4' and 'plus 4' should not be used as it refers to the operation 'add 4'. Zero is neither positive nor negative.

Maths Interact

▶ The relationship between positive and negative numbers is shown both on horizontal and vertical number lines as an animation. The animation also shows the directions corresponding to numbers getting bigger or smaller.

▶ The animation shows how a number line may be used to carry out addition and subtraction of positive and negative numbers.

Teaching points

● Ordering positive and negative integers on a number line.

● ⁻n should be read as 'negative n' and not 'minus n' which strictly means 'subtract n'.

● Addition and subtraction of directed numbers.

Key words

| integer |
| positive |
| negative |
| plus |
| minus |
| sign |

Notes

All positive numbers could be written in the form ⁺n.

Question ❹ uses *University Challenge*, in which it is possible to score negatively. This question is included to provide a context for looking at negative numbers and the addition required is intended to be done intuitively at this stage.

Question ❺ looks briefly at the difference between a positive and a negative temperature as an example of negative numbers in context. This is also covered in the previous knowledge on the unit opening page.

Question ❻ also requires the pupils to think of a gap across zero intuitively. If you wish, you could leave questions ❹ to ❻ until you have covered the second topic on addition and subtraction of directed numbers.

Pupils need to understand that the numbers in a magic square add up to the same value on any row, column or diagonal in order to be able to do question ❿.

Question ⓫ is a SAT question which also links to this previous knowledge but it is more difficult and needs the pupils to properly understand addition and subtraction of directed numbers.

Homework

Unit Questions –

3 Calculations

FRAMEWORK OBJECTIVES
Pages 40, 88, 102

▶ Number facts
▶ Estimates and approximations

Resources

Available on **Teacher Resource CD-ROM 7ᶜ:**

Extra Practice N1-3
Homework Sheet N1-3
Starter N1-3-1
Plenary N1-3-1

Starters

Pupils stand up and secretly pick a number between 1 and 30. Write different number properties on the board such as 'in the 3 times table', 'in the 5 times table ', 'even' etc. If the property fits a pupil number, the pupil sits down. Last one standing is the winner – the class checks the winner's number against the properties on the board.

Plenaries

Give a pupil a starting number that is even. Move around the class in a clockwise direction, doubling as you go, e.g. start 12, next pupil says 24, next 48, etc. If you change direction, the pupils have to halve the number. Repeat with an odd starting number.

Key Words

complement

double

halve

approximate

square

square root

round, estimate

calculation

Teaching points

● Complements 100, 50 and 1.
● Doubling and halving integers and decimals.
● Using a knowledge of times tables and division facts.
● Considering best approximations.
● Reading scales on a number line.

Notes

Question ❶ uses the fact that a century is equal to 100, and may need to be explained to some pupils.

Question ❹ uses previous knowledge of doubling single-digit numbers. Pupils are asked to double two-digit numbers including decimals. Parts **d**, **j** and **o** are linked: the answer to one part will help with the other parts.

Question ❻ uses repeated doubling. Less confident pupils may need to use a calculator.

Question ❿ requires a good knowledge of multiplication facts up to 10×10 to state associated division facts. Weaker pupils may need some number cards.

Question ⓫ parts **i** to **l** require knowledge of square roots. It is worth showing the pattern made by squared numbers in the times tables and explaining how squared numbers are written and that the opposite of squaring is square rooting.

Question ⓬ expects pupils to round to the nearest hundred before finding the total.

Question ⓭ considers different degrees of approximation. Pupils should round both numbers to the same level of accuracy, before comparing the totals.

Questions ⓮ and ⓯ show scales graduated in ten divisions. Pupils should use this to work out the size of each division and find the value the arrow is pointing to.

Question ⓴ is an open ended question with an infinite range of answers, good for a plenary question.

Homework

Unit Questions ❾ – ⓬

4 Adding and subtracting

FRAMEWORK OBJECTIVES

Pages 2, 6, 84, 104, 108

▶ Standard column procedures
▶ Calculator skills

Resources

Available on **Teacher Resource CD-ROM 7ᶜ:**

Worksheet N1-4-1 **8** and **15**
Worksheet N1-4-2
Extra Practice N1-4
Homework Sheet N1-4
Starter N1-4-1
Plenary N1-4-1

Other resources required

10 faced or ordinary dice for question 9

Starters

Play Question **9** with the class. Put the template on the board for pupils to copy onto their wipeboards or exercise books. Play the game (using the template on the board) against the pupils to see who can make the largest total. Stress how the template looks – it is vital to respect place value when using column addition and subtraction.

Plenaries

Check misconceptions: The pupils must set the calculations out correctly – i.e. respecting the place value by having the decimal points in line and filling in extra zeros if necessary.

e.g. 20.17 + 4.6

```
   20.17          not        20.17
  +4.60                        4.6
  ------                     ------
   24.77                     204.23
                                  1
```

Key Words

decimal number

add, addition

subtract, subtraction

calculator:

clear, display

enter, key

Teaching points

- Column addition and subtraction.
- Use of a calculator.
- The importance of lining up the decimal points in each of the numbers when adding or subtracting and filling in missing digits with zeros, especially within subtraction questions where the top number has a missing digit at the end.

Notes

Question **9** **Make it large** is a game that requires pupils to explain a winning strategy. The random generation of the digits means that you can only use your judgement. Higher digits should be placed in the columns on the left.

Question **10** **Zero hero** is a calculator game that asks pupils to explain a winning strategy. This strategy depends on how intelligent your opponent is! The key to winning is to be Player 1 so that you enter the number. If both players make a digit zero on every turn, then Player 1 wins if they key in a number with an even number of non-zero digits. However, players don't have to make a digit zero on each turn and to win Player 1 must ensure that they always leave an even number of possible turns after every turn. This can be achieved by entering a number with an even number of digits and always leaving a digit of 1 if the opponent does not clear a column to zero on any turn. If the opponent leaves 1 in any column then Player 1 needs to make a different column 1. The number will become an even string of 1s after a turn by Player 1 which means the removal of the final digit will fall to Player 1.

Homework

Unit Questions **13** – **15**

1 Place value *Answers*

1   **a** 4 tenths   **d** 7 hundredths
    b 5 thousandths   **e** 8 thousandths
    c 6 tenths

2   **a** 0.04   **d** 0.25
    b 0.005   **e** 6.07
    c 0.015   **f** 3.004

3   **a** Eight tenths
    b Twenty-seven hundredths
    c Sixteen thousandths
    d Two hundred and seventy-five thousandths
    e Six and seven hundredths

4   **a** Three and seven thousandths
    b Four and thirty-nine thousandths
    c Four and thirty-nine hundredths
    d Seven and nine tenths
    e Six and five hundred and thirty-three thousandths

5   **a** $7\frac{27}{1000}$
    b $18\frac{181}{1000}$

6

	words	fraction	decimal
a	three tenths	$\frac{3}{10}$	0.3
b	seven hundredths	$\frac{7}{10}$	**0.7**
c	three thousandths	$\frac{3}{1000}$	0.003
d	eighty-one thousandths	$\frac{81}{1000}$	**0.081**
e	nine and eleven thousandths	$9\frac{11}{1000}$	**9.011**
f	nine and two hundred and three thousandths	$9\frac{203}{1000}$	**9.203**

7   **a** 80   **g** 6.5
    b 0.2   **h** 0.07
    c 700   **i** 4.5
    d 82   **j** 0.034
    e 6000   **k** 0.004
    f 30   **l** 0.045

8   **a** **0.4** $\times$ 10 = 4
    b 4 $\times$ **100** = 400
    c 0.4 $\div$ 10 = **0.04**
    d **4** $\div$ 100 = 0.04

9

	0.06	0.6	60
a	8.3	**83**	**8300**
b	**0.29**	2.9	**290**
c	**0.005**	**0.05**	5

10

$7 \div 100 = 0.07$	$0.7 \times 1000 = 700$
$7 \div 10 = 0.7$	$7 \times 10 = 70$

So the odd one out is

$\ldots \times 1000 = 700$

11 16 Hertz

12   **a** $\boxed{7}$. $\boxed{4}\;\boxed{3}$ **b** $\boxed{3}$. $\boxed{4}\;\boxed{7}$

13   **a** 0.125
    b Because there are fewer digits. Also because 5 is smaller than 125, for example.

14   **a** 1.47 2.307 2.377 2.47 2.477
    b 37.477
       38.377
       38.477
       38.479
       39.177

15   **a** False   **d** True
    b False   **e** True
    c True   **f** False

16   **a** 23.7 < 23.705
    b 0.907 < 0.97
    c 6.089 < 6.809

17   **a** 0.04 m
    b 30.1 cm
    c 0.007 kg
    d 750.5 g
    e 330 mℓ
    f 4801 mℓ

18   **a** To change metres to kilometres … **divide by 1000**
    b To change kilograms to grams … **multiply by 1000**

19   **a** 0.5 kg, 0.05 kg, 5 g
    b 2000 mℓ, 0.2 ℓ, 20 mℓ
    c 7.001 km, 7000 m, 70 m, 0.007 km
    d 4.4°C, 4°C, ⁻4°C, ⁻4.4°C

20 1.067 kg, 1.67 kg, $1\frac{3}{4}$ kg, 1780 g

2 Negative numbers — *Answers*

1

$^-8\ ^-7\ ^-6\ ^-5\ ^-4\ ^-3\ ^-2\ ^-1\ 0\ 1\ 2\ 3\ 4\ 5\ 6\ 7\ 8$

e   a c   d   b

2
a $2 > -4$ c $1 > -7$ e $-2 < 0$
b $-3 < 1$ d $0 > -9$ f $-12 < -2$

3 a

$^-4\ ^-3\ ^-2\ ^-1\ 0\ 1\ 2\ 3\ 4\ 5\ 6\ 7$

$^-4\ \ \ \ ^-2\ ^-1\ 0\ \ \ \ \ \ 3\ \ \ \ \ \ \ \ 7$

b $^-4, ^-2, ^-1, 0, 3, 7$

4 a $^-5$ b 5

5 a $9°C$ b $25°C$ c $16°C$ d $35°C$

6 6 floors

7 a

$+1\ +1\ +1\ +1$
$^-8\ ^-7\ ^-6\ ^-5\ ^-4\ ^-3\ ^-2\ ^-1\ 0\ 1\ 2\ 3\ 4\ 5\ 6\ 7\ 8$
$^-6 + 4 = ^-2$

b

$-1\ -1\ -1\ -1$
$^-8\ ^-7\ ^-6\ ^-5\ ^-4\ ^-3\ ^-2\ ^-1\ 0\ 1\ 2\ 3\ 4\ 5\ 6\ 7\ 8$
$7 + ^-4 = 3$

8
a $^-8$ e $^-16$ i 8 m $^-21$
b $^-9$ f $^-17$ j 13 n $^-54$
c 4 g $^-18$ k $^-14$ o $^-19$
d 4 h $^-6$ l 18 p $^-16$

9
a 2 d 2 g 15
b 6 e 10 h $^-3$
c $^-17$ f 5 i $^-2$

10
a

$^-2$	$^-6$	$^-7$
$^-10$	$^-5$	0
$^-3$	$^-4$	$^-8$

b

$^-6$	$^-1$	$^-8$
$^-7$	$^-5$	$^-3$
$^-2$	$^-9$	$^-4$

c

$^-1$	$^-8$	0
$^-2$	$^-3$	$^-4$
$^-6$	2	$^-5$

11 a $^-19$ b 16 c $^-22$

12 e.g. Eleven minus eighteen.
No she could have chosen any two numbers with a difference of $^-7$.

13
a
$6 + 2 = 8$
$6 + 1 = 7$
$6 + 0 = 6$
$6 + ^-1 = 5$
$6 + ^-2 = 4$
$6 + ^-3 = 3$
$6 + ^-4 = 2$
$6 + ^-5 = 1$
$6 + ^-6 = 0$
$6 + ^-7 = -1$

b
$6 - 3 = 3$
$6 - 2 = 4$
$6 - 1 = 5$
$6 - 0 = 6$
$6 - ^-1 = 7$
$6 - ^-2 = 8$
$6 - ^-3 = 9$
$6 - ^-4 = 10$
$6 - ^-5 = 11$
$6 - ^-6 = 12$

14
a e.g. $^-1 + ^-1$
b e.g. $^-3 + 1$
c Possibilities include:
$^-1 + ^-6$
$^-2 + ^-5$
$^-3 + ^-4$
$^-7 + 0$
$^-8 + 1$
$^-9 + 2$
$^-10 + 3$

15
a Possibilities include:
$10 - 14$, $9 - 13$, $0 - 4$, $-1 - 3$
b 4

16 a £230   b $^-$£100

3 Calculations — *Answers*

1 17

2 a 60 b 30 c 5 d 81 e 95

3 a 0.8 b 0.3 c 0.28 d 0.91

4
a 12 c 84 e 1660 g 15 600 i 12.06
b 60 d 600 f 4800 h 0.8 j 1.54

5 $20 \rightarrow 40 \rightarrow 80 \rightarrow 160 \rightarrow 320$

6 6

7
a 3 c 21 e 415 g 3900 i 3.015
b 15 d 150 f 1200 h 0.2 j 0.385

8 17

9 $40 \rightarrow 20 \rightarrow 10 \rightarrow 5 \rightarrow 2.5$

10

5	×	8	=	40
40	÷	5	=	8
40	÷	8	=	5

11
a $2 \times 3 < 56 \div 7$
b $1 \times 5 > 2$ squared
c $5 \times 7 < 6$ squared
d $2 \times 7 > 3^2$
e $5^2 > 3 \times 8$
f $3 \times 6 > 4^2$
g $9^2 > 10 \times 8$
h $49 \div 7 < 5 \times 10$
i $\sqrt{25} > 40 \div 10$
j $72 \div 8 < \sqrt{100}$
k $81 < 50 \div 5$
l $16 \div 4 < \sqrt{36}$

Number 1

12 a

Year 7	Year 8	Year 9	Year 10	Year 11
250	200	200	300	200

b 1150 (250 + 200 + 200 + 300 + 200)

13 a 3300 + 1900 = 5200
3000 + 2000 = 5000

b 3300 + 1900

14 a 5.5   **b** 23.5   **c** 3.25   **d** 3.7

15 a 20   **d** 114
b 35   **e** 137
c 66   **f** 179

16 11.5, 4.5

17 2.4 mℓ

18 a 9.2   **b** 24

19 ⁻5

20 Possibilities include:
19, 21
18, 22
17, 23
16, 24
15, 25
14, 26
13, 27
12, 28
11, 29
10, 30

---

4   Adding and subtracting   *Answers*

1 a
```
   236
+   37
   273
    1
```
f
```
  369.1
    3.9
+  58.3
  431.3
  12 1
```

b
```
  36.3
+  4.5
  40.8
   1
```
g
```
  53.49
+ 36.63
  90.12
  11 1
```

c
```
  73.6
+  8.7
  82.3
  11
```
h
```
  378.26
   80.4
+   5.68
  464.34
  11 1 1
```

d
```
  256.3
+  97.8
  354.1
  1 1 1
```
i
```
  583.47
    0.64
+   91.4
  675.51
   1  1 1
```

e
```
  417.2
   83.4
+  45.6
  546.2
  1 1 1
```

2 a
```
     7 1
   4̸8̸5
  −  37
    448
```
d
```
    5 14 1
   6̸2̸5.3
  −  92.8
    532.5
```

b
```
    7 1
   6̸8.3
  −  6.6
    61.7
```
e
```
    5 1 71
   6̸3.8̸0
  − 26.63
    37.17
```

c
```
     6 12 1
   5̸7̸3.3
  −  57.8
    515.5
```
f
```
    8 12 13 1
   9̸3.4̸0
  − 64.76
    28.64
```

3 a 421   **g** 259
b 82   **h** 389.4
c 40.38   **i** 25.72
d 238.3   **j** 295.65
e 19.29   **k** 535.99
f 410.11   **l** 700.27

4 a
```
  3 4 . 2 7
−   7 . 9
  4 2 . 1 7
```

b
```
  2 2 . 8 1
−   8 . 4 6
  3 1 . 2 7
```

c
```
  6 3 . 8 2
−   9 . 1 6
  5 4 . 6 6
```

d
```
  4 2 . 6
−   8 . 7 1
  3 3 . 8 9
```

5 60.5 seconds

6 a £5.67
b £4.33

7 Pupils doing questions **1** to **3** with a calculator.

8 a
```
          564.12
       242.39  321.73
     111.1  131.29  190.44
   46.92  64.18  67.11  123.33
```

b
```
          96.27
       59.67  36.6
     37.25  22.42  14.18
   24.77  12.48  9.94  4.24
 20.17  4.6  7.88  2.06  2.18
```

c
```
          234.67
       126.57  108.1
     78.72  47.85  60.25
   54.94  23.78  24.07  36.18
```

d
```
             450.97
         261.22  189.75
       181.28  79.94  109.81
    146.55  34.73  45.21  64.6
 120.17  26.38  8.35  36.86  27.74
```

9 Game. See Notes on page 15 for strategy hints.

10 Game. See Notes on page 15 for strategy hints.

Answers

1 a Three tenths
  b Four hundredths
  c Eight tenths
  d Five thousandths

2 a 0.4   b 3.06   c 0.13

3 a $6 \times 10 = $ **60**
  b $8.4 \times 10 = $ **84**
  c $0.43 \times 100 = $ **43**
  d $4.18 \times 100 = $ **418**
  e $72 \div 10 = $ **7.2**
  f $5.7 \div 10 = $ **0.57**
  g $324 \div 100 = $ **3.24**
  h $34.7 \div 100 = $ **0.347**

4 a 0.125   b 0.475

5 a 0.06 m   b 60 g   c 0.033 ℓ

6 a 12.00   b 19.15   c 13.20

7 a ⁻5   i ⁻1
  b ⁻5   j 9
  c 6   k 16
  d 2   l 4
  e ⁻6   m 4
  f ⁻13   n ⁻43
  g ⁻11   o ⁻29
  h ⁻5   p ⁻39

8 a Possibilities include:
    $1 + 2$
    $⁻3 + 6$
    $⁻4 + 7$
    $⁻5 + 8$
    $⁻6 + 9$
    $⁻7 + 10$
  b Possibilities include:
    $⁻7 + 1$
    $⁻8 + 2$
    $⁻9 + 3$
    $⁻10 + 4$
    $⁻11 + 5$

9 a (1) 40
    (2) 60
    (3) 15
    (4) 69
    (5) 96
  b (1) 0.6
    (2) 0.4
    (3) 0.25
    (4) 0.68
    (5) 0.95

10 a (1) 16   (2) 4
  b (1) 100   (2) 25
  c (1) 76   (2) 19
  d (1) 1400   (2) 350
  e (1) 5200   (2) 1300
  f (1) 0.56   (2) 0.14
  g (1) 7.2   (2) 1.8
  h (1) 1.28   (2) 0.32

11 a $42 \div 7 = $ **6** $42 \div 6 = 7$
  b $63 \div 9 = 7$ $63 \div 7 = $ **9**

12 a $3100 - 1400 = 1700$
    $3200 - 1300 = 1900$
  b $3100 - 1400$

13 a
```
    4  5  7
 +     6  8
 ─────────
    5  2  5
    1  1
```
  b
```
    6  1 . 7
 +  2  5 . 4
 ──────────
    8  7 . 1
         1
```
  c
```
    5  4 . 3  6
 +      3 . 1  8
 ──────────────
    5  7 . 5  4
            1
```
  d
```
    3  4  6 . 6  0
 +      7  1 . 1  5
 ──────────────────
    4  1  7 . 7  5
               1
```
  e
```
    3  2 . 6  0
    1  7 . 1  6
 +      1 . 4  6
 ──────────────
    5  1 . 2  2
    1  1  1
```
  f
```
    2  3  1 . 3  8
    5  2  3 . 4  0
 +      6  2 . 7  0
 ──────────────────
    8  1  7 . 4  8
    1  1  1
```
  g
```
    ²⁷ ²8
 −  2  6  6
 ──────────
       6  2
```
  h
```
    5  ³⁴ ¹⁵⁶ . ¹2
 −  2  1  7 . 7
 ──────────────
    3  2  8 . 5
```
  i
```
    5  ⁶⁷ . ¹⁶⁷ ¹2
 −  3  4 . 8  4
 ──────────────
    2  2 . 8  8
```
  j
```
    ⁵⁶ ³ ¹⁷8 . 2  8
 −        4  6 . 9  0
 ──────────────────
    5  9  1 . 3  8
```
  k
```
    ²³ ¹³⁴ ¹6 . ¹⁷0
 −        5  6 . 3  5
 ──────────────────
    2  8  7 . 3  5
```
  l
```
    ⁷8  ²2  8 . ⁵⁶ ¹0
 −        7  2 . 3  6
 ──────────────────
    7  5  6 . 2  4
```

14 $5.4 + 4.8 + 3.6 + 3.1 + 2.9 + 2.4$
    $+ 1.0 + 0.7 + 0.2 + 0.1 = 24.2$

15

			403.88			
		162.06		241.82		
	70.75		91.31		150.51	
16.62		54.13		37.18		113.33

			221.99			
		90.98		131.01		
	40.52		50.46		80.55	
24.74		15.78		34.68		45.87

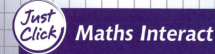

Maths Interact

Pupil Book page 25

Pupils should already know how to:

- **recognise numbers in words and figures**

  A number is presented in words and the object is to click the corresponding number shown in figures.

- **write tenths and hundredths as decimals**

  A decimal is described in words and the response is to enter this number in figures using decimal notation.

- **calculate a temperature rise and fall across 0°**

  Fill in the missing figures to complete statements about temperature change.

- **find squares to 10 × 10**

  A matching game in which numbers and their squares are shown on cards. Clicking a pair of matching cards causes them to disappear.

- **multiply and divide a whole number by 10**

  A random selection of ten calculations is shown on the screen. All of the answers are whole numbers.

Pupil Book page 46

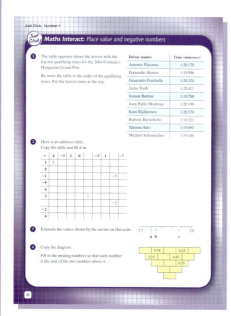

Place value and negative numbers

Maths Interact summary

1 Drivers with the top ten qualifying times for a grand prix are presented. The results are to be rearranged based on the times.

2 Numbers are entered to complete an addition table for positive and negative values.

3 A decimal number scale is shown and arrows indicate the positions of three unknown values. These values must be estimated within a small tolerance.

4 Values are entered to complete a decimal addition wall. In some cases, the positions of the unknown values require a subtraction to be carried out.

Pupil Book answers

1

Michael Schumacher	1:19.146
Rubens Barrichello	1:19.323
Takuma Sato	1:19.693
Jenson Button	1:19.700
Fernando Alonso	1:19.996
Antonio Pizzonia	1:20.170
Juan Pablo Montoya	1:20.199
Giancarlo Fisichella	1:20.324
Jarno Trulli	1:20.411
Kimi Räikkönen	1:20.570

2

+	4	⁻3	2	0	⁻2	⁻5	1	⁻4	⁻7
1	5	⁻2	3	1	⁻1	⁻4	2	⁻3	⁻6
0	4	⁻3	2	0	⁻2	⁻5	1	⁻4	⁻7
⁻1	3	⁻4	1	⁻1	⁻3	⁻6	0	⁻5	⁻8
⁻9	⁻5	⁻12	⁻7	⁻9	⁻11	⁻14	⁻8	⁻13	⁻16
6	10	3	8	6	4	1	7	2	⁻1
3	7	0	5	3	1	⁻2	4	⁻1	⁻4
2	6	⁻1	4	2	0	⁻3	3	⁻2	⁻5
⁻2	2	⁻5	0	⁻2	⁻4	⁻7	⁻1	⁻6	⁻9
4	8	1	6	4	2	⁻1	5	0	⁻3

3 a 3.72   b 3.73   c 3.775

4

3.16	9.74	4.74	0.23	3.15
	12.9	14.48	4.97	3.38
		27.38	19.45	8.35
			46.83	27.8
				74.63

Shape, Space and Measures 1 2 3 4 5

Year 6	1 3-D shapes	Shape, Space and Measures 3
• Perimeter	2 Length and perimeter	• 2-D representations of 3-D shapes
• Area	3 Area	**Year 8**
• Metric units		• Plans and elevations
		• Units of measurement
		• Area and volume

Framework teaching programme

198–201 **Use 2-D representations to visualise 3-D objects**

234–241 **Perimeter, area and volume**

18–21 **Solving problems**

Overview

This unit builds on the work in Year 6 on perimeter and area and units of each. Pupils use 2-D representations of 3-D objects including isometric views to consider the properties of 3-D shapes. Units of perimeter and perimeter problems are introduced in section 2, with area covered in section 3. Section 3 also introduces the concept of surface area.

1 3-D shapes

▶ Describing 3-D shapes
▶ Using isometric paper to draw 3-D objects
▶ Nets of cubes and cuboids

2 Length and perimeter

▶ Recognising and using units of length
▶ Calculating perimeter
▶ Finding the perimeter of combined shapes

3 Area

▶ Area of a rectangle and a right-angled triangle
▶ Areas of shapes made from rectangles
▶ Surface area of cubes and cuboids

 Maths Interact

See page 28
and Pupil Book 7^C pages 47 and 68.

New concepts

Surface area

1   3-D shapes

FRAMEWORK OBJECTIVES
Pages 198, 200

▶ Describing 3-D shapes
▶ Using isometric paper to draw 3-D objects
▶ Nets of cubes and cuboids

Resources

Available on **Teacher Resource CD-ROM 7^C:**

Worksheet S1-1-1 ❶ and ❽
Extra Practice S1-1
Homework Sheet S1-1
Starter S1-1-1
Plenary S1-1-1
Dotty isometric paper
Squared paper

Other resources required

Multilink cubes

Starters

Ask the pupils to close their eyes and imagine a cube made of cardboard. The sun is shining on the cube and the heat begins to melt the glue holding the sides together. Slowly but surely the sides begin to fall away from each other and the cube flattens out. Pupils open their eyes and draw what they have seen. Has everyone drawn the same picture? Is there only one answer? (No, 11. See Answers for ⑯ **a**.)

Plenaries

Pick a pupil and tell him/her one of the key words from the list. The pupil has to guess the name of the solid in five questions and is only allowed to answer Yes or No. Repeat with another pupil or play in pairs.

Just Click   Maths Interact

▶ An isometric grid is shown on the screen. The pencil tool may be used to draw 3-D shapes on the grid. Drawing is made easier by a 'snap' function which makes the end points of lines snap to the nearest point where the grid lines meet.

Teaching points

● Definition of face, edge and vertex.
● Names of solids.
● Properties of pyramids and prisms
  – a pyramid tapers to a single vertex.
  – a prism has the same cross-section throughout.
● Strictly a prism must have a polygonal cross-section so a cylinder is not a prism.
● Use of isometric paper.
● Definition of a net of a solid.

Key Words

2-D, 3-D

pyramid

prism

sphere

cube, cuboid

tetrahedron

cylinder

hemisphere

face, vertex, vertices, edge, net

Notes

In question ❶ you could go through the cube explaining how each value has been found before setting the rest of the question. Question ❽ goes on to allow pupils to discover Euler's theorem.

The Worksheet for questions ❶ and ❽ will probably not be needed at this level but you could use it to save pupils drawing the tables.

The second topic requires pupils to draw shapes on dotty isometric paper. The drawing of shapes on lined isometric paper is covered in **Shape, Space and Measures 3**.

Topic 3 on nets doesn't emphasise the accuracy of the net but all the nets drawn in the book are full sized and you can emphasise the importance of accuracy with more able pupils at this stage.

This section should be accessible to all pupils but you will need to provide Multilink cubes for those pupils with less developed spatial awareness.

Homework

Unit Questions ❶ – ❹

2   Length and perimeter

FRAMEWORK OBJECTIVES

Pages 18, 90, 230, 234, 236

▶ Recognising and using units of length
▶ Calculating perimeter
▶ Finding the perimeter of combined shapes

Resources

Available on **Teacher Resource CD-ROM 7^C:**

Extra Practice S1-2
Homework Sheet S1-2
Starter S1-2-1
Plenary S1-2-1

Starters

Use Questions ❶ and ❷ from the textbook as a verbal starter to estimate heights and lengths and check pupils appreciate when to use mm, cm, m and km.

Plenaries

How tall are you in metric units? Use the fact that a classroom door is approximately 2 m as a guide.

Key Words

millimetre

centimetre

metre

kilometre

length

distance

side

perimeter

Teaching points

- Selecting appropriate metric units to make a measurement.
- Definition of perimeter.
- Using a word formula to calculate the perimeter of a rectangle.
- Using opposite sides to find the missing sides in a shape made using rectangles.
- Using the properties of squares and equilateral triangles to find the perimeter of a shape.

Notes

The red topic considers the appropriate use of metric units. It is worth emphasising the relative size of each unit and when they are used. The term 'length' is used to describe small measurements. The term 'distance' is used to describe large measurements.

The formula for the perimeter of a rectangle has been described in words. The formula has been deliberately missed out, because algebraic substitution is not covered until **Algebra 2**.

Question ❿ uses parallel sides to find the length of an unknown side.

The properties of a square and an isosceles triangle are needed to answer Question ⓫.

Homework

Unit Questions ❺ – ❽

3 Area and volume

FRAMEWORK OBJECTIVES
Pages 90, 234, 236, 238, 240

▶ Area of a rectangle and right-angled triangle
▶ Area of shapes made from rectangles
▶ Surface area of cubes and cuboids

Resources

Available on **Teacher Resource CD-ROM 7^C:**

Extra Practice S1-3
Homework Sheet S1-3
Starter S1-3-1
Plenary S1-3-1

Key Words

area:
square millimetre, square centimetre, square metre
rectangle
right-angled triangle
cube
cuboid
surface
surface area

Starters

Pupils draw a 3 × 3 grid and fill in the cells using any numbers between 1 and 25 (numbers can be used more than once). Call out times tables facts such as 2 × 5, 3 × 4, 6 × 4, etc. First pupil to cross off all their numbers is the winner (only one number crossed off at a time). Repeat with numbers between 40 and 100, calling out halving and doubling facts – e.g. half of 130, 90 ÷ 2, double 23 etc.

Plenaries

● *A 4 × 4 square is PERFECT. Why?* (Perimeter = area)
Can you find any perfect rectangles? (e.g. 3 × 6)
● Check misconceptions: units for perimeter are the same as for length e.g. cm, m, etc. Units for area are squared, e.g. cm², m², etc. and for volume are cubed e.g. cm³, m³, etc.

Teaching points

● Units of area as square units.
● The formulae for the areas of rectangles and right-angled triangles.
● To find the area of compound shapes divide the shape into simple parts and find the total of the areas of the parts.
● To find the area of more complicated shapes, either divide the area into simple parts as for compound shapes or surround the shape with a rectangle and subtract the area of the extra parts that you add.
● The surface area of a solid is the total area of all the faces of the solid.
● The concept of volume.
● The formula for the volume of a cuboid.

Notes

Pupils are expected to understand the algebraic formulae in this section. You may therefore wish to cover **Algebra 2** section 1 before undertaking this work.

Conversion of square units is not covered here but you may wish to introduce the concept that, for example, there are 100 mm² in 1 cm².

Questions ❻ and ❼ require perimeter from the last section together with area. Question ❼ is at Level 6 and you may wish to omit this with less confident pupils.

Question ⓯ can be done using the formula for the surface area of a cuboid. Less able pupils at this level will probably benefit from sketching the net and calculating the area of each face first.

To find the surface area of a solid it is usually best to sketch the net of the solid and work out the area of each face in turn and then find the total of these areas.

Homework

Unit Questions ❾ – ⓫

1 3-D shapes
Answers

1

	Cube	Cuboid	Square-based pyramid	Tetrahedron	Triangular prism
Faces	6	6	5	4	5
Edges	12	12	8	6	9
Vertices	8	8	5	4	6

2 a Circle   b 2   c None (0)

3 a A sphere has **one** curved face.
It has no **edges** or **vertices**.
b A hemisphere has one curved face and one **flat** face.
It has one **edge** and no **vertices**.

4 a Sphere   d Triangular prism
b Cuboid   e Square-based pyramid
c Cylinder   f Cube

5 Cuboid

6 faces, 8 vertices, 12 edges

6 a Triangle   b 7 faces, 15 edges, 10 vertices
c 8 faces, 18 edges, 12 vertices

7 a 2   b 4 If he could look down from above.

8 a

	Faces	Vertices	Edges
Cube	6	8	12
Cuboid	6	8	12
Square-based pyramid	5	5	8
Tetrahedron	4	4	6
Triangular prism	5	6	9

b Cube 14, Cuboid 14, Square-based pyramid 11,
Tetrahedron 8, Triangular prism 11
c faces + vertices − 2 = edges

9 a 6   b 6   c 5

10 a e.g.
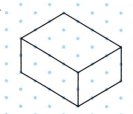
b 5 cuboids drawn and labelled with height, width and length.

11 a

b 24

12
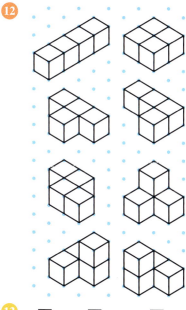

13
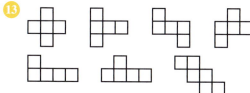

14 a 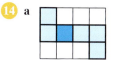   b

15
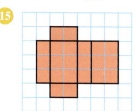

16 a Five from:

b One net for each of the cuboids in Question **10** b

17 a Any net of a cube
b e.g.

	4		
5	6	2	1
	3		

2   Length and perimeter   *Answers*

1
  a True
  b False   mm → m
  c True
  d False   km → m
  e True

2
  a m   **c** m   **e** mm   **g** m
  b cm   **d** km   **f** cm or mm **h** km

3
This morning I travelled 1.5 **km** to school. On the way I passed a tall building, it was over 20 **m** high. I stopped at the shop and bought a 15 **cm** ruler. Outside I splashed in a shallow puddle, it was 20 **mm** deep.

4
  a 12 cm
  b 12 cm

5
Height = 2.7 cm
Width = 7.2 cm
Perimeter = 19.8 cm

6
Two of:
10 cm × 1 cm rectangle
9 cm × 2 cm rectangle
8 cm × 3 cm rectangle
7 cm × 4 cm rectangle
6 cm × 5 cm rectangle
Pupils may include sides with non-integer lengths.

7
  a 22 cm
  b 24 cm
  c 26 cm
  d 30 cm

8
  a One of the shapes has angled sides which makes the edges longer.
  b Any two different shapes with base 1 cm and height 3 cm.

9
The larger shape is made up of two smaller shapes joined together. The part of the perimeter of each shape where they now join cannot be counted.

10
  a 60 cm
  b 38 cm
  c 45.2 cm

11
  a 30 cm   **b** 33 cm   **c** 32 cm

3   Area   *Answers*

1
  a 12 cm^2 **c** 175 mm^2 **e** 3.5 m^2 (35 000 cm^2)
  b 40 cm^2 **d** 15 m^2 **f** 200 mm^2 (2 cm^2)

2
  a 12 cm^2 **c** 48 mm^2 **e** 14 m^2
  b 20 cm^2 **d** 9 m^2 **f** 6 cm^2 (600 mm^2)

3 96 m^2

4 62 370 mm^2

5 480 mm^2

6
  a, b Rectangles can be: 12 cm × 1 cm
                             6 cm × 2 cm
                             3 cm × 4 cm
  c Any rectangle drawn in **a** and **b** split evenly in two to make a triangle.

7 A, C, B   length of side A = $\sqrt{36}$ = 6 cm
                 length of side C = $\frac{36}{4}$ = 9 cm

8
Area of rectangle A = **4 × 8**
                      = **32** cm^2
Height of rectangle B = **12 − 4**
                      = **8** cm
Width of rectangle B = **8 − 5**
                      = **3** cm
Area of rectangle B = **8 × 3**
                      = **24** cm^2
Area of shape = **32 + 24**
               = **56** cm^2

9
  a 75 cm^2 **b** 72 cm^2

10
Area of outer rectangle = **6 × 14**
                      = **84** cm^2
Area of hole = **3 × 5**
              = **15** cm^2
Green area = **84 − 15**
             = **69** cm^2

11 a 42 cm²   **b** 588 cm²

12 a $\frac{1}{2} \times 1 \times 1 + \frac{1}{2} \times 1 \times 2 + \frac{1}{2} \times 2 \times 2 + \frac{1}{2} \times 1 \times 2 = 4.5$ cm²
   b $3 \times 3 - (\frac{1}{2} \times 1 \times 1 + \frac{1}{2} \times 1 \times 2 + \frac{1}{2} \times 1 \times 2 + \frac{1}{2} \times 2 \times 2)$
      = 4.5 cm²

13 a 20 m²   **b** 24 m

14 148 cm²

15 76 cm²

16 a 2106.6 cm²   **b** 352.48 cm²   **c** 1149.12 cm²

17 $(80 \times 25 + 30 \times 25) \times 2 + 150 \times 30 + 150 \times 25$
             $+ 150 \times 50 + 150 \times 25$
             $+ 150 \times 80 + 150 \times 50$
                 $= 44\,500$ cm²

18 5.08 m² or 50 800 cm²

19 Cuboid A = 38 cm²
    Cuboid B = 32 cm²
    ∴ Not the same area.

Unit Questions: Shape, Space and Measures 1 — *Answers*

1 a 5
   b 9
   c 6

2 a Cylinder
   b Sphere
   c Cuboid

3

4 a, **b**, **c**

5 a 4 mm, 4 cm, 4 m, 4 km
   b 20 mm, 40 cm, 30 m, 10 km
   c 7 mm, 80 cm, 50 m, 2 km
   d 3 mm, 90 cm, 1 m, 4 km

6 a 10 cm
   b 14 cm

7 a 76 cm
   b 60 cm

8 a 35 cm
   b 35 cm
   c 63 cm

9 a 140 cm²
   b 70 cm²

10 a 100 cm²
    b 900 cm²

11 a 14 cm²
    b 70 cm²
    c 20 cm²
    d 208 cm²

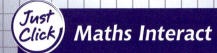

Maths Interact

Pupil Book page 47

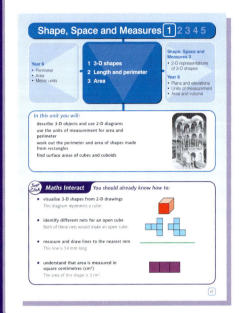

Pupils should already know how to:

- **visualise 3-D shapes from 2-D drawings**

  A 2-D drawing is shown together with a selection of 3-D images. Students have to decide which of the images may be represented by the drawing.

- **identify different nets for an open cube**

  Patterns of five squares are shown in a variety of configurations. The object is to identify which ones are nets of an open cube.

- **measure and draw lines to the nearest mm**

  The program features a whiteboard ruler that may be dragged and rotated. The ruler is used to measure the length of a line drawn on screen.

- **understand that area is measured in square cm (cm²)**

  A shape is presented on screen along with a grid of squares that may be positioned over the shape to determine its area.

Pupil Book page 68

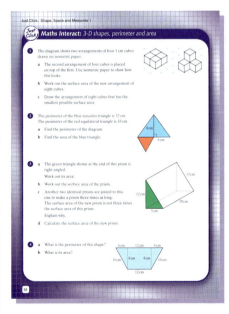

3-D shapes, perimeter and area

Maths Interact summary

1. The screen shows two arrangements of cubes on an isometric grid. Cubes may be dragged to make a new arrangement satisfying the given conditions.

2. A problem solving activity involving area and perimeter. Information is presented in written form and on a diagram.

3. This activity involves calculating areas based on a 2-D representation of 3-D shapes.

4. Each question presents a trapezium with lengths labelled. The perimeter and area are to be found in each case.

Pupil Book answers

1. a
   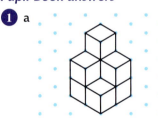

   b Surface area = 28 cm²

   c

2. a 38 cm   b 48 cm²

3. a 30 cm²   b 660 cm²
   c Four of the 'ends' are not on the outside of the new prism and so do not contribute to the new surface area.
   d 1860 cm²

4. a 56 cm   b 144 cm²

Number 1 2 3 4 5

Year 6
- Fractions
- Decimals
- Percentages

Number 1
- Decimals

1 **Fractions and decimals**

2 **Working with fractions**

3 **Percentages**

4 **Mental methods**

Number 4
- Ratio
- Proportion

Framework teaching programme

60–77	Fractions, decimals and percentages
92–101	Mental methods of calculation with fractions, decimals and percentages
110–111	Checking results
28–31	Solving problems

Overview

This unit develops the work on fractions, decimals and percentages that pupils saw in Year 6 and the decimals from **Number 1**. Mental openers can be used to see how much support individual pupils need with the revision topics from Year 6 that appear at the start of the unit. This unit links to the work on ratio and proportion that occurs in **Number 4**. The calculation of a fraction of an amount using a unitary fraction is covered here. Non-unitary fractions are introduced in **Number 5** where there is also a revision of the equivalence of decimals, fractions and percentages.

1 Fractions and decimals
▶ Fractional notation
▶ Small number as a fraction of a larger one
▶ Equivalent fractions and cancelling fractions
▶ Terminating decimals to fractions
▶ Comparing fractions

2 Working with fractions
▶ Adding and subtracting fractions
▶ Multiplying a fraction by an integer
▶ Finding fractions of amounts

3 Percentages
▶ Percentages
▶ Equivalence of percentages, decimals and fractions
▶ Percentages of amounts

4 Mental methods
▶ Addition and subtraction techniques
▶ Multiplication and division techniques

 Maths Interact

See page 38
and Pupil Book 7^C pages 69 and 92.

New concepts

Addition and subtraction of fractions

Calculating a fraction of an amount

Finding percentages of amounts

1 Fractions and decimals

Resources

Available on **Teacher Resource CD-ROM 7^c:**

Worksheet N2-1-1 ⑪
Extra Practice N2-1
Homework Sheet N2-1
Starter N2-1-1
Plenary N2-1-1

FRAMEWORK OBJECTIVES

Pages 60, 62, 64

▶ Fractional notation
▶ Small number as a fraction of a larger one
▶ Equivalent fractions and cancelling fractions
▶ Terminating decimals to fractions
▶ Comparing fractions

Key Words

fraction

numerator

denominator

equivalent

cancel, cancelling

decimal fraction

Starters

Use the fraction wall on page 71 of the Pupil Book to go around the class and ask each pupil a question such as: *Give me a fraction greater than $\frac{1}{3}$, Give me a fraction equal to $\frac{1}{4}$, Give me a fraction greater than $\frac{2}{5}$, Give me a fraction less than $\frac{3}{7}$, Give me a fraction equal to $\frac{4}{6}$,* etc.

Plenaries

Check vocabulary:

● n**U**merator and **D**enominator
  P   O
                  W
                  N

● Check misconceptions:
  Decimal equivalent of fractions, e.g. $\frac{1}{4} = 0.25$ and not 1.4, $\frac{2}{10} = 0.2$ and not 2.10

Teaching points

● Using fractions to describe simple parts of shapes.
● Writing a small number as a fraction of a larger number.
● Units must be the same if writing one quantity as a fraction of another quantity.
● Equivalent fractions.
● Cancelling fractions.
● Converting decimals to fractions.
● Using a fraction wall to compare the size of fractions.

Notes

In question ④ some pupils will think that one quarter of the shape is shaded.

In fact, you can establish that approximately $\frac{3}{8}$ of the shape is shaded if you use this diagram.

It would be exactly $\frac{3}{8}$ of course if the triangle were equilateral and the vertical lines split the base into exact quarters.

Question ⑭ requires pupils to write the fractions as equivalent fractions to see the larger one. You could make seeing the answer much more difficult for more able pupils by using the fractions $\frac{3}{5}$ and $\frac{2}{3}$. You could do this question in the blue section with less able pupils and allow them to use a fraction wall.

Question ⑳ will benefit from discussion with more able pupils. In any fraction $\frac{a}{b}$, with a and b taken from a list of consecutive integers, the greatest possible value is obtained by using the largest possible integer for a and the smallest possible for b, the least possible value is obtained by using the smallest possible integer for a and the largest possible for b, and the greatest possible value that is less than one is obtained by using the largest possible integer for b and the next largest for a.

Homework

Unit Questions ❶ – ❹

2 Working with fractions

FRAMEWORK OBJECTIVES
Pages 66, 68

▶ Adding and subtracting fractions
▶ Multiplying a fraction by an integer
▶ Finding fractions of amounts

Available on **Teacher Resource CD-ROM 7ᶜ:**

Worksheet N2-2-1 **1** and **3**
Extra Practice N2-2
Homework Sheet N2-2
Starter N2-2-1
Plenary N2-2-1

Plenaries

- Check misconceptions: Add only the numerators when the denominators are common, e.g. $\frac{3}{8} + \frac{2}{8} = \frac{5}{8}$ and not $\frac{5}{16}$. Encourage the pupils to say the question as three **eigths** + two **eigths** = five **eigths** in the same way that three **bananas** + two **bananas** gives five **bananas**.

- When the denominators are different, a common denominator must be found, e.g. $\frac{3}{8} + \frac{1}{4} = \frac{3}{8} + \frac{2}{8} = \frac{5}{8}$ and not $\frac{4}{12}$ by simply adding numerators and denominators. Possible analogy is three **sheep** + one **kangaroo** does not equal four **shangaroos** or four **kaneeps**.

Maths Interact

▶ Select Add to see how diagrams may be used to represent addition of fractions. Select Subtract to see how diagrams may be used to represent subtraction of fractions.

▶ This animation shows the process of multiplying a fraction by an integer.

▶ The process of calculating a fraction of an amount is presented as an animation.

Teaching points

- Simple addition and subtraction of fractions.
- Multiplying fractions by integers and finding fractions of quantities.

Key Words

fraction

numerator

denominator

integer

Notes

More formal methods for addition and subtraction will be covered in Year 8.

Multiplying fractions by integers and finding fractions of quantities involving improper fractions is covered in **Number 5**. Fractional answers are covered in Year 8.

The worksheet for questions **1** and **3** should be used by less able pupils at this level to ensure that they concentrate on the concepts rather than drawing diagrams.

Question **4** introduces a cross-curricular link with music and requires pupils to add the fractions of a beat for the various musical notes. You may wish to use the more challenging question from the extension book with the more able pupils.

Question **10** is challenging despite the fact that there is no need to use fractional notation. To make the largest solution the smallest integer in the list must be used as the divisor and the smallest solution is obtained by using the largest integer in the list as the divisor. You could encourage your best pupils to write the solutions using fractional notation.

Question **13** doesn't depend on which way the second turn is made although pupils will probably consider the two turns in the same direction.

Homework

Unit Questions **5** – **8**

3 Percentages

FRAMEWORK OBJECTIVES
Pages 70, 72, 98

▶ Percentages
▶ Equivalence of percentages, decimals and fractions
▶ Percentages of amounts

Resources

Available on **Teacher Resource CD-ROM 7^C:**

Worksheet N2-3-1 **8**
Extra Practice N2-3
Homework Sheet N2-3
Starter N2-3-1
Plenary N2-3-1

Starters

Shout out a fraction such as $\frac{1}{4}$, and ask the class to shout back the hundredth equivalent fraction, e.g, $\frac{25}{100}$. $\frac{1}{2}$ would give $\frac{50}{100}$, $\frac{1}{5}$ would give $\frac{20}{100}$, etc. Explain that the answers are all special fractions – in the denominator 100, the zero and one change places to give the % sign $\frac{1}{4}$ is 25%, $\frac{1}{2}$ is 50%, etc.

Plenaries

Ask the class: *Which is bigger – A. 10% of £15 or B. 15% of £10?* Pupils show their answers using wipeboards or a show of hands. Ask the pupils to discuss strategies and justify answers (the two answers are the same). *Does this always work?* Try 10% of £25 and 25% of £10, 25% of £20 and 20% of £25, etc. (use the common percentages of 10%, 20%, 25% and 50%).

Key Words

percentage (%)
fraction
lowest terms
decimal
amount

Teaching points

- Percentage as parts out of 100.
- Writing percentages as fractions and decimals by dividing the percentage by 100.
- Knowledge of simple equivalent percentages, fractions and decimals.
- Finding percentages of amounts both with and without a calculator. Without a calculator jot down the value of 10% and then use this to find 5% and/or 1% to enable the percentage required to be built up.

Homework

Unit Questions **9** – **12**

Notes

Pupils should be encouraged to explain their solutions as much as possible throughout this section. Emphasise the overall equivalence between percentage, fraction and decimal throughout. You may wish to cover

Questions **1** and **2** orally with more able pupils.

Question **3j** requires pupils to write $33\frac{1}{3}\%$ as the fraction $\frac{1}{3}$ and this may need some explanation. To see that

$33\frac{1}{3}\% = \frac{1}{3}$, first write $33\frac{1}{3}\% = \frac{33\frac{1}{3}}{100}$ and then multiply

numerator and denominator by 3 to get $\frac{100}{300} = \frac{1}{3}$. This will need careful explanation and you may wish to go on to consider other percentages of this type at this stage, e.g $66\frac{2}{3}\%$, $12\frac{1}{2}\%$ etc.

Question **4** parts **g** to **j** require pupils to deal with converting percentages to decimals where there is a fractional part to the percentage. Concentrate on getting

the pupils to convert the fraction to a decimal and then divide by 100.

So, for example, $12\frac{1}{2}\% = 12.5\% = 0.125$

The emphasis in the orange topic is the application of known simple equivalents and you should make sure that you allow the pupils plenty of opportunity to discuss the simple equivalents required. Using the calculator to calculate percentages of quantities and amounts should be relatively straightforward once the entry of the percentage into the calculator is understood. The use of a percentage key on a calculator should be discouraged although pupils may want to know how to use this key if their calculator has one.

Questions **11** and **12** require the pupils to explain their solutions and you will probably want to take plenty of oral answers with most pupils before asking pupils to write an explanation down. The most able pupils will be able to explain their method clearly but an oral explanation for some pupils will suffice here.

4 Mental methods

FRAMEWORK OBJECTIVES
Pages 92, 94, 96, 100

▶ Addition and subtraction techniques
▶ Multiplication and division techniques

Resources

Available on **Teacher Resource CD-ROM 7ᶜ:**

Worksheet N2-4-1
Worksheet N2-4-2
Extra Practice N2-4
Homework Sheet N2-4
Starter N2-4-1
Plenary N2-4-1

Starters

Draw '↑', '↓' and two boxes on the board – put a starting decimal in one box (such as 5.3) and a 'jump' decimal in the other box (such as 0.3). Point to either the up or down arrow and go around the class with pupils giving the next number in the sequence, e.g. 5.3, 5, 4.7, 4.4, etc. Change the direction of the sequence at any time by pointing at the appropriate arrow.

Key Words

add, addition

subtract, subtraction

double, halve

multiply, multiplication

divide, division

partition, partitioning

Teaching points

● Addition and subtraction methods including partitioning.
● Multiplication and division strategies including the use of factors, partitioning and doubles and halves. The use of partitioning for division is shown but is not covered in the exercise (there is a question in the Extension book).

Notes

Most of these methods should be accompanied by suitable jottings and not attempted entirely mentally. You should check that pupils are able to use the methods shown for whole number calculations as well as for decimals.

This is a carefully structured exercise, which allows pupils to practise each of the methods given. There are a few worded questions that require pupils to choose the best way of working out the problem and these will be more difficult for some pupils.

The **3 in a row** game on Worksheet N2-4-2 requires pupils to work in pairs and provides considerable practice of the main multiplication tricks within the game.

Homework

Unit Questions ⑬ – ⑯

1 Fractions and decimals — *Answers*

1
a $\frac{3}{7}$
c $\frac{9}{16}$
e $\frac{5}{16}$
b $\frac{2}{5}$
d $\frac{5}{12}$
f $\frac{3}{8}$

2
a $\frac{3}{7}$
b $\frac{3}{4}$
c $\frac{7}{9}$

3 In the fraction $\frac{7}{12}$, 7 is the numerator and 12 is the denominator

4 No. The parts are not of equal size.

5

6
a $\frac{1}{4}$
c $\frac{1}{3}$
e $\frac{2}{7}$
g $\frac{3}{16}$
b $\frac{1}{5}$
d $\frac{1}{6}$
f $\frac{3}{14}$
h $\frac{2}{11}$

7
a (1) $\frac{1}{4}$
(2) $\frac{1}{2}$
(3) $\frac{1}{8}$
(4) $\frac{1}{10}$
b (1) $\frac{1}{2}$
(2) $\frac{3}{4}$
(3) $\frac{1}{4}$
(4) $\frac{1}{8}$

8
a $\frac{1}{2}$
c $\frac{1}{12}$
e $\frac{2}{3}$
b $\frac{1}{2}$
d $\frac{3}{4}$
f $\frac{5}{12}$

9
a $\frac{15}{60}(\frac{1}{4})$
e $\frac{35}{100}(\frac{7}{20})$
i $\frac{750}{1000}(\frac{3}{4})$
b $\frac{20}{60}(\frac{1}{3})$
f $\frac{17}{100}$
j $\frac{200}{3000}(\frac{1}{15})$
c $\frac{20}{120}(\frac{1}{6})$
g $\frac{30}{100}(\frac{3}{10})$
d $\frac{30}{240}(\frac{1}{8})$
h $\frac{800}{1000}(\frac{8}{10})$

10
a 5 thumbs = $\frac{5}{12}$ foot
b 12 thumbs = 1 foot
c 6 thumbs = $\frac{6}{12} = \frac{3}{6} = \frac{1}{2}$ foot
d 8 thumbs = $\frac{2}{3}$ foot

11
North: $\frac{1}{2}$, $\frac{5}{10}$, $(\frac{6}{12})$, $\frac{3}{4}$
West: $\frac{2}{3}$, $\frac{8}{12}$, $(\frac{4}{6})$
East: $\frac{9}{12}$, $(\frac{6}{8})$
South: $(\frac{3}{12})$, $\frac{2}{8}$, $\frac{1}{4}$

12
a $\frac{10}{14} = \frac{5}{7}$
b $\frac{6}{9} = \frac{2}{3}$
c $\frac{24}{32} = \frac{12}{16} = \frac{6}{8} = \frac{3}{4}$
d $\frac{12}{48} = \frac{6}{24} = \frac{3}{12} = \frac{1}{4}$
e $\frac{12}{16} = \frac{3}{4}$
f $\frac{45}{75} = \frac{3}{5}$

13
a $\frac{2}{3} = \frac{6}{9}$
b $\frac{1}{3} = \frac{5}{15}$
c $\frac{3}{4} = \frac{18}{24}$
d $\frac{3}{5} = \frac{18}{30}$
e $\frac{5}{12} = \frac{15}{36} = \frac{30}{72}$
f $\frac{3}{8} = \frac{12}{32} = \frac{24}{64}$

14 More pupils play football. $\frac{2}{3}$ is larger than $\frac{2}{5}$. ($\frac{2}{3} = \frac{10}{15}$, $\frac{2}{5} = \frac{6}{15}$)

15
a $0.5 = \frac{5}{10} = \frac{1}{2}$
b $0.7 = \frac{7}{10}$
c $0.31 = \frac{31}{100}$
d $0.35 = \frac{35}{100} = \frac{7}{20}$
e $2.24 = 2\frac{24}{100} = 2\frac{12}{50}$
f $1.65 = 1\frac{65}{100} = 1\frac{13}{20}$

16
a $\frac{3}{10}$
b $\frac{8}{10} = \frac{4}{5}$
c $\frac{1}{2}$
d $\frac{31}{100}$
e $1\frac{35}{100} = 1\frac{7}{20}$
f $5\frac{45}{100} = 5\frac{9}{20}$
g $2.26 = 2\frac{26}{100} = 2\frac{13}{50}$
h $1.375 = 1\frac{375}{1000} = 1\frac{3}{8}$

17
a 0.1
b (1) 0.3 (3) 0.2
(2) 0.7 (4) 0.6

18
a $\frac{3}{4}$
c $\frac{5}{6}$
e $\frac{3}{5}$
b $\frac{7}{8}$
d $\frac{6}{7}$
f $\frac{3}{7}$

19
a $\frac{1}{2} > \frac{1}{3}$
d $\frac{2}{3} > \frac{1}{2}$
b $\frac{2}{7} > \frac{1}{5}$
e $\frac{2}{3} < \frac{5}{7}$
c $\frac{1}{4} < \frac{3}{8}$
f $\frac{3}{8} > \frac{1}{3}$

20
a $\frac{2}{6}$
b $\frac{5}{6}$
c $\frac{6}{2}$

2 Working with fractions — *Answers*

1
a $\frac{4}{12}$ (or $\frac{1}{3}$)
b $\frac{2}{12}$ (or $\frac{1}{6}$)
c $\frac{8}{12}$ (or $\frac{2}{3}$)

2
a $1\frac{1}{2}$
b $\frac{3}{8}$
c $\frac{6}{10}$ or $\frac{3}{5}$

3
a $\frac{3}{5}$
c $\frac{4}{6}$ or $\frac{2}{3}$
e $\frac{3}{4}$
b $\frac{4}{7}$
d $\frac{5}{9}$
f $\frac{1}{2}$

4
a $\frac{1}{2}$
c $1\frac{5}{8}$
e $1\frac{3}{16}$
b $\frac{7}{8}$
d 1
f $2\frac{1}{16}$

5
a (1) 6 (2) 6 (3) 6 (4) 6
b They are all the same sum.

6
a 18
c 10
b 21
d 24

7 Kevin 40, Steven 32

8
a 6
c 4
b 12
d 9

9
a (1) $8 \times 7 \div 3 = 18.\dot{6}$
(2) $3 \times 7 \div 8 = 2.625$
b Using the largest numbers for the product and the smallest for the divisor results in the largest possible answer. Reversing this process gives the smallest possible answer.

10　**a**　(1)　20 mℓ concentrate
　　　　(2)　100 mℓ water
　　b　(1)　30 mℓ concentrate
　　　　(2)　150 mℓ water
　　c　(1)　110 mℓ concentrate
　　　　(2)　550 mℓ water

11　300 g beef
　　2 tablespoons tomato puree
　　100 mℓ water
　　4 sheets lasagne pasta
　　400 mℓ cheese sauce
　　50 g grated cheese
　　$\frac{2}{3}$ pack of lasagne mix

12　No. Rachel has only turned 350°
　　and not a full circle of 360° if both
　　turns are in the same direction. The
　　two turns are not equal so do not
　　cancel each other out if she turns
　　the other way the second time.

13　**a**　30 mins　**b**　75 mins　**c**　$\frac{3}{10}$

14　C, D, A, B

15　C because $\frac{2}{5}$ of £50 is £20.
　　A is only £19.
　　B is only £18.

3　Percentages　　　　　　　　　　　　　　*Answers*

1　**a**　(1) 36%　(2) 64%
　　b　(1) 87%　(2) 13%
　　c　(1) 26%　(2) 74%
　　d　(1) 92%　(2) 8%
　　e　(1) 24%　(2) 76%
　　f　(1) 60%　(2) 40%

2　**a**　60%　　　　　**b**　40%

3　**a**　$\frac{27}{100}$　　　　**f**　$\frac{3}{20}$
　　b　$\frac{3}{10}$　　　　**g**　$\frac{13}{20}$
　　c　$\frac{3}{5}$　　　　**h**　$\frac{1}{4}$
　　d　$\frac{4}{5}$　　　　**i**　$\frac{3}{4}$
　　e　$\frac{1}{20}$　　　　**j**　$\frac{1}{3}$

4　**a**　0.17　　　　**f**　0.08
　　b　0.4　　　　**g**　0.375
　　c　0.62　　　　**h**　0.125
　　d　0.46　　　　**i**　0.035
　　e　0.05　　　　**j**　0.355

5　**a**　To change a percentage into a decimal you divide by **100**.
　　b　(1) 1　(2) 2　(3) 1.5　(4) 2.25

6　**a**　25% = $\frac{1}{4}$　　　　**e**　75% = $\frac{3}{4}$
　　b　10% = $\frac{1}{10}$　　　　**f**　40% = $\frac{2}{5}$
　　c　**50% = $\frac{1}{2}$**　　　　**g**　$33\frac{1}{3}$% = $\frac{1}{3}$
　　d　20% = $\frac{1}{5}$　　　　**h**　$66\frac{2}{3}$% = $\frac{2}{3}$

7　**a**　50%　　**c**　75%　　**e**　40%　　**g**　80%
　　b　25%　　**d**　20%　　**f**　60%　　**h**　10%

8　**a**　
```
0    0.25   0.5   0.75   1

0    25%   50%   75%   100%

0     1/4   1/2   3/4    1
```

b
```
0      0.333...  0.666...    1

0      33⅓%    66⅔%    100%

0       1/3     2/3      1
```

c
```
0  0.1 0.2 0.3 0.4 0.5 0.6 0.7 0.8 0.9  1

0  10% 20% 30% 40% 50% 60% 70% 80% 90% 100%

0  1/10 1/5 3/10 2/5 1/2 3/5 7/10 4/5 9/10  1
```

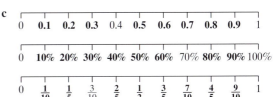

9　**a**　5.04 m　　　　**f**　429 mm
　　b　32.43 kg　　　**g**　£784.42
　　c　£428.40　　　**h**　2019.6 litres
　　d　510 g　　　　**i**　£320
　　e　$2329.60　　　**j**　£681.50

10　**a**　10% of £400 = 400 ÷ **10** = **£40**
　　　　1% of £400 = **400** ÷ **100** = **£4** (or 40 ÷ 10 = £4)
　　b　(1) £80　(3) £12　(5) £152
　　　　(2) £20　(4) £92　(6) £188

11　**a**　£82.50
　　b　10% of £550 = 550 ÷ 10　　= 55
　　　　5% of £550 = 　55 ÷ 2　　= 27.50
　　　　　　　　　　　 55 + 27.50 = 82.50

12　**a**　£12 + £6 + £3 = £21
　　b　Dividing by 10 gives 10%, halving the answer gives 5%,
　　　　halving again gives 2.5%
　　　　10% + 5% + 2.5% = 17.5%

13　**a**　304 kg　　　**b**　221 kg

4   Mental methods   *Answers*

1 **a** 3.9, 4, 4.1
     e 10, 9.9, 9.8
   b 16.1, 16.2, 16.3
     f 2.02, 2.01, 2
   c 13, 13.1, 13.2
     g 3.99, 4, 4.01
   d 12.1, 12, 11.9
     h 100, 99.99, 99.98

2 **a** 173

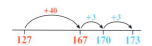

   b (1) 17.3   (3) 127   (5) 12.7   (7) 1.27
       (2) 1.73   (4) 46   (6) 4.6   (8) 0.46

3 **a**

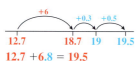

    12.7 + 6.8 = 19.5

   b

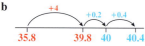

    35.8 + 4.6 = 40.4

   c

    32.5 − 5.9 = 26.6

   d

    56.3 − 9.7 = 46.6

4 Ben could add 9.7 and 6.6 to check that it gives 16.3.

5 **a** $24.6 + 4.9 = 24.6 + 5 - 0.1$
                 $= 29.6 - 0.1$
                 $= 29.5$
   b $6.8 + 7.9 = 6.8 + 8 - 0.1$
              $= 14.8 - 0.1$
              $= 14.7$
   c $67.3 - 39 = 67.3 - 40 + 1$
              $= 27.3 + 1$
              $= 28.3$
   d $98.2 - 69 = 98.2 - 70 + 1$
              $= 28.2 + 1$
              $= 29.2$

6 **a** $14.6 + 6.8 = 14.6 + 7 - 0.2$
              $= 21.6 - 0.2$
              $= 21.4$
   b $15.8 + 7.8 = 15.8 + 8 - 0.2$
              $= 23.8 - 0.2$
              $= 23.6$
   c $47.3 - 38 = 47.3 - 40 + 2$
              $= 7.3 + 2$
              $= 9.3$
   d $84.2 - 58 = 84.2 - 60 + 2$
              $= 24.2 + 2$
              $= 26.2$

7 **a** $13.5 + 13.6 = 13.5 + 13.5 + 0.1$
                 $= 2.7 + 0.1$
                 $= 27.1$
   b $12.2 + 12.4 = 12.2 + 12.2 + 0.2$
                 $= 24.4 + 0.2$
                 $= 24.6$
   c $9.3 + 8.9 = 9 + 0.3 + 9 - 0.1$
               $= 18 + 0.3 - 0.1$
               $= 18.2$
   d $30.7 + 29.8 = 30 + 0.7 + 30 - 0.2$
                 $= 60 + 0.7 - 0.2$
                 $= 60.5$

8 $20.4 - 14.8 = 5.6$
    $20.4 - 5.6 = 14.8$
    $5.6 + 14.8 = 20.4$

9 1.6 kg

10 **a** $4.1 \times 30 = 4.1 \times 10 \times 3$
             $= 41 \times 3$
             $= 123$
   b $6.7 \times 40 = 6.7 \times 10 \times 4$
             $= 67 \times 4$
             $= 268$
   c $3.7 \times 70 = 3.7 \times 10 \times 7$
             $= 37 \times 7$
             $= 259$
   d $8.2 \times 50 = 8.2 \times 100 \div 2$
             $= 820 \div 2$
             $= 410$

11 **a** $18.6 \div 6 = 18.6 \div 3 \div 2$
             $= 6.2 \div 2$
             $= 3.1$
   b $42.4 \div 8 = 42.4 \div 4 \div 2$
             $= 10.6 \div 2$
             $= 5.3$
   c $80.1 \div 9 = 80.1 \div 3 \div 3$
             $= 26.7 \div 3$
             $= 8.9$
   d $66.4 \div 8 = 66.4 \div 2 \div 2 \div 2$
             $= 33.2 \div 2 \div 2$
             $= 16.6 \div 2$
             $= 8.3$

12 **a** $3.7 \times 11 = (3.7 \times 10) + (3.7 \times 1)$
             $=\quad 37 \quad + \quad 3.7$
             $= 40.7$
   b $4.8 \times 12 = (4.8 \times 10) + (4.8 \times 2)$
             $=\quad 48 \quad + \quad 9.6$
             $= 57.6$
   c $3.3 \times 9 = (3.3 \times 10) - (3.3 \times 1)$
             $=\quad 33 \quad - \quad 3.3$
             $= 29.7$
   d $2.6 \times 8 = (2.6 \times 10) - (2.6 \times 2)$
             $=\quad 26 \quad - \quad 5.2$
             $= 20.8$

13   **a**   5 × 3 = 15   **c**   25 × 6 = 150   **e**   7 × 5 = 35   **15**   £184
     b   13 × 4 = 52   **d**   3 × 9 = 27   **f**   65 × 2 = 130

14   60.8 ÷ 8 = 7.6   **16**   £43.20
     60.8 ÷ 7.6 = 8
     8 × 7.6 = 60.8

Unit Questions: **Number 2**   *Answers*

1

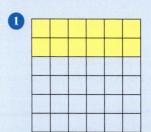

Any 12 squares coloured in.
One third of 36 is 12.

2   **a** $\frac{70}{100} = \frac{7}{10}$ **c** $\frac{15}{60} = \frac{1}{4}$
     b $\frac{250}{1000} = \frac{1}{4}$ **d** $\frac{750}{1000} = \frac{3}{4}$

3   **a** $\frac{5}{10}$
     b $\frac{6}{12}, \frac{7}{14}, \frac{8}{16}, \frac{9}{18}$
     c $\frac{4}{12}, \frac{5}{15}, \frac{6}{18}, \frac{7}{21}, \frac{8}{24}, \frac{9}{27}$
     d $\frac{3}{12}, \frac{4}{16}, \frac{5}{20}, \frac{6}{24}, \frac{7}{28}, \frac{8}{32}, \frac{9}{36}$

4   **a** $\frac{2}{5}$ **d** $\frac{1}{4}$
     b $\frac{3}{5}$ **e** $\frac{7}{20}$
     c $\frac{1}{2}$ **f** $1\frac{3}{4}$

5   **a** $3\frac{1}{2}$ **b** $\frac{3}{5}$ **c** $\frac{7}{13}$

6   **a**   16   **c**   10
     b   30   **d**   18

7   **a**   60 cm
     b   750 g
     c   40 minutes

8   This puzzle is easy

9   **a**   (1) 67%   (2) 33%
     b   (1) 42%   (2) 58%
     c   (1) 16%   (2) 84%

10   **a**   (1) $\frac{7}{20}$ (2) 0.35
     b   (1) $\frac{4}{5}$ (2) 0.8
     c   (1) $\frac{11}{50}$ (2) 0.22
     d   (1) $\frac{3}{4}$ (2) 0.75

11   **a**   £70   **e**   £140
     b   £35   **f**   £154
     c   £7   **g**   £259
     d   £14   **h**   £623

12   21

13   **a**   3, 3.1, 3.2
     b   10.01, 10, 9.99

14   **a**   245
     b   (1) 24.5
           (2) 2.45
           (3) 187
           (4) 5.8
           (5) 1.87
           (6) 0.245

15   **a**   18.6   **f**   14.3
     b   61.1   **g**   29.8
     c   13.1   **h**   13.4
     d   78.4   **i**   61.3
     e   39.2
     Working must be shown

16   **a**   102   **f**   7.4
     b   30.8   **g**   9.1
     c   340   **h**   33
     d   80   **i**   60
     e   70
     Working must be shown

Maths Interact

Pupil Book page 69

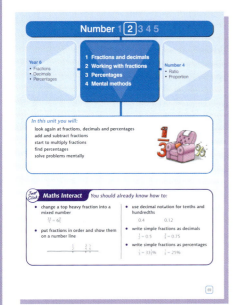

Pupils should already know how to:

- **change a top heavy fraction into a mixed number**

  Select Examples to determine the method using diagrams. Select Practice for questions without diagrams.

- **put fractions in order and show them on a number line**

  Three random fractions are presented for each question. They may be dragged into position on a number line for comparison.

- **use decimal notation for tenths and hundredths**

  A decimal is described in words and the response is to enter this number in figures using decimal notation.

- **write simple fractions as decimals**

  A matching game in which fractions and equivalent decimals are shown on cards. Clicking a pair of matching cards causes them to disappear.

- **write simple fractions as percentages**

  This is a variation of the matching game above in which fractions are matched to the corresponding percentages.

Pupil Book page 92

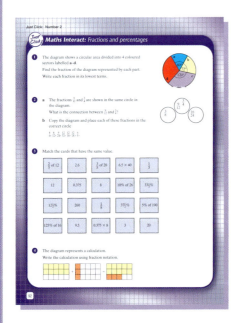

Fractions and percentages

Maths Interact summary

1. A circle is divided into coloured sectors. The angle of the sector is known and the object is to determine the fraction of the circle in its simplest form.

2. Three circles are shown, each one containing a single fraction. Further fractions may be dragged into place so that all fractions in a given circle are equivalent.

3. A matching game in which percentages of amounts and their values are shown on cards. Clicking a pair of matching cards causes them to disappear.

4. Addition of fractions is represented on a diagram. The corresponding calculation is to be set out using standard notation.

Pupil Book answers

1. a $\frac{1}{6}$ c $\frac{1}{3}$
   b $\frac{1}{5}$ d $\frac{3}{10}$

2. a $\frac{9}{12}$ and $\frac{3}{4}$ are equivalent fractions.
   b Group 1: $\frac{9}{24}, \frac{3}{8}, \frac{12}{32}$
   Group 2: $\frac{12}{16}, \frac{3}{4}, \frac{9}{12}$
   Group 3: $\frac{4}{6}, \frac{8}{12}, \frac{16}{24}, \frac{12}{18}, \frac{6}{9}$

3. $\frac{2}{3}$ of 12 = 8,   2.6 = 10% of 26,
   $\frac{3}{5}$ of 20 = 12,   6.5 × 40 = 260,
   $\frac{1}{3}$ = 33$\frac{1}{3}$%,   0.375 = 37$\frac{1}{2}$%,
   12$\frac{1}{2}$% = $\frac{1}{8}$,
   5% of 190 = 9.5,
   125% of 16 = 20,
   0.375 × 8 = 3

4. $\frac{2}{3} + \frac{1}{5} = \frac{13}{15}$

Handling Data 1 2 3

Year 6
- Line graphs
- Frequency tables
- Bar charts

1 Averages and range
2 Interpreting diagrams
3 Probability
4 Probability experiments

Handling Data 2
- Questionnaire design
- Line graphs
- Frequency diagrams
- Pie charts

Framework teaching programme

256–261 Calculate averages and range
268–271 Interpret diagrams

276–283 Understand the probability scale
Collect data from a simple experiment

Overview

This unit consists of three main teaching sections, covering averages and range, interpreting diagrams and introduction to the language of probability. The fourth section is different in style and provides practical probability experiments. The averages section includes median, mode and mean from simple data, and modal class and mean from a frequency table. The Interpreting diagrams section concentrates on single distributions.

1 Averages and range
▶ Finding the median of a set of data
▶ Finding the mode and the modal group
▶ Finding the range of a set of data
▶ Finding the mean of a set of data
▶ Finding the mean from a frequency table

2 Interpreting diagrams
▶ Interpreting bar charts
▶ Interpreting line graphs
▶ Interpreting pie charts
▶ Doing calculations from pie charts

3 Probability
▶ Using probability scales
▶ Using numbers to describe probabilities
▶ Calculating simple probabilities
▶ Deciding if events are equally likely

4 Probability experiments
▶ Four probability experiments

 Maths Interact
See page 46
and Pupil Book 7^C pages 93 and 118.

New concepts

Median
Mean, including from a frequency table

Probability scale from 0 – 1

1 Averages and range

Resources

Available on **Teacher Resource CD-ROM 7^C:**

Extra Practice D1-1
Homework Sheet D1-1
Starter D1-1-1
Starter D1-1-2
Starter D1-1-3
Plenary D1-1-1
Plenary D1-1-2
Plenary D1-1-3

FRAMEWORK OBJECTIVES
Pages 256, 258, 260

▶ Finding the median of a set of data
▶ Finding the mode and the modal group
▶ Finding the range of a set of data
▶ Finding the mean of a set of data
▶ Finding the mean from a frequency table

Starters

Give the salaries for the members of a small company; Director: £120 000, Supervisor: £21 000, three Machine Operatives: £14 000 each, Cleaner: £6000.
Ask pupils to calculate the mean, median and mode. *If the workers were campaigning for a pay rise, which average would they use and why? Likewise, which average would the Director use to argue against the rise?*

Check common problem areas:

● Finding the median for an even number of numbers. *What is the quick way of finding the midpoint of two numbers?* (Add them together and halve the result.)

Teaching points

● Finding the median of a set of data including from an even number of data values.
● Finding the mode of a set of data including the fact that the mode can be used for non-numerical data (such as modal colour).
● Finding the range of a set of data.
● Finding the mean of a set of data.
● Finding the mean from a frequency table by adding an extra column to the table.

Key Words

average
data
frequency
mean
median
mode
modal value
modal class
range
table

Notes

This section covers all three types of average as well as the range. The main stumbling points are probably finding the median of a set of data where there are an even number of data values. This involves finding the two 'middle' values with the median being the mean of these two. It can help pupils to write out the list of values and then to cross out values from each end of the list to find the middle one(s).

Finding the mean from a frequency table is also quite difficult. It is important that pupils understand what they are doing when they calculate the total in the extra column in the table. In the example on page 95, it is important to stress that there were **8** matches with **2** goals, which is a total of **16** goals.

Homework

Unit Questions –

2 Interpreting diagrams

FRAMEWORK OBJECTIVES
Pages 268, 270

▶ Interpreting bar charts
▶ Interpreting line graphs
▶ Interpreting pie charts
▶ Doing calculations from pie charts

Resources

Available on **Teacher Resource CD-ROM 7ᶜ:**

Extra Practice D1-2
Homework Sheet D1-2
Starter D1-2-1
Plenary D1-2-1
Plenary D1-2-2

Key Words

bar chart

line graph

pie chart

percentage

Starters

Use graphs and charts taken from newspapers and magazines to demonstrate different types of statistical diagrams. These could be collected by pupils as a previous homework. Interpret them as a class and look for common points to note, such as axes not starting at zero in order to maximise the effect of changes.

Teaching points

- Interpreting bar charts, including compound bar charts where colours are used to split a bar into a number of sections such as male and female.

- Interpreting line graphs, including time series graphs.

- Interpreting pie charts, especially trying to say what percentage or fraction of the chart a sector represents.

- Calculations from pie charts, particularly finding the percentage of a total. This skill is covered in **Number 2** but may need some revision.

Notes

The real skill in reading bar charts is looking carefully at the vertical scale. Most pupils find this relatively straightforward. The same skill is involved in reading line graphs. The effect of changing the vertical scale is picked up in *How to solve it*.

The work on pie charts is quite demanding. It involves estimating percentages and fractions which is worth practising. Pupils need to understand that pie charts always represent how a whole is divided up. Finding a percentage of a total was covered in **Number 1** but may need some revision.

Homework

Unit Questions ❽ – ❾

3 Probability

Resources

Available on **Teacher Resource CD-ROM 7^C:**

Extra Practice D1-3

Homework Sheet D1-3

Starter D1-3-1

Starter D1-3-2

Plenary D1-3-1

Plenary D1-3-2

FRAMEWORK OBJECTIVES

Pages 276, 278, 280

▶ Using probability scales
▶ Using numbers to describe probabilities
▶ Calculating simple probabilities
▶ Deciding if events are equally likely

Key Words

probability

scale

tally

impossible

likely

certain

unlikely

event

Starters

Have a probability scale (with words and/or numbers) ready drawn on the board. Get pupils to write down and illustrate an event on a piece of paper. Then ask them to come and stick it on the line where they think it should go. Discuss. This makes good display material.

Teaching points

- Using probability scales, initially with word descriptions to mark points.
- Using probability scales mainly with fractions but also with decimals and percentages.
- Calculating simple probabilities and writing them mainly as fractions.
- Situations where the probabilities of events are not equal or the situation is not fair.

Notes

The first two topics deal with simple probability scales. This starts with words and then moves on to using fractions, decimals and percentages. The vast majority of questions stick with fractions but there are a couple using percentages and decimals. The third topic deals with calculating probabilities. The stress should be on the fact that the base of the fraction is always the total number of possible outcomes. No formal definition of probability is given in the book as this can become very wordy or sound very complicated. Pupils mustn't write probabilities in the form '1 in 4'. The final topic stresses that not all situations produce equally likely events. The examples are based around situations where there is an element of personal choice.

Homework

Unit Questions ⑩ – ⑫

4 Probability experiments

▶ Four probability experiments

Teaching points

- Experiments can be used to estimate probabilities.
- A repeated experiment often gives a different result.
- The rules of a game may not be fair.
- Biasing a dice affects the result of an experiment.

Notes

This section is not in the usual format for the book. It consists of a double page spread of four probability experiments.

The value of these is to show pupils that what probability predicts in theory does not always happen in reality. They also get over the concept that a repeated experiment will probably have a different outcome. The experiments are also used to introduce the idea of bias.

A worksheet is available for Experiment 4 if you do not want pupils to draw their own nets of dice.

As development for future GCSE coursework, one or more of these experiments could be formally written up if time permits.

Resources

Available on **Teacher Resource CD-ROM 7^C:**

Worksheet D1-4-1

Homework Sheet D1-4

Starter D1-4-1

Plenary D1-4-1

Other resources required

coloured counters	**dice**
envelopes	**blu-tak**
sellotape	**glue**
scissors	

Just Click Maths Interact

▶ A biased dice is shown for which 4 of the scores are equally likely. The dice is rolled once each time the Dice button is clicked until 10 scores have been obtained. The results are shown in a table and the object is to try to decide which score is favoured by the bias.

Once 10 scores have been obtained, a further 10 results are generated, each time the dice button is clicked, up to a maximum of 100.

Clicking New produces a dice with a different bias.

Key Words

probability
tally
table
record
bias
fair

Homework

Experiments could be written up as a homework task.

1 Averages and range

1 a 16   b 178   c 32   d 61.5

2 16.15

3 150

4 a 4, 4, 4, 5, 5, 5, 5, 6, 6, 6, 6, 6, 6, 6, 7, 7, 7, 7, 8, 8, 8, 9, 9
   b 6

5 Hatchback

6 a 410   b France

7 a 27
   b £0
   c £4.90
   d The median average is better as 18 out of 27 pupils earned more than £0.

8 £0.50–£0.99

9 16–20

10 33 cm

11 a 6   b 2

12 107 seconds

13 a 24.4   c 33
   b 139.333…   d 0.56

14 42 minutes

15 a 5.6875
   b 5.7
   c Go up because the judge awarded a higher score than the mean.

16 a Tanya's taxi   13.2 minutes
     Carrie's taxi   12 minutes
   b Tanya   3 minutes
     Carrie   15 minutes
   c Tanya's taxi as the range is smaller.

17 325

18 66

19 2

20 40.22 As this is larger than the stated mean, the machine is likely to be working properly.

21 Better than average as more golfers are taking 4 or less shots.

22 a Mean   29
     Median   29
     Mode   30
   b Use the mode as this shows the largest number of buttons in the packet.

2 Interpreting diagrams

1 a 19   b 24   c 13   d 82

2 a 34   b 42   c 56

3 a False. 7R raised £38.
   b Can't tell
   c True
   d True: £211 ÷ 6 more than £30
   e False. £211 in total.

4 a 10%
   b Y10, Y11
   c Sweets
   d Cannot tell which class spends the most as the results are in percentages and do not give the actual amounts of money spent.
   e £1.20

5 a 5%   c 2001–2002
   b 29%   d At first, DVDs were expensive and not widely available.

6 Temperature rises steadily until July then remains constant between July and August and then starts to fall.

7 Answers should be around:
   a 45%   b 55%   c 65%   d 35%

8 a Answers should be around:

	17–20	21–30	31–40	41–50	51–60	Over 60	Total
Females	52%	18%	15%	5%	5%	5%	100%
Males	59%	24%	8%	4%	3%	2%	100%

   b A larger percentage of male drivers pass their test between the ages of 17–20 than female drivers.

9 Answers should be around:
   a Vodafone 35%   b Vodafone 158
     O_2 30% O_2 135
     Orange   20%   Orange   90
     Virgin   10%   Virgin   45
     Other   5%   Other   22

10 Pupil's own reports. Could include:
Zaxton spent   £20.8 million more on education
              £10.4 million less on social services
              £41.6 million more on police
              £41.6 million less on transport
              £10.4 million less on publicity

3 Probability — *Answers*

1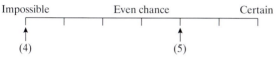

(1), (2) and (4) Individual

2 **a** and **c**
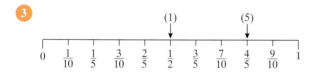

(1), (2) and (3) Pupil's own answers.
b Pupil's probability descriptions.

3

(2), (3) and (4) Pupil's own answers.

4 **b** Answers marked on probability scale.
(1) 40%   (2) 10%   (3) 80%   (4) 50%

5 $\frac{1}{300}$

6 $\frac{1}{4}$

7 **a** $\frac{2}{11}$ **b** $\frac{2}{11}$ **c** $\frac{2}{11}$ **d** $\frac{4}{11}$

8 **a** $\frac{1}{6}$ **b** $\frac{1}{2}$ **c** $\frac{4}{6}$ or $\frac{2}{3}$ **d** $\frac{1}{2}$

9 **a** $\frac{3}{8}$ **c** 0   **e** $\frac{1}{2}$ **g** $\frac{3}{8}$
 b $\frac{1}{8}$ **d** $\frac{6}{8}$ or $\frac{3}{4}$ **f** $\frac{3}{4}$ **h** $\frac{3}{8}$

10 2 fours, 2 other even numbers and 2 odd numbers.

11 **a** Red triangle: There are only 9 cards left to choose from, 3 of which are triangles.
b Yellow hexagon. There is only one of them.
c 0. There are no more yellow hexagons to choose from.
d Red triangle. There are 3 triangle cards out of the 8 cards that are left.
e Green circle. There are 2 out of 4 cards with circles on.

12 $\frac{7}{12}$. There is a greater than half chance she will choose a packet that she likes.

13 **a** $\frac{9}{49}$ **c** $\frac{20}{49}$ **e** $\frac{24}{49}$ **g** $\frac{15}{49}$
 b $\frac{10}{49}$ **d** $\frac{39}{49}$ **f** $\frac{25}{49}$ **h** $\frac{7}{49}$ or $\frac{1}{7}$

14 **a** A larger proportion of the total tickets sold are green than either blue or red.
b Green $\frac{300}{650} = \frac{6}{13}$ Blue $\frac{200}{650} = \frac{4}{13}$ Red $\frac{150}{650} = \frac{3}{13}$

15 No. Practice times suggest that Edmund is more likely to win.

16 No. Probability of having an accident affected by tiredness, alcohol, driver age and experience and the number of miles driven each year.

17 **a** Because there is more red than any other colour.
b Red $\frac{1}{2}$, blue $\frac{1}{3}$, green $\frac{1}{6}$

18 Jane is incorrect.
Richard is incorrect the proportions are the same.
Katy is correct.
Divide both the red and the blue counters evenly between the bags.

Unit Questions: **Handling Data 1** — *Answers*

1 **a** 45   **b** 46.5   **c** 143   **d** 81.5

2 **a** 53   **b** Walk

3 £80, £220

4 85.196 kg

5 16

6 2

7 79%

8

	Books	Clothes	Tins	Cardboard	Plastic	Glass	Paper
Recycle already	10%	35%	30%	15%	25%	45%	65%
Willing to start	25%	35%	45%	30%	35%	25%	20%

9 **a** Plain   **b** $\frac{1}{10}$

10 Strawberry 7   Orange 2
Raspberry 3   Lemon 0

11 **a** $\frac{2}{7}$ **b** $\frac{1}{6}$

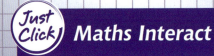

Maths Interact

Pupil Book page 93

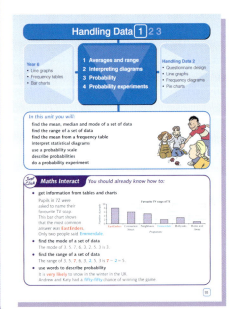

Pupils should already know how to:

- **get information from tables and charts**

  Select Table or Chart to be presented with information in that form. Questions are then asked that require some interpretation of the information shown.

- **find the mode of a set of data**

  A table of 20 randomly chosen values is presented in a table. The object is to find the mode or modal values.

- **find the range of a set of data**

  A table of 20 randomly chosen values is presented in a table. The object is to find the range.

- **use words to describe probability**

  A randomly selected event is presented using a simulation of a fruit machine display. The object is to discuss the likelihood of the event.

Pupil Book page 118

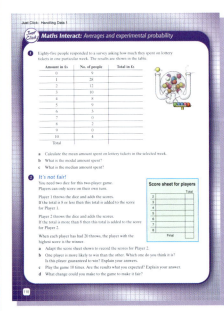

Averages and experimental probability

Maths Interact summary

1 The results of a survey on the amount of money that people spend on lottery tickets are shown in a table. The mean, median and mode are to be found from the table.

2 The rules for a two-player dice game are given. The scoring system is different for the two players and pupils are encouraged to discuss the likely outcome. A simulation of 10 games may then be played.

Pupil Book answers

1 a mean = £2.74
  b mode = £1
  c median = £2

2 a

Score	Tally	Total
9		
10		
11		
12		
Game total		

b The rules favour Player 1. If play continued indefinitely then, on average, every 36 throws Player 1 would score 26 times making a total of 152 and giving an average score per throw of $\frac{152}{36}$. Player 2, however, would only score 10 times with a total of 100 giving an average of $\frac{100}{36}$. Neither player is guaranteed to win in a game with 20 throws.

c Pupil's answer

d One way to make the game fair is to count scores of 3 and 5 for Player 2 instead of Player 1. This gives an expected average of $\frac{126}{36}$ for both players.

Algebra 1 **2** 3 4 5

Algebra 1
- Using letters for unknowns

1 Writing letters
2 Collecting like terms
3 Substitution

Algebra 4
- Multiplying out brackets
- Constructing and solving linear equations

Framework teaching programme

112–119 Formulae and expressions
138–143 Using formulae

26–27 Solving problems

Overview

This unit continues the work on algebraic notation from **Algebra 1**. The unit develops the use of correct notation and leads to the correct order for algebraic operations including brackets. This unit also introduces collecting like terms, multiplying out a bracket and substitution into expressions and formulae. The unit ends by deriving simple expressions and formulae.

1 Writing letters

▶ Using correct algebraic notation
▶ Understanding the correct order of algebraic operations
▶ Using inverse operations

2 Collecting like terms

▶ Collecting like terms
▶ Multiplying out a bracket
▶ Simplifying algebraic fractions

3 Substitution

▶ Substituting into simple linear expressions
▶ Substituting into formulae expressed in words and symbols
▶ Deriving expressions and formulae

 Maths Interact

See page 54
and Pupil Book 7^C pages 119 and 136.

New concepts

The order of algebraic operations
Multiplying out an expression in a bracket by a single term

Substitution into expressions and formulae

Algebra 2

1   Writing letters

FRAMEWORK OBJECTIVES
Pages 112, 114

▶ Using correct algebraic notation
▶ Understanding the correct order of algebraic operations
▶ Using inverse operations

Resources

Available on **Teacher Resource CD-ROM 7^C:**

Extra Practice A2-1
Homework Sheet A2-1
Starter A2-1-1
Plenary A2-1-1

Plenaries

- Ensure that pupils know the difference between the words 'equation' and 'expression'.
- Check misconceptions: $7 - n \neq n - 7$
  $$n \div 3 = \frac{n}{3}, \textbf{not } \frac{3}{n}.$$

Key Words

expression

brackets

equals (=)

term

equation

inverse

Teaching points

- The meaning of algebraic expressions involving the four rules.
- Correct algebraic notation for products, quotients and squares.
- The use of brackets when addition or subtraction is required before multiplication.
- The equivalence of equations such as $c = a + b, c = b + a, a + b = c$ and $b + a = c$.
- The order of operations – multiplication and division take precedence over addition and subtraction.
- Anything included in brackets is to be done first.
- Addition and subtraction are inverse operations.
- Multiplication and division are inverse operations.

Notes

The red topic is a revision of the last topic in **Algebra 1**.

The order of algebraic operations is covered in the orange topic although BODMAS is not properly covered until **Number 3**.

Questions ❻ and ❼ are based on the SATs questions in **Algebra 1**.

Inverse operations are covered in the yellow topic. Two stage inverses are introduced using questions ⑫ and ⑬. Question ⑫ does not require any algebraic explanation but the fact that the inverse of two operations is the inverse of each operation in the reverse order is required in Question ⑬, which will be demanding for many pupils at this level.

Homework

Unit Questions ❶ – ❺

48

2 Collecting like terms

FRAMEWORK OBJECTIVES
Pages 116

▶ Collecting like terms
▶ Multiplying out a bracket
▶ Simplifying algebraic fractions

Resources

Available on **Teacher Resource CD-ROM 7ᶜ:**

Worksheet A2-2-1 **3**
Extra Practice A2-2
Homework Sheet A2-2
Starter A2-2-1
Plenary A2-2-1
Plenary A2-2-2
Plenary A2-2-3

Key Words

term

simplify

expression

brackets

cancel, cancelling

lowest terms

Starters

Pupils collect like terms almost every day of their lives without realising it. Ask some pupils to empty their pockets of money. Look for cases where you can demonstrate, for example, $10p + 5p + 2p = 17p$. Talk about having a mixture of UK pennies and American cents and that these cannot be combined.

Plenaries

Check misconceptions:
$14b - 5 \neq 9b$
$2x - 7x \neq 5x$
$2(a + b) \neq 2a + b$
$6m - m \neq 6$

Teaching points

- Terms involving the same combination of letters are like terms.

- pq and qp terms are like terms.

- Adding and subtracting like terms to simplify expressions.

- Multiplying out a bracket by a single positive term.

- $\dfrac{x}{x} = 1$ as anything divided by itself is 1.

- Simplifying algebraic fractions by cancelling.

Notes

Colour is used to highlight like terms in question **1** but is removed in Question **2**.

Remind pupils about perimeter before question **5**, which also requires pupils to draw a shape given its perimeter as an algebraic expression. Clearly there are many possible answers for this and you should discuss several different answers.

Multiplying a bracket using a partitioning diagram is covered in question **9**, which also introduces multiplying a bracketed expression by a letter term rather than just a number.

Worksheet A2-2-1 can be used to save pupils drawing the brick diagrams in question **3** and allow them just to fill the diagrams in.

Homework

Unit Questions **6** – **9**

3 Substitution

FRAMEWORK OBJECTIVES

Pages 138, 140

▶ Substituting into simple linear expressions
▶ Substituting into formulae expressed in words and symbols
▶ Deriving expressions and formulae

Resources

Available on **Teacher Resource CD-ROM 7ᶜ:**

Extra Practice A2-3

Homework Sheet A2-3

Starter A2-3-1

Plenary A2-3-1

Plenary A2-3-2

Starters

Have three expressions, such as $3x - 2$, $x + 3$ and $2x + 1$ written on the board ready. The whole class stand up. Give a pupil a number (for x) and ask them to substitute it into any one of the three expressions (tell them which one). If they give the correct answer, they get to sit down and pick the next student, number and expression. If they give an incorrect answer, they still sit down but the previous pupil gets to choose the next pupil again. Encourage pupils to stick to whole numbers between 1 and 15, or simple decimals.

Just Click — Maths Interact

▶ Substitution of a value for a variable is presented as an animation. The animation is controlled through the use of the animation player.

▶ A formula for the number of months in a given number of years is presented in words. A formula for the volume of a cuboid is given in symbols. The use of these formulae is presented as an animation.

▶ The formula for the number of months in a given number of years is now re-written in symbols and used within an animation.

Teaching points

● Substitute values into an expression or formula by replacing the letter with the number.
● Writing and using expressions and formulae.

Key Words

expression

variable

value

evaluate

substitute

formula, formulae

Notes

Pupils need to understand that the letters used in an expression are variables and as such, the same expression can be evaluated using any value.

When evaluating expressions and formulae stress that a substitution is taking place and use the football analogy to help. A common error made by pupils when substituting values is to leave the letter substituted in the expression or formula i.e. when substituting $x = 3$ into the expression $x + 5$, pupils often write their answer as $3x + 5 = 8$.

Finally, when using algebra to write a formula, pupils need to be encouraged to select the most appropriate letters. Usually the most obvious will suffice.

Homework

Unit Questions ⑩ – ⑬

1 Writing letters — Answers

1
a $y + 5$
b $x - 8$
c $5z$
d $\frac{p}{4}$
e $2k + 7$
f $\frac{a}{2}$
g $2j - 3$
h $\frac{16}{q}$
i w^2
j $4d + 7$
k $\frac{e}{2} - 8$
l $\frac{g}{4} + 6$
m t
n $5(b - 3)$
o $3(a + b)$
p $r(s - 2)$

2 a $4n$ b $6y$ c $5a$

3
a $2n, 3$
b $3x, 4y, {}^-2z$
c $5x, {}^-3y, {}^-6z, 8$

4
a $y = x$
b $s = t - r$ or $r = t - s$
c $a = b + c$ or $a - c = b$

5
a $3n$ means 3 times n.
$n + 3$ means add 3 to n.
b $2p$ means 2 times p.
p^2 means multiply p by p.
c $3(n + 1)$ means add 1 to n and then multiply by 3.
$3n + 1$ means multiply n by 3 and then add 1.

6 Harry is **one year younger than Bob**.
Jay is **twice as old as Bob**.

7
a $a + 4, 3a$
b $b - 4, 3(b - 4)$
c $\frac{c}{3}, \frac{c}{3} + 4$

8
a Multiply n by 2 and then add 3.
b Add 3 to n and then multiply by 2.
c Divide n by 12 then add 5.
d Divide n by 8 then subtract 4.
e Multiply n by 3 then add 5.
f Subtract 2 from n then multiply by 4.
g Multiply n by 4 then subtract this from 5.
h Divide n by 6 then subtract this from 12.

9
a $2 + 3 = 5$ $4 + 5 = 9$ $7 + 3 = 10$ $a + b = b + a$
$3 + 2 = 5$ $5 + 4 = 9$ $3 + 7 = 10$
b $2 \times 3 = 6$ $4 \times 5 = 20$ $7 \times 3 = 21$ $a \times b = b \times a$
$3 \times 2 = 6$ $5 \times 4 = 20$ $3 \times 7 = 21$ $ab = ba$
c $2 + (3 + 4) = 9$ $5 + (2 + 1) = 8$ $a + (b + c) = (a + b) + c$
$(2 + 3) + 4 = 9$ $(5 + 2) + 1 = 8$
d $2 \times (3 \times 4) = 24$ $5 \times (2 \times 4) = 40$ $a \times (b \times c) = (a \times b) \times c$
$(2 \times 3) \times 4 = 24$ $(5 \times 2) \times 4 = 40$ $a(bc) = (ab)c$

10
a subtract 4
b add 8
c divide by 4
d multiply by 7
e -3
f $+2$
g $\div 5$
h $\times 10$

11
a If $p + q = 6$ then $p = 6 - q$ and $q = 6 - p$
b If $r \times s = 14$ then $r = \frac{14}{s}$ and $s = \frac{14}{r}$
c If $p = 6 - q$ then $q = 6 - p$ and $p + q = 6$
d If $r = \frac{12}{s}$ then $s = \frac{12}{r}$ and $r \times s = 12$

12 8

13 Subtract 3 from 48 then divide by 5.

2 Collecting like terms

1
a $9g$
b $4p$
c $8u$
d v
e $9ab$
f $4rs$
g $9ut$
h $7bc$
i $9g + 9h$
j $4j + 6k$
k $10d + 2e$
l $5w + 5e$
m $9xy + 8gh$
n $9pq + 10st$
o $12uv + 10$
p $nm + 5$

2
a $7a$
b $6b$
c $8c$
d d
e $6ef$
f $6g + 2h$
g $3i + 4j$
h $8kl + 2$
i $5p + 9q + r$
j $9rs + 4t + 6$

3
a
	$2a + 2b$		
	$a + b$	$b + a$	
a	b	a

b
	$2a + 4b$		
	$a + 2b$	$a + 2b$	
a	$2b$	a

c
	$d + 2e + f$	
$d + e$	$e + f$	
d	e	f

d
	$5pq + 4rs$	
$4pq + 2rs$	$2rs + pq$	
$4pq$	$2rs$	pq

4
a $2a$
b $7b$
c $a + 2b$
d $2xy$
e p
f $3pq$

5
a (1) $3a + b$
(2) $2a + 2b$
(3) $8a + 6$
b e.g. rectangle 6 by $3a$ or triangle with sides $3a$, $3a$ and 12.

6
a $8k + 7$
b $2k + 5$
c $5t + 7$
d $3b + 17$

7
a $4x + 4y$
b $3a + 3b$
c $5p - 5q$
d $6f - 6g$
e $4x + 8y$
f $6a + 9b$
g $15c - 5d$
h $10g + 15h$
i $12j - 18k$
j $6x + 15$
k $20x - 16$
l $5xy + 15$
m $21 - 7y$
n $12 - 10rs$
o $40xy - 30yz$

8
a $3ac$
b $4de$
c $5tu$
d $6sv$
e $5abc$
f $6fgh$

9
a
	y	z
x	xy	xz

$x(y + z) = xy + xz$

c
	$2m$	n
p	$2mp$	np

$p(2m + n) = 2mp + np$

b
	s	t
r	rs	rt

$r(s + t) = rs + rt$

d
	$3p$	$4q$
n	$3np$	$4nq$

$n(3p + 4q) = 3np + 4nq$

10
a $5a + 5b$
b $3a + 6b$
c $4a - 4b$
d $6a + 3$
e $ab + 4ac$
f $4ab + ac$

11
a 1
b 2
c 3
d $2a$
e $3b$
f $4c$

12
a $\dfrac{3a}{4}$
b $\dfrac{2a}{3}$
c $\dfrac{2}{3}$
d $\dfrac{3}{8}$
e $\dfrac{4}{5}$
f $\dfrac{6}{7}$
g $\dfrac{1}{2}$
h $\dfrac{x}{2}$
i $\dfrac{2q}{3}$

3 Substitution — *Answers*

1
a 21   d 4   g 8   j 4   m 0
b 25   e 8   h 30   k 4   n 5
c 7   f 15   i 6   l 7

2
a 15   c 8   e 28   g 12
b 22   d 30   f 0   h 119

3
a (1) 12   (2) 12   (3) 12   (4) 12
b They are all the same.
c $4b$

4
a (1) 40   (2) 23   (3) 63   (4) 32
b $4(w + 3) = 4w + \mathbf{12}$

5 8; If $2n = 16$ then $n = 8$ (or equivalent).

6 31

7 a 35   b 56   c 84   d 210

8 a 4   b 6   c 10   d 21

9 a £28   b £19.20   c £17.88

10 a 35 cm^2 b 9 cm^2 c 552 mm^2 d 38.54 cm^2

11 a 35   b 114   c 11

12
a 75 units^2 c 265.08 units^2
b 147 units^2 d 439.23 units^2

13
a $d = 365y$ c $y = \dfrac{m}{12}$
b $p = 4l$ d $c = pl$

14
a (1) $r + 10$
   (2) $2r$
   (3) $2r - 5$
b $T = r + r + 10 + 2r + 2r - 5 = 6r + 5$

15 a $m = \dfrac{5}{8}k$

16 a $2c + 2d + e$ b $2h$

Unit Questions: **Algebra 2** — *Answers*

1
a $w - 3$ c $4y$ e b^2 g $\dfrac{d}{4} - 2$
b $x + 7$ d $\dfrac{z}{2}$ f $3c + 5$ h $\dfrac{e}{2} + 7$

2 a $5n$ b $4z$ c $7a$

3
a Multiply c by 2 then subtract 4.
b Multiply t by 5 then add 2.
c Multiply d by 4 then add 7.
d Add 4 to w and then multiply by 3.
e Divide g by 4 then add 9.
f Divide h by 6 then subtract 2.
g Subtract 7 from v then multiply by 5.
h Multiply n by 9 then add 2.

4
a subtract 5   c divide by 6   e -7 g $\div 3$
b add 2   d multiply by 4   f $+1$ h $\times 8$

5
a If $g + h = 8$ then $g = 8 - \mathbf{h}$ and $h = \mathbf{8 - g}$
b If $y \times z = 20$ then $y = \dfrac{20}{z}$ and $z = \dfrac{20}{y}$

6
a $9j$ e $13p + 11t$ i $2f + 1$
b $2w$ f $4d + 7e$ j $3p + 10$
c $9cd$ g $19st + 8ef$ k $7t + 5$
d $6st$ h $ab + ef$ l $10d$

7
a $2bc$ c tu e $3abc$
b $5de$ d $3sw$ f $5fgk$

8
a $3a + 3b$ d $7f - 14$ g $am + 2an$
b $4c + 12$ e $12h + 6j$ h $3bp - 2bq$
c $4d - 4e$ f $10 - 4k$

9
a $\dfrac{3}{8}$ c $\dfrac{5y}{6}$ e $\dfrac{6a}{7}$ g $\dfrac{3t}{4}$
b $\dfrac{1}{2}$ d $\dfrac{d}{3}$ f $\dfrac{q}{4}$ h $\dfrac{8y}{9w}$

10
a 14   d 6   g 4   j 6
b 9   e 16   h 4   k 21
c 21   f 17   i 22   l 15

11
a £225   c £276.20
b £323   d £453

12 a 60   b 20   c 90

13
a (1) $w + 12$
   (2) $3w$
   (3) $3w - 4$
b $T = w + w + 12 + 3w + 3w - 4 = 8w + 8$

Just Click — Maths Interact

Pupil Book page 119

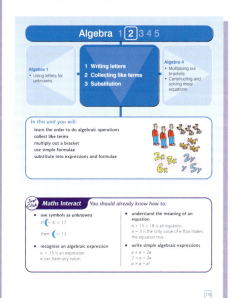

Pupils should already know how to:

- **use symbols as unknowns**

  Symbols representing unknown values are used to make very simple statements. The value of the symbol is to be found in each case.

- **recognise an algebraic expression**

  A very simple expression is defined in terms of a single variable. Choose a value for the variable and then enter the value of the expression.

- **understand the meaning of an equation**

  Letters representing unknown values are used to make very simple equations. Pupils are asked to find the value of the letter that makes the equation true.

- **write simple algebraic expressions**

  Expressions are presented, or described, that may be written simply using standard algebraic notation for multiples and powers of a variable. The standard screen keypad has been modified to allow the expressions to be entered.

Pupil Book page 136

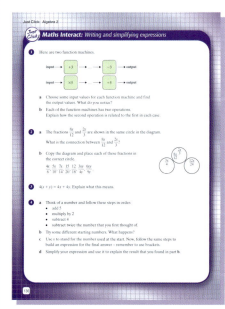

Writing and simplifying expressions

Maths Interact summary

1 A two stage function machine is used to demonstrate the effect of applying an operation followed by its inverse.

2 Three circles are shown, each one containing a single algebraic fraction. Further algebraic fractions may be dragged into place so that all fractions in a given circle are equivalent.

3 Enter a value for x and a value for y. An animated sequence then demonstrates that $4(x + y)$ has the same value as $4x + 4y$.

4 An animation demonstrates that a particular sequence of steps produces the same Finish number for any Start number. Algebra is used to explain the result.

Pupil Book answers

1 **a** The output is the same number as the input.

   b The second operation is the inverse of the first.

2 **a** The fractions are equivalent

   b Group 1: $\dfrac{2x}{3}$, $\dfrac{4x}{6}$, $\dfrac{8x}{12}$, $\dfrac{12x}{18}$, $\dfrac{6xy}{9y}$

   Group 2: $\dfrac{15x}{20}$, $\dfrac{3xy}{4y}$, $\dfrac{3x}{4}$

   Group 3: $\dfrac{5x}{10}$, $\dfrac{12x}{24}$, $\dfrac{7x}{14}$

3 If you add x and y and then multiply by 4, this is the same as multiplying x by 4, y by 4 and adding the two together.

4 **a** Pupil's work.

   b The answer is always 6.

   c $2(x + 5) - 4 - 2x$

   d The expression simplifies to 6. Regardless of which number you start with the x terms cancel out leaving 6 as the answer.

Year 6
- Using a protractor
- Drawing angles
- Plotting coordinates
- Checking that angles in a triangle total 180°

1 **Angles**
2 **Triangles and quadrilaterals**

Shape, Space and Measures 3
- Constructions

Shape, Space and Measures 4
- Reflections
- Rotations
- Translations

Framework teaching programme

178–189 Geometrical reasoning applied to lines, angles and shapes

232–233 Understanding angle

218–219 Using coordinates in all four quadrants

Overview

This unit consists of two main teaching sections covering angle and angle facts, and properties of triangles and quadrilaterals and the use of coordinates in all four quadrants.

1 Angles
- ▶ Measuring angles
- ▶ Estimating angles
- ▶ Calculating angles on a line and at a point
- ▶ Calculating angles in a triangle
- ▶ Using vertically opposite angle

2 Triangles and quadrilaterals
- ▶ Recognising different triangles
- ▶ Recognising different quadrilaterals
- ▶ Coordinates in four quadrants
- ▶ Solving problems with coordinates

 Maths Interact

See page 60
and Pupil Book 7^C pages 137 and 156.

New concepts

Calculating angles at a point
Vertically opposite angles are equal

Coordinates in four quadrants

1 Angles

FRAMEWORK OBJECTIVES
Pages 178, 180, 182, 232

▶ Measuring angles
▶ Estimating angles
▶ Calculating angles on a line and at a point
▶ Calculating angles in a triangle
▶ Using vertically opposite angle

Resources

Available on **Teacher Resource CD-ROM 7ᶜ:**

Extra Practice S2-1
Homework Sheet S2-1
Starter S2-1-1
Plenary S2-1-1

Other resources required

protractors or angle measurers

Starters

Ask the pupils to close their eyes and hold out their right arm horizontally and extend their index finger. Gives instructions such as spin 90° clockwise, 45° anticlockwise, etc. Every now and again ask the pupils to open their eyes to see if their finger is pointing in the same direction as the rest of the class. Who is better at estimating angles – boys or girls?

Plenaries

Key misconception: Reading protractors – encourage the pupils to estimate the angle before measuring it, especially whether they think the angle is acute, obtuse or reflex, This should then help if they are confused about whether to read off 60° or 120° from the protractor.

Just Click — Maths Interact

▶ An angle of random size is shown on screen and the object is to estimate its size within a tolerance of 3°. Feedback is given to allow an estimate to be improved until the desired level of accuracy is achieved.

Teaching points

- Measuring angles with a protractor.
- Labelling angles with letters.
- Estimating the size of angles and classifying them as acute, right, obtuse or reflex.
- Calculating angles around a point and knowing that they total 360°.
- Calculating angles in triangles.
- Knowing that vertically opposite angles are equal.

Key Words

angle

triangle

angles at a point

straight line

vertically opposite

intersect

Notes

Much of the early part of this chapter will have been covered before. However, careful use of a protractor or angle measurer is always worth practising. The calculation of angles requires some algebra and this can be done either formally as linear equations or less formally as a mental exercise. Questions ⑫ – ⑱ use concepts seen in the whole section and allow pupils to solve some general angles questions after question ⑪, which specifically deals with opposite angles.

Question ⑯ relies on pupils realising that the 54° angle can either be one of the equal angles or the distinct angle in the isosceles triangle. Question ⑰ introduces the idea of two lines in 3-D space being skew so that they are neither parallel nor intersect. Very few pupils will get this immediately but it is a good discussion point.

Angles can be written in a number of ways. In the book the three letter convention is used. The three letters are written down in order from the end of one arm of the angle through the apex to the other arm. This angle is therefore ∠ABC. This can also be written as AB̂C or sometimes as just ∠B.

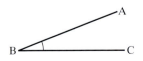

Homework

Unit Questions ❶ – ❻

2 Triangles and quadrilaterals

FRAMEWORK OBJECTIVES
Pages 186, 218

▶ Recognising different triangles
▶ Recognising different quadrilaterals
▶ Coordinates in four quadrants
▶ Solving problems with coordinates

Resources

Available on **Teacher Resource CD-ROM 7ᶜ:**

Worksheet S2-2-1 ⑤
Extra Practice S2-2
Homework Sheet S2-2
Starter S2-2-1
Plenary S2-2-1
Squared paper

Other resources required

rulers   protractors

mirrors (optional)

Key Words

triangle	rectangle
isosceles	parallelogram
equilateral	rhombus
scalene	trapezium
right-angled	kite
quadrilateral	vertex
square	vertices

Starters

Use Question ⑤ from the Pupil Book to introduce the key words for this section.

Plenaries

Pupils draw a set of axes from 0 to 5 on both axes. They place a battleship (4 crosses in a line), frigate (3 crosses in a line) and 2 dinghies (single cross) somewhere on their grid. The crosses are placed only at whole numbers – e.g. battleship at $(1, 0)$, $(2, 0)$, $(3, 0)$, $(4, 0)$. Go around the class asking pupils to shout out a pair of coordinates trying to sink other pupils' ships. Pupils are out when all parts of their ships have been sunk. (Draw an empty grid on the board to show where the shots hit.)

Check misconception: plotting coordinates – $(2, 4)$ is 2 across and 4 up and not 2 up and 4 across. Remember – x is a cross, wise up!

Teaching points

- To recognise the different properties of triangles.
- To recognise the basic quadrilaterals.
- To use coordinates in all four quadrants.
- To solve coordinate problems using the geometric properties of shapes.

Notes

The teaching in the first part of this section looks at common shapes and their properties. Lines of reflection symmetry are dealt with in **Shape, Space and Measures 3**. Time should be spent demonstrating the links between the rectangle and the parallelogram and the rhombus and the square.

When introducing coordinates sayings such as 'along the corridor and up the stairs' or 'walk before you climb' may be used to help pupils identify which coordinate is written first. When plotting a point, say $(3, 4)$, pupils will often mark a cross at the point $(3, 0)$ and another at $(0, 4)$ and then join these with a line. Pupils must understand that each bracketed pair of numbers defines a single point on the grid.

Homework

Unit Questions ⑦ – ⑩

Shape, Space and Measures 2

1 Angles — *Answers*

1
a (1) 50° (2) ∠ABC
b (1) 125° (2) ∠WXY
c (1) 255° (2) ∠TSR
d (1) 113° (2) ∠JKL
e (1) 323° (2) ∠LMN
f (1) 97° (2) ∠PQR
g (1) 307° (2) ∠FDE
h (1) 292° (2) ∠NMO

2 Angles should be close to those given.
a (1) Acute (2) 25°
b (1) Obtuse (2) 160°
c (1) Obtuse (2) 145°
d (1) Reflex (2) 250°
e (1) Reflex (2) 310°
f (1) Obtuse (2) 95°
g (1) Acute (2) 35°
h (1) Reflex (2) 272°
i (1) Obtuse (2) 138°
j (1) Reflex (2) 342°

3 Angles should be close to those given.
a (blue) (1) ∠ABC (2) 80°
  (red) (1) ∠ACB (2) 45°
b (blue) (1) ∠QPR (2) 75°
  (red) (1) ∠QSR (2) 105°
c (blue) (1) ∠WVZ (2) 90°
  (red) (1) ∠VZY (2) 120°

4
a 160° f 72.5°
b 130° g 85°
c 85° h 67°
d 161° i 100°
e 125°

5
a $a = 110°$ d $d = 50°$ g $g = 60°$
b $b = 145°$ e $e = 72°$ h $h = 57°$
c $c = 133°$ f $f = 39°$ i $i = 104°$

6 a $a = 110°$ b $b = 60°$ c $c = 56°$

7
a $a = 60°$ d $d = 43.3°$
b $b = 120°$ e $e = 32°$
c $c = 45°$ f $f = 90°$
  $g = 36°$

8
a $a = 65°$ c $c = 70°$ e $e = 53°$
b $b = 35°$ d $d = 45°$ f $f = 49°$

9
a $a = 32°$ c $c = 72°$
b $b = 63°$ d $d = 45°$

10
a $a = 58°, x = 122°$ d 139°
b $b = 48°, y = 101°$ e 119°
c $c = 87°, z = 93°$ f 121°

11
a $w = 36°$ c $a = 152°$
  $x = 144°$ $b = 28°$
  $y = 144°$ $c = 28°$
b $p = 147°$
  $q = 33°$
  $r = 33°$

12 a 2 hours b 3 hours c 5 hours

13 91.3125 days

14 16°

15
a False. There are 180° in a triangle, and there has to be three angles. Two right angles already add up to 180° so this would be impossible.
b True
c False. Angles of a triangle add up to 180° and a reflex angle is more than 180°.
d True

16 Pupil's diagrams showing triangles with angles 54°, 54°, 72° and 54°, 63°, 63°

17 Lines could be drawn parallel in two dimensions or in three dimensions.

18
a $x = 50°$
b $c = 60°$
  $d = 60°$
  $e = 60°$
  $f = 60$
c $a = 34°$
  $b = 72°$
  $c = 74°$
  $d = 106°$
d $e = 67°$
  $f = 113°$
  $d = 67°$
  $g = 67°$
  $h = 67°$
  $i = 113°$

2 Triangles and quadrilaterals — *Answers*

1
a $a = 4$ cm, $b = 4$ cm, $c = 4$ cm
The triangle has **3** equal sides.
It is called an **equilateral** triangle.
b $d = 60°, e = 60°, f = 60°$
The triangle has **3** equal angles.
An **equilateral** triangle has **3** equal sides and **3** equal angles.

2
a $j = 5$ cm, $k = 5$ cm, $l = 3$ cm
The triangle has **2** equal sides.
It is called an **isosceles** triangle.
b $m = 73°, n = 73°, p = 34°$
The triangle has **2** equal angles.
An **isosceles** triangle has **2** equal sides and **2** equal angles.

3 AB = **6 cm** BC = **3 cm** AC = **4 cm**
∠BAC = **25°** ∠ABC = **37°** ∠ACB = **118°**
A scalene triangle has **no** equal sides and **no** equal angles.

4
a No. An equilateral triangle has 3 angles of equal size (60°).
b Yes. An isosceles triangle has 2 sides that are the same length and 2 angles of equal size. The angles would be 90°, 45°, 45°.

5
Three sides of different lengths – Scalene Triangle
Four equal sides and four equal angles – Square
Two different pairs of equal sides and four equal angles – Rectangle
Two different pairs of equal sides and two different pairs of equal angles – Parallelogram
Exactly three equal angles – Equilateral triangle

6
a There are 2 different pairs of parallel equal sides.
b All angles are equal in a rectangle. There are 2 pairs of equal angles in a parallelogram.

7 a (2, 2) (1, 4) (5, 6) b (6, 4)

8 b
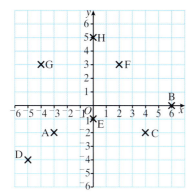

9 a, b
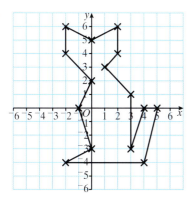

c Cat

10 a–c
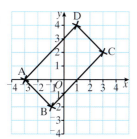

d (1, 4)

11 a–c
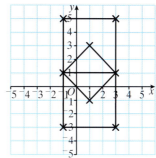

12 a–b
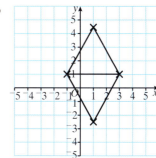

c (1, 4.5)(1, ⁻2.5) (*y* values correct to 1 d.p.)

13 Game

14 a (1) Any point on line *x* = ⁻1 with *y* < 1
(2) (⁻1, 1)
(3) (⁻1, 4)

b No. A rectangle has 2 pairs of sides of equal length.

15 c Possible positions include:
(1, ⁻1)   (1, 0)   (1, 1)   (1, 3)

d They have the same *x*-coordinate.

Unit Questions: **Shape, Space and Measures 2**   *Answers*

1 a Acute, ∠ABC, 75°
b Obtuse, ∠EFG, 127°
c Reflex, ∠RST, 305°

2 a 115° ∠BAC, 65° ∠ACD
b 65° ∠PRS, 115° ∠RSQ

3 a 129°   **b** 71°   **c** 48°

4 a 49°   **b** 41°   **c** 69°

5 a *r* = 153°, *s* = 27°, *t* = 153°

6 a 20 mins   **c** 45 mins
b 7.5 mins

7 a False   **c** False
b True   **d** False

8 a Parallelogram
b Trapezium
c Rhombus

9 a, b
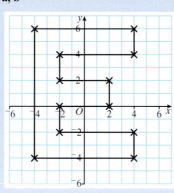

c The letter E

10 a, b
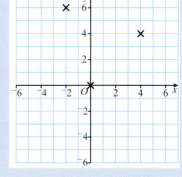

c (1) (6, ⁻2)
(2) (⁻6, 2)
(3) e.g. (4, 0)

59

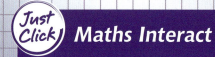

Maths Interact

Pupil Book page 137

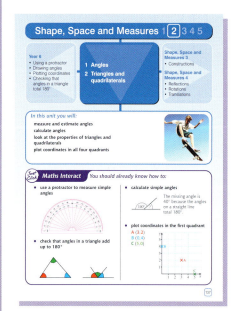

Pupils should already know how to:

- **use a protractor to measure simple angles**

  The program features a whiteboard protractor that may be dragged and rotated. The protractor is used to measure an angle between 0° and 180° drawn at random on the screen.

- **check that angles in a triangle add up to 180°**

  A triangle is shown and its interior angles are coloured. The coloured angles may be dragged on to a straight line to demonstrate that their sum is 180°.

- **calculate simple angles**

  Each question shows two angles on one side of a straight line. One angle is given and the other is to be calculated.

- **plot coordinates in the first quadrant**

  Coordinates of three points A, B and C are given. Clicking on a grid marks the positions of these points. Once all three have been placed their positions may be adjusted.

Pupil Book page 156

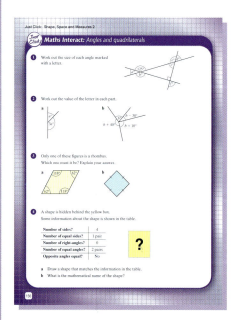

Angles and quadrilaterals

Maths Interact summary

① Angle properties of straight lines and triangles are needed to calculate unknown angles shown on a diagram.

② This activity is essentially about the application of algebra to problem solving within the context of finding unknown angles.

③ A quadrilateral is shown in which the lengths of the sides may be changed without changing its angles. A second quadrilateral is then shown in which the angles may be changed while the sides remain fixed in length. Pupils are expected to deduce which of two given shapes must be a rhombus.

④ A shape is hidden from view but information about the shape is shown. Pupils have to draw a shape that matches the information and write down its name. The Show button reveals the shape.

Pupil Book answers

① **a** 55° **c** 35° **e** 145°
   b 125° **d** 35° **f** 90°

② **a** $a = 45°$
   b $b = 85°$

③ Shape **b** must be the rhombus. In shape **a**, only the angles are given and this tells us nothing about the lengths of the sides. In shape **b**, the sides are fixed with equal length and so the shape is always a rhombus even though the angles may change.

④ **a**

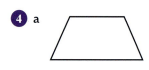

   b Trapezium.

Handling Data 1 2 3

Handling Data 1
- Interpreting diagrams

Handling Data 2
1 Collecting information
2 Drawing diagrams
3 Interpreting diagrams

Handling Data 3
- Statistics project

Framework teaching programme

248–255	Collect and organise data	268–271	Interpret graphs and diagrams
262–265	Construct graphs and diagrams	24–25	Solving problems

Overview

1 Collecting information
- ▶ Different types of data
- ▶ Open and closed questions
- ▶ Choosing a sample
- ▶ Two-way tally charts
- ▶ Frequency tables

2 Drawing diagrams
- ▶ Discrete and continuous data
- ▶ Bar charts and bar-line graphs
- ▶ Frequency diagrams

3 Interpreting diagrams
- ▶ Interpreting graphs and diagrams
- ▶ Drawing conclusions based on the shape of graphs

 Maths Interact

See page 70
and Pupil Book 7^C pages 159 and 180.

New concepts

Open and closed questions	Frequency diagrams
Discrete and continuous data	Grouping data

1 Collecting information

Resources

Available on **Teacher Resource CD-ROM 7ᶜ**:

Extra Practice D2-1

Homework Sheet D2-1

Starter D2-1-1

Starter D2-1-2

Plenary D2-1-1

Framework objectives

Pages 248, 250, 252

▶ Different types of data
▶ Open and closed questions
▶ Choosing a sample
▶ Two-way tally charts
▶ Frequency tables

Key Words

questionnaire

tally chart

frequency table

class interval

experiment

survey

table

data

Starters

Put four headings, widely spaced out, on the board – 'WALK', 'BUS', 'CYCLE', 'HELICOPTER'. Ask pupils to come out and line up neatly under the heading which describes the way they travel to school – a human bar chart is formed. Hopefully, some come by car which opens the discussion for the need for 'OTHER'.

Plenaries

Discuss what is wrong with the following question – 'Really smart people think smoking should be banned. Do you?' (biased question). Ask the pupils to improve the question with a series of questions – Do you want smoking banned in public places? Why? (give options), etc.

Teaching points

- Statistics can be used to solve problems.
- There are three types of data: primary, secondary and experimental.
- Questions can be open or closed.
- Closed questions are easier to analyse using statistics.
- It is often necessary to take a sample from a population.
- Use tally charts to record answers to questions and the results of surveys.
- Data can be grouped and put into a frequency table.

Notes

The aim of this section is to build up skills of planning and organising a survey or questionnaire. Pupils find question writing very difficult and the section aims to show them how to make good choices of closed questions and sensible groups for data recording.

Sampling is not done in any detail at this stage. Types of sampling will be dealt with in Year 9. It is enough for Year 7 pupils to understand that it is not possible to interview everyone in the country to ask them what TV programme they watched last night so a representative sample must be used. They should begin to think about what should be taken into account when devising a sample and the size of the sample.

The tally tables used are two-way tables. Question ⓭ uses two colours to emphasise the two categories of the data.

Homework

Unit Questions –

2 Drawing diagrams

FRAMEWORK OBJECTIVES
Pages 262, 264

▶ Discrete and continuous data
▶ Bar charts and bar-line graphs
▶ Frequency diagrams

Resources

Available on **Teacher Resource CD-ROM 7ᶜ:**

Extra Practice D2-2
Homework Sheet D2-2
Starter D2-2-1
Plenary D2-2-1

Plenaries

- Check misconceptions: All statistical diagrams should have a title, labelled axes and a key if appropriate. Bar charts must have the labels centrally under the bars.
- Check vocabulary: Frequency

Maths Interact

Just Click

▶ Examples of discrete and continuous data are shown on the screen at random. Each example may be dragged into the area labelled Discrete or the area labelled Continuous. The primary purpose of the activity is to facilitate class discussion. A Check button provides feedback on the decisions made.

Teaching points

- Data can be described as discrete or continuous.
- Discrete data can only take specific values, which do not necessarily have to be whole numbers.
- Continuous data can take any value in a specified range.
- Bar charts and bar-line graphs are used to display discrete data.
- Bar charts and bar-line graphs have gaps between their bars.
- Frequency diagrams are used to display continuous data.
- Frequency diagrams do not have gaps between their bars.

Key Words

| bar graph |
| frequency diagram |
| bar-line graph |
| discrete |
| continuous |

Notes

The concepts of discrete and continuous data are very difficult. The danger is always that pupils will come to think of discrete data as whole numbers and continuous data as decimal values. Shoe size is therefore a good example of discrete data because it goes up in halves. Good examples of continuous data are heights, weights and ages.

Bar charts and bar-line graphs are covered very briefly as it is assumed that pupils will be confident about drawing them at this stage. The rules of equal width bars and titles and labels should be emphasised.

Frequency diagrams are introduced as a way of displaying continuous data. The main differences between them and bar charts are that they have a continuous graph-type scale on the horizontal axis and they have no gaps between the bars. In later years, this idea will be developed into histograms.

In question 🔟, class groups described with inequalities are introduced. This is worth spending some time on with the group.

Homework

Unit Questions ❺ – ❼

3 Interpreting diagrams

FRAMEWORK OBJECTIVES
Pages 24, 268, 270

▶ Interpreting graphs and diagrams
▶ Drawing conclusions based on the shape of graphs

Resources

Available on **Teacher Resource CD-ROM 7ᶜ:**

Extra Practice D2-3
Homework Sheet D2-3
Starter D2-3-1
Plenary D2-3-1

Starters

Ask 16 pupils to name their favourite flavour crisp – produce a tally chart on the board. Pupils fold a circular piece of paper in half four times. When unfolded, 16 sectors are produced and a pie chart can be constructed for the tally chart. (If circular paper is not available, number fans spread out can be used for 10 people.)

Plenaries

Use Question **8** to check understanding of a pie chart. The total amount must be known before statements about how many are in each category can be made.

Key Words

bar chart

pie chart

frequency

mean

represent

interpret

Teaching points

- Each part of the data is represented by a single bar.
- The heights of all the bars added together give the total frequency.
- The mean value is calculated by dividing the total frequency by the number of separate bars.
- Pie charts allow comparisons of sectors. Sometimes the exact quantity represented by each sector is not always known because the total frequency is not given.
- When the categories in a compound bar chart do not total 100% the missing percentage is a null response.
- Compound bar charts are most effective split into either two or three different categories.
- Comparative bar charts represent a merger of two or three separate bar charts to allow direct comparisons of the same data from different sources.
- Always read the title and the axes labels carefully. Consider what the graph does tell you.
- Do not make assumptions about the data.

Homework

Unit Questions **8** – **9**

Notes

This section considers interpreting bar and pie charts and making conclusions from the shape of the graphs.

The dotted line in question **3** cannot represent the mean value because the line is lower than each separate data value. The mean value would be between the highest and the lowest bar.

It is worth emphasising that the total frequency is often omitted from pie charts; in this instance only the relative size of the sectors can be compared. This is the case in question **6**.

Question **8** considers that equal sized sections on different pie charts do not always represent the same quantities.

An extension to question **9** would be to make a poster to promote healthy living. The bar chart should be analysed to decide which issue to draw attention to.

An extension to question **11** would be to ask the question, 'Does this graph provide evidence for Global Warming?'

The significance of the scale on a bar chart is emphasised in question **12**. This idea is extended in *How to solve it*, where altering the scale of the axis distorts the graph and changes the presentation of the data, making it misleading.

To answer question **15** pupils will need to estimate the amount of the pie chart that is red. Reminders that $\frac{4}{10} = 40\%$ may be needed here.

1 Collecting information

1 a Number of miles travelled
b Temperatures for June, July and August over several years
c Speed of reactions of boys and girls measured by testing
d Size of print, number of pages and legibility tests
e Populations and sizes of European countries
f Type and number of vehicles passing school, measured throughout day

2 a Primary
b Secondary
c Experimental
d Primary
e Secondary. Use viewing figures published.
f Secondary

3 Each face of the dice could represent one of the toys. She could then throw the dice to see how many throws it took before all six faces showed.

4 a Use secondary data from the Internet.
b Use numbered counters and draw them from a bag, recording the results.

5 a Less than 2 hours
Between 2 and 4 hours
More than 4 hours
d Less than 1 mile
Between 1 and 2 miles
More than 2 miles
b More than
Less than
The same
Don't know
e Orange
Vodafone
Virgin
O$_2$
Other
c 0–5
6–10
11–15
16–20
21+

6 There are too many different football clubs.

7 a Leading question. It implies the respondent should agree.
b Biased. Implies that tabloid newspapers are poorer quality.
c Biased. Use of "unhealthy" implies banning a good idea.
d Embarrasing. People will not tell truth.
e Embarrasing. People will not tell truth.

8 a Do you think local trains keep good time
Always ☐ Sometimes ☐ Never ☐ Don't know ☐
b Do you think that service in local shops is
Good ☐ OK ☐ Bad ☐ Don't know ☐
c Do you think children's behaviour over the past 20 years has
got better ☐ got worse ☐ stayed same ☐ don't know ☐
d Pupils' own responses with boxes to tick

9 a Nearest cm
b Nearest km
c Nearest hour

10 He should choose 50 boys and 50 girls, some from each year group.

11 No. Most people who work do not shop during the morning.

12 The people he would ask would do sport and would want better sporting facilities.

13 a, b

Year	Bus	Car	Cycle	Walk
7	II	I	II	I
8	IIII	II	I	II
9	II	II	I	IIII

14 a, b

	A*	A	B	C	D	E	F	G
Male	I	I	I	II	IIII	I	II	I
Female	I	I	II	IIII	I			I

15

	1996	1998	2000	2001	2001/02	2002/03
Lot more	46%	30%	33%	25%	30%	38%
Little more	29%	29%	34%	31%	34%	35%

16 a

Journey length (miles)	0–5	6–10	11–13	16–20	21–25
No. of families					

b

No. of words	0–5	6–10	11–15	16–20	21–25	26–30	31–35	36–40	41–45
No. of sentences									

c

Age	20–29	30–39	40–49	50–59	60–69
No. of teachers					

d

Length (mm)	0–50	51–100	101–150	151–200	201–250
No. of worms					

17 a, b

Distance (m)	1–3.9	4–6.9	7–9.9	10–12.9	13–15.9
Tally	|||	||||	||| ||||	|||	||

c

Distance (m)	1–3.9	4–6.9	7–9.9	10–12.9	13–15.9
Tally	3	4	8	3	2

18
- Draw a series of lines of known length.
- Use a sample size greater than 30, split into equal age ranges.
- Ask the people to estimate line length, taking a correct guess to be within 0.5 cm–1.5 cm.
- Tally the responses.
- Calculate the error in measurement for each person.
- Draw a bar chart to display the results.

2 Drawing diagrams   *Answers*

1
a Discrete	c Discrete	e Continuous
b Continuous	d Continuous	f Continuous

2 a Discrete   b Discrete

3 Either response is possible:

Continuous – your actual age measured in real time which is a continuous scale.

Discrete – your rounded age to the complete years you have been alive.

4
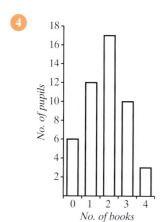

5
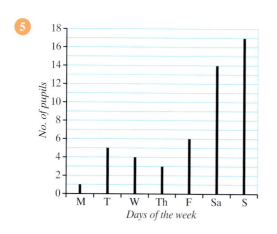

6
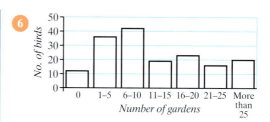

7
Activity	Tally	Frequency
Chess			1
Computers	||||	5
Dancing			1
Music	||||	4
Reading	|||	3
Skateboarding	|||	3
Sport	|||| |||	8
Swimming	|||	3

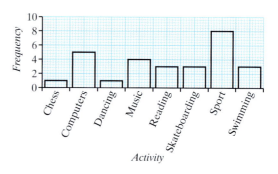

8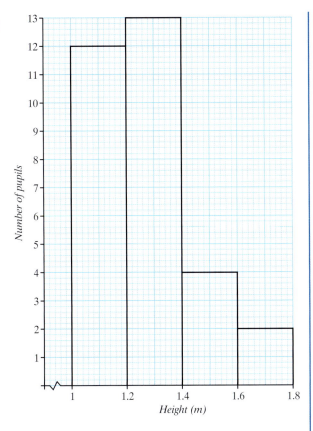
Number of pupils / *Height (m)*

9 **a** and **b**

time (sec)	38–43	43–48	48–53	53–58	58–63
tally	⊮ ⊪⊪	⊮ ⊮	⊮ ⊪⊪⊪	⊪	⊪
frequency	8	10	9	2	1

c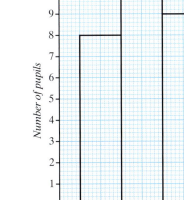
Number of pupils / *Time (seconds)*

10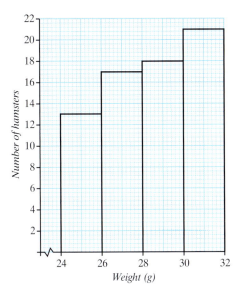
Number of hamsters / *Weight (g)*

11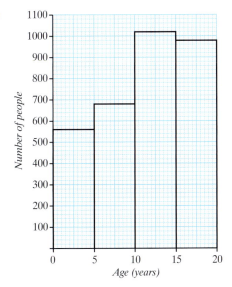
Number of people / *Age (years)*

12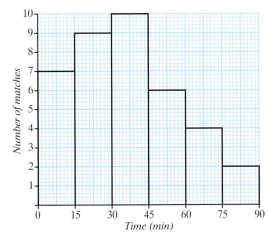
Number of matches / *Time (min)*

3 Interpreting diagrams

Answers

1 **a** None

    b 8

    c Christmas presents

    d 24

    e 4

2 **a** Tuesday

    b 3 minutes

    c Bus arrived on time

3 Hamish's mean is less than all rainfall values.

4 **a**

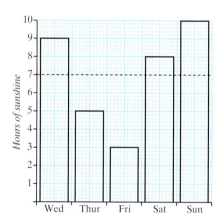

    b 7 mm

    c See bar chart.

5 **a** More youth projects

    b 20%

    c 125

6 **a** News of the World

    b 2 times

    c Does not state how many papers were sold in total.

7 **a**

1 person	6 000 000
2 people	7 000 000
3 people	3 000 000
4 people	2 800 000
5 people	1 000 000
6 people	200 000

8 The two countries have different populations, therefore 10% of 10 million is not the same as 10% of 4 million.

9 **a** 140   **b** 20%   **c** 20%

10 **a** 35%

     b Secondary schools tend to be further away from homes than primary schools.

11 **a** Anglian

     b North West. Both years have highest rainfall.

     c The red bars are almost all higher than the blue bars.

     d South West

12 **a** Different scales of amount have been used.

     b King Edward £400

         Queen Elizabeth £1000

13 **a** False

     b False

     c True

14 **a** £950

     b Sunday

     c More hot drinks are sold than cold ones.

15 A 40% of 200 = 80

     B 40% of 100 = 40

     C 50% of 90 = 45

     D   5% of 100 = 50

     Therefore B represents the smallest number of pupils.

1 **a** Number of births per year for the past 100 years.
  b Number of books borrowed from a library by boys and girls.

2 **a** It is dependent on what the news is showing.
  b Do you feel happy when you watch the news?

3 Select business places to conduct the survey.
Survey a larger sample of people.
Ask "Do you use a bicycle to get to work?"

4 **a, b**

	Can Swim	Can't Swim
Boy	IIII III	IIII
Girl	IIII I	IIII I

  c 11

5 **a** Sweets are sold in weights of any value within a certain range.
  b You can only have whole numbers of sweets.

6 **a and b**

speed (mph)	tally	frequency
28	III	3
29	IIII	4
30	IIII I	6
31	IIII	4
32	III	3

  c

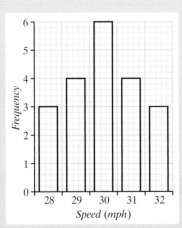

  d No. Cars surveyed are travelling close to the speed limit.

7

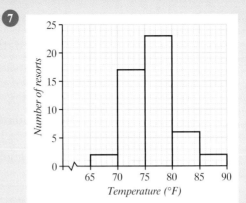

8 **a** Fossil fuels   92 400
       Hydro and biomass   12 000
       Renewable   8400
       Nuclear   7200
  b 11 times

9 **a** 2002
  b 2004
  c Increased to maximum in 2002 then decreased. In 2004 5% more boys were overweight than in 1999.
  d There is not enough information. The graph does not state how many children aged 2–18 there are in each year.

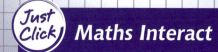

Maths Interact

Pupil Book page 159

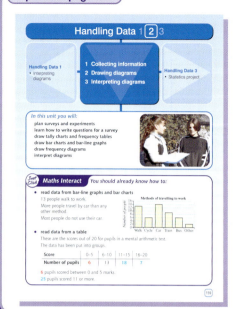

Pupils should already know how to:

- **read data from bar-line graphs and bar charts**

  Information about methods of travel to work is presented in the form of a bar-line graph or bar chart, at random, and this is to be interpreted by the pupils.

- **read data from a table**

  Test scores are presented in tabular form and questions are asked that require the data to be taken from the table.

Pupil Book page 180

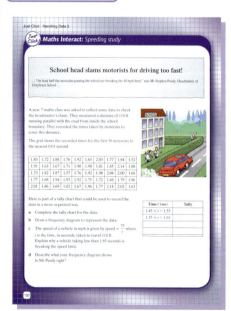

Speeding study

Maths Interact summary

1 A fictitious newspaper headline about speeding motorists sets the scene for organising and analysing data from a table, applying a formula, presenting the results in a bar chart and testing a hypothesis.

Pupil Book answers

1 a

Time (seconds)	Tally
$1.45 \leqslant t < 1.55$	II
$1.55 \leqslant t < 1.65$	III
$1.65 \leqslant t < 1.75$	ЖГ ЖГ
$1.75 \leqslant t < 1.85$	ЖГ ЖГ III
$1.85 \leqslant t < 1.95$	ЖГ ЖГ I
$1.95 \leqslant t < 2.05$	ЖГ IIII
$2.05 \leqslant t < 2.15$	II

b

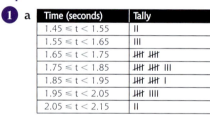

Number of motorists vs *Time in seconds*

c A vehicle that takes 1.85 seconds to travel the distance is travelling at a speed of 40.541 mph (3 d.p.). A vehicle that takes less time to cover the same distance must be going faster. If a car is breaking the speed limit with a time of 1.85 seconds, then it must be breaking the speed limit with a shorter time.

d 28 out of 50 motorists (56%) are taking less than 1.85 seconds and so are speeding. Mr Peedy is right, more than half the motorists are speeding.

Number 1 2 **3** 4 5

Year 6
- Estimation
- Multiplication and division
- Using a calculator
- Measures

Number 1
- Place value

1. **Rounding**
2. **Multiplying**
3. **Dividing**
4. **Order of operations**
5. **Measures**

Number 3
- Calculations
- Multiplication and division of decimals
- Calculator methods

Framework teaching programme

Overview

This unit consists of five teaching sections covering place value, multiplication and division, order of operations and the use of metric and imperial units. This unit follows from the work in **Number 1** on place value and addition and subtraction of whole numbers and decimals. This unit includes an introduction to BODMAS. Multiplication and division of decimals is left for **Number 5**.

1 Rounding
- ▶ Rounding positive whole numbers
- ▶ Checking answers using approximations
- ▶ Rounding decimals to the nearest whole number and to 1 d.p.
- ▶ Sensible answers to problems

2 Multiplying
- ▶ Simple methods of multiplication
- ▶ Long multiplication

3 Dividing
- ▶ Simple methods of division
- ▶ Writing answers to division questions properly
- ▶ Estimation for division questions

4 Order of operations
- ▶ Carrying out calculations using BODMAS
- ▶ Using a calculator

5 Measures
- ▶ Metric units and conversion within the metric system
- ▶ Metric equivalents of imperial measures
- ▶ Reading scales

 Maths Interact

See page 82
and Pupil Book 7^C pages 181 and 208.

New concepts

Rounding decimals to 1 decimal place   Order of operations – BODMAS

1 Rounding

FRAMEWORK OBJECTIVES

Pages 42, 44, 110

▶ Rounding positive whole numbers

▶ Checking answers using approximations

▶ Rounding decimals to the nearest whole number and to 1 d.p.

▶ Sensible answers to problems

Resources

Available on **Teacher Resource CD-ROM 7ᶜ:**

Extra Practice N3-1

Homework Sheet N3-1

Starter N3-1-1

Plenary N3-1-1

Starters

Pick a number, then give pupils five clues, e.g. (1) To the nearest hundred the number is 400.
(2) It's less than 394. (3) To the nearest 10 it's 390. (4) It's even.
(5) Two of the digits are the same.
Answer: 388. Pupils make up their own five clues that involve rounding and produce a unique number.

Plenaries

Check misconceptions: Check rounding – e.g. 476 to the nearest hundred is 500 and not 5; 342 to the nearest ten is 340 and not 34. **Stress that the digits do not lose value.**

Key Words

round

approximately

nearest

to one decimal place
(to 1 d.p.)

Teaching points

● Rounding to the nearest 10, 100 and 1000.

● Checking answers by using approximations.

● Rounding decimals to the nearest whole number and to 1 d.p.

● Using context to check if an answer is sensible.

Notes

When checking answers, pupils should be encouraged to approximate values sensibly to the nearest 10, 100 or 1000 before undertaking any calculations.

When rounding to 1 decimal place pupils need to write 'to 1 d.p.' after their answers.

A common misconception when rounding to 1 d.p. is to add 1 on to the whole number part instead of the first decimal place when rounding up, i.e. 4.67 becomes 5.6 to 1 d.p. instead of 4.7

One of the major difficulties with contextual rounding is realising that rounding up is often required even when the answer would round down using the rules of rounding and vice versa. In the example in the green topic the division would give 2.25 which would round to 2 to the nearest whole number but the contextual answer is 3.

Homework

Unit Questions **❶** – **❻**

2 Multiplying

FRAMEWORK OBJECTIVES
Pages 82, 84, 104

▶ Simple methods of multiplication
▶ Long multiplication

Resources

Available on **Teacher Resource CD-ROM 7ᶜ:**

Worksheet N3-2-1
Extra Practice N3-2
Homework Sheet N3-2
Starter N3-2-1
Plenary N3-2-1

Starters

Pupils draw a 3×3 grid and fill in the cells using any numbers between 1 and 25 (numbers can be used more than once). Call out times tables facts such as 2×5, 3×4, 6×4, etc. First pupil to cross off all their numbers is the winner (only one number crossed off at a time). Repeat with numbers between 35 and 80 for the cells.

Plenaries

Start with a 1–100 square. Choose a 2×2 square, e.g.

15	16
25	26

Multiply the opposite corners – $15 \times 26 = 390$ and $16 \times 25 = 400$ (discuss strategies). Let the pupils pick another 2×2 square – is the second answer always 10 more than the first answer? Why? $[n(n + 11) - (n + 1)(n + 10) = 10]$

Key Words

multiply, multiplication

product

partitioning

commutative

Teaching points

- Multiplication is the same as repeated addition.
- Use of partitioning and the commutative law of multiplication.
- Use of compensation method – multiplying x by 99 is the same as multiplying x by 100 and subtracting 1 lot of x.
- Multiplying by zero always gives a zero answer.
- Multiplying by one leaves the amount unchanged.
- Long multiplication using the grid method, Galosian multiplication and the traditional method.
- Estimating answers by rounding the numbers to the nearest 10, 100 or 1000.

Notes

Decimal multiplication is not covered in this section. Mental decimal multiplication has been covered in **Number 2** and decimal multiplication is covered in **Number 5**. The emphasis in this section is on integer products, although money questions are covered using £ and p to avoid decimal products. You could emphasise to pupils the equivalence of multiplying by £1.99 and by (£2 − £0.01) if you wish to keep the units the same.

So $29 \times 1.99 = 29 \times (2 - 0.01) = 29 \times 2 - 29 \times 0.01 = 58 - 0.29 = 57.71$ but with money it is easier to mix the units and use £ and p with most pupils.

In the orange topic encourage pupils to thoroughly practise each of the methods given before they choose a method that they like best.

Homework

Unit Questions **7** – **8**

3 DstDividing

FRAMEWORK OBJECTIVES
Pages 82, 84, 106

▶ Simple methods of division
▶ Writing answers to division questions properly
▶ Estimation for division questions

Starters

Pupils draw a 3 × 3 grid and fill in the cells using any numbers between 1 and 12 (numbers can be used more than once). Call out 3, 4 or 5 division facts such as 24 ÷ 3, 16 ÷ 4, 25 ÷ 5, etc. First pupil to cross off all their numbers is the winner (only one number crossed off at a time).

Plenaries

Pupils work in pairs to try to solve a calculation such as 416 ÷ 13 by treating 416 as the target. Pupil 1 starts by multiplying 13 by an integer (multiple of 10) e.g. 130. This is the pair's running total. Pupil 2 has a go, maybe 20 × 13 = 260, to give a running total of 390. Pupil 1 has another go to try to get the target of 416. The pupils continue until their running total hits the target. The pair who does it in the fewest moves is the winner.

Key Words

divide

estimate

remainder

quotient

divisor

division

exact

inverse

Teaching points

- Division is the same as repeated subtraction.
- The method for division by subtraction of sensible multiples of the divisor.
- You cannot divide by zero.
- Dividing by one leaves the amount unchanged.
- Writing a quotient using a remainder, a fraction or a decimal.
- Estimating answers by rounding the dividend to a simple multiple of the divisor.
- Estimating answers by rounding both the dividend and the divisor.

Notes

Decimal division is not covered in this section but will be done in **Number 5**.

Traditional short and long division are not included in the *Framework* and so the method has not been covered in this section.

The sensible rounding of quotients depending on context is covered in the orange topic.

In Question ⑧ you may need to remind pupils about how to calculate a mean.

Estimation is potentially confusing for pupils as there is no single correct answer for each question. An estimate is good if it gives an answer that is close to the exact answer and there are different ways to do estimates especially for division. You could ask pupils to compare all of the exact answers to the estimates in question ⑪ and decide how good their estimates are.

Homework

Unit Questions ⑨ – ⑪

4 Order of operations

FRAMEWORK OBJECTIVES
**Pages 86, 104,
108, 110**

▶ Carrying out calculations using BODMAS
▶ Using a calculator

Resources

Available on **Teacher Resource CD-ROM 7^c:**

Extra Practice N3-4
Homework Sheet N3-4
Starter N3-4-1
Plenary N3-4-1

Starters

Ask the pupils to write down the answers to the following three questions:
$4 + 5 \times 6$, $20 \div 10 + 2$, $20 + 10 \div 2$.
Do the questions on a scientific calculator – match the answers with those of the pupils. Probably only question 2 will match. Discussion about order – BODMAS.

Plenaries

Put the following on the board:
$3\ 4\ 5\ 2 = 17$
$3\ 4\ 5\ 2 = 4$
$3\ 4\ 5\ 2 = 13$
$3\ 4\ 5\ 2 = 1$

Ask the pupils to insert brackets and the four operations between the numbers to make the statements correct.

[Answer: $3 + 4 + 5 \times 2 = 17$
$3 + 4 - 5 + 2 = 4$
$3 + 4 \times 5 \div 2 = 13$
$(3 + 4) \div (5 + 2) = 1$]

Maths Interact

Just Click

▶ The BODMAS rule is defined and applied to some examples in this animation. The animation player may be used to control the presentation.

▶ The need to understand the rules of BODMAS when using a scientific calculator is demonstrated in this animation.

Teaching points

- Identifying the order of operations.
- Using BODMAS.
- Using a calculator efficiently.

Key Words

order of operations

brackets

Notes

Pupils need to be aware that the order of operations is important. Most mistakes are made as a result of pupils simply working from left to right when answering a BODMAS question.

It is essential that the pupils become confident in the use of a calculator. Pupils need to be aware of when to use the subtraction key and when to use the sign change key. The memory facility of the calculator has not been explicitly taught as sensible use of brackets renders it unnecessary for this exercise. The use of the memory key is, however, taught in **Number 5**.

Another common problem arises when pupils try to calculate using the square root key on a calculator. They will need to be reminded to use a bracket to enter a calculation like $\sqrt{3^2 + 7}$. So the key sequence for this is

to give 4 and not simply

which gives the answer 10

Homework

Unit Questions ⑫ – ⑬

5 Measures

Resources

Available on **Teacher Resource CD-ROM 7ᶜ**:

Extra Practice N3-5
Homework Sheet N3-5
Starter N3-5-1
Plenary N3-5-1
Plenary N3-5-2

FRAMEWORK OBJECTIVES

Pages 228, 230

▶ Metric units and conversion within the metric system
▶ Metric equivalents of imperial measures
▶ Reading scales

Starters

Divide the board into two – label one side 'Metric' and the other side 'Imperial'. In groups, pupils brainstorm as many units as possible that fit in either column. After a few minutes, bring together all the suggested measurements and label them either l, m or c (length, mass or capacity).

Plenaries

Write the words 'Oct' and 'Dec' in bubbles on the board. Ask the pupils to write as many words (using a dictionary if necessary) as possible which start with 'Oct' and 'Dec' (e.g. Octopus, Octagon, Decade, Decathlon, etc.) *What do most of the words have in common?* (The numbers 8 and 10.) *Why is **Oct**ober the 10th month not the 8th and **Dec**ember the 12th and not the 10th?* Ask the pupils to investigate the origins of July and August (inserted by Julius Caesar and Augustus into the original 10-month calendar).

Key Words

millimetre	second
centimetre	minute
metre	hour
kilometre	day
gram	week
kilogram	month
millilitre	year
centilitre	century
litre	millennium

Teaching points

- Using and converting between metric units of length, mass, time, area and capacity.
- Approximate equivalents between metric and imperial units.
- Reading scales.

Homework

Unit Questions ⑭ – ⑰

Notes

The greatest difficulty for pupils with the red topic is whether to multiply or divide when converting between metric units. This is covered in the *How to solve it* section at the end of the unit. Encourage pupils to see that there are more small units than large units so you multiply going from a larger unit to a smaller one.

Pupils also find it difficult to remember conversion facts. Encourage them to see the links between the units for mass, length and capacity by concentrating on the prefixes. So, for example, k always means 1000.

The conversion facts linking seconds, minutes, hours, days and weeks have been omitted from the teaching as they are in common usage. When teaching units of time, pupils need to be aware of the number of days in the different months. This is not covered within the teaching of this section. You can obviously remind pupils about the rhyme:

30 days have September, April, June and November, all the rest have 31, excepting February alone, which has but 28 days clear and 29 in each leap year.

For pupils who cannot remember this, the use of the knuckles on pupils' hands provides a simple way to be able to work out the days in each month.

If you clench your fists and turn your hands so the backs of the hands are facing you, and count the months in order starting from the left, the knuckles are months with 31 days and the gaps are all 30 except for February. You still have to remind pupils that February has 28 days except in a leap year when it has 29 days. Leap years are 2008, 2012, 2016 etc.

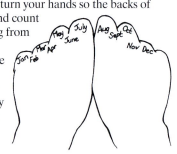

When reading scales encourage pupils to think carefully about the value of each division.

1 Rounding — *Answers*

1 60 kg

2 **a** 200 litres **b** 180 litres

3 **a** (1) 19 750
    (2) 19 700
    (3) 20 000
 b 20 000

4 Bungalow £113 000
 Detached £173 000
 Semi-detached £99 000
 Terrace £88 000
 Flat or maisonette £122 000

5 $70 \times 60 = 4200$

6 692 or 702 because $4 \times 3 = 12$; therefore the answer has to end in 2.

7 $50 \times 20 = 1000$ Kevin was wrong. 244 is too small.

8 $7 \times 8 = 56$, therefore the answer should end in 6.

9 $\dfrac{800}{400} = 2$

10 3.1

11 Breeding cattle 16
 Dairy 4
 Beef 3
 Pigs 10
 Sheep 65

12

		a	b
100 m:	10.08 s	10 s	10.1 s
400 m:	46.10 s	46 s	46.1 s
Long jump:	7.74 m	8 m	7.7 m
High jump:	2.24 m	2 m	2.2 m
Shot putt:	21.55 m	22 m	21.6 m
Javelin:	76.35 m	76 m	76.4 m

13 **a** 7 **b** 7.6 **c** 8 **d** £7.60

13 66p for one person and 67p for two people. Jay cannot share the money equally.

13 14

2 Multiplying — *Answers*

1 **a** (1) $7 \times \mathbf{16} = (7 \times \mathbf{10}) + (7 \times \mathbf{6})$
        $= 70 + \mathbf{42}$
        $= \mathbf{112}$
    (2) $8 \times \mathbf{17} = (8 \times \mathbf{10}) + (8 \times \mathbf{7})$
        $= 80 + \mathbf{56}$
        $= \mathbf{136}$
    (3) $7 \times \mathbf{22} = (7 \times \mathbf{20}) + (7 \times \mathbf{2})$
        $= 140 + \mathbf{14}$
        $= \mathbf{154}$
    (4) $8 \times \mathbf{24} = (8 \times \mathbf{20}) + (8 \times \mathbf{4})$
        $= 160 + \mathbf{32}$
        $= \mathbf{192}$
 b (1) 84 (4) 138 (7) 156
    (2) 112 (5) 248 (8) 294
    (3) 136 (6) 378 (9) 480

2 **a** (1) $6 \times \mathbf{14} = 6 \times \mathbf{7} \times \mathbf{2}$
        $= 42 \times \mathbf{2} = \mathbf{84}$
    (2) $5 \times \mathbf{18} = 5 \times \mathbf{9} \times \mathbf{2} = 5 \times \mathbf{2} \times \mathbf{9}$
        $= \mathbf{10} \times \mathbf{9} = \mathbf{90}$
    (3) $5 \times \mathbf{26} = 5 \times \mathbf{13} \times \mathbf{2} = 5 \times \mathbf{2} \times \mathbf{13}$
        $= \mathbf{10} \times 13 = \mathbf{130}$
    (4) $\frac{1}{2} \times \mathbf{9} \times \mathbf{6} = \frac{1}{2} \times \mathbf{6} \times \mathbf{9}$
        $= 3 \times \mathbf{9}$
        $= \mathbf{27}$
 b (1) 96 (3) 140 (5) 160
    (2) 170 (4) 15 (6) 44

3 **a** 693 **c** 1683 **e** 686 **g** 776
 b 891 **d** 3366 **f** 1470 **h** 1358

4 **a** $32 \times \mathbf{£1.99} = 32 \times \mathbf{£2} - 32 \times \mathbf{1p} = \mathbf{£64} - \mathbf{32p} = \mathbf{£63.68}$
 b $45 \times \mathbf{£1.99} = 45 \times \mathbf{£2} - 45 \times \mathbf{1p} = \mathbf{£90} - \mathbf{45p} = \mathbf{£89.55}$
 c $14 \times \mathbf{£2.99} = 14 \times \mathbf{£3} - 14 \times \mathbf{1p} = \mathbf{£42} - \mathbf{14p} = \mathbf{£41.86}$
 d $24 \times \mathbf{£1.98} = 24 \times \mathbf{£2} - 24 \times \mathbf{2p} = \mathbf{£48} - \mathbf{48p} = \mathbf{£47.52}$

5

245×1	=	245
13×99	=	1287
28×98	=	2744
25×99	=	2475

6 **a** £35.64 **b** £25.74

7 £155.81

8 **a** $300 \times 60 = 18\,000$

×	200	70	3	
60	12 000	4200	180	16 380
4	800	280	12	+ 1 092
				17 472

$273 \times 64 = 17\,472$

9 **a** $300 \times 50 = 15\,000$

    b

    314 × 48 = 15 072

10 **a** (1) $200 \times 80 = 16\,000$ (2) 16 948
    b (1) $300 \times 60 = 18\,000$ (2) 18 154
    c (1) $400 \times 90 = 36\,000$ (2) 35 931
    d (1) $200 \times 50 = 10\,000$ (2) 9541
    e (1) $600 \times 40 = 24\,000$ (2) 21 957

    f (1) $200 \times 70 = 14\,000$ (2) 15 696
    g (1) $400 \times 80 = 32\,000$ (2) 32 424
    h (1) $500 \times 50 = 25\,000$ (2) 23 376
    i (1) $80 \times 70 = 5600$ (2) 5727
    j (1) $80 \times 40 = 3200$ (2) 3268
    k (1) $30 \times 70 = 2100$ (2) 2346
    l (1) $80 \times 30 = 2400$ (2) 2418
    m (1) $70 \times 700 = 49\,000$ (2) 48 983
    n (1) $50 \times 400 = 20\,000$ (2) 19 136
    o (1) $50 \times 800 = 40\,000$ (2) 40 425
    p (1) $60 \times 300 = 18\,000$ (2) 20 601

11 8760 hours

---

3 Dividing   *Answers*

1 **a**

```
    684
   −600    6 × 100
    84
   −60     6 × 10
    24
   −24     6 × 4
     0
Answer:      114
```
    $684 \div 6 = 114$

    b

```
    424
   −400    8 × 50
    24
   −24     8 × 3
     0
Answer:      53
```
    $424 \div 8 = 53$

2 **a** 116   **c** 63   **e** 237   **g** 126
    b 137   **d** 157   **f** 268   **h** 134

3 **a** $7426 \div 47 = 158$ **b** $7426 \div 158 = 47$

4 **a**

```
    559
   −520    13 × 40
    39
   −39     13 × 3
     0
Answer:      43
```
    $55 \div 13 = 43$

    b

```
    348
   −240    12 × 20
    108
   −60     12 × 5
    48
   −48     12 × 4
     0
Answer:      29
```
    $348 \div 12 = 29$

5 **a** 37   **c** 64   **e** 23   **g** 123
    b 42   **d** 37   **f** 34   **h** 115

6 £48

7 **a** (1) 6 r 1 (2) $6\frac{1}{4}$ (3) 6.25
    b (1) 10 r 2 (2) $10\frac{2}{5}$ (3) 10.4
    c (1) 13 r 1 (2) $13\frac{1}{4}$ (3) 13.25
    d (1) 7 r 4 (2) $7\frac{1}{2}$ (3) 7.5

    e (1) 8 r 1 (2) $8\frac{1}{4}$ (3) 8.25
    f (1) 6 r 6 (2) $6\frac{3}{4}$ (3) 6.75
    g (1) 4 r 6 (2) $4\frac{1}{2}$ (3) 4.5
    h (1) 3 r 4 (2) $3\frac{1}{4}$ (3) 3.25

8 **a** £11 771   **b** £12 000

9 **a** 7   **b** 13   **c** 23

10 14

11 Pupils may have different estimates.
    a (1) $420 \div 7 = 60$ (2) 58
    b (1) $560 \div 8 = 70$ (2) 69
    c (1) $270 \div 9 = 30$ (2) 31
    d (1) $280 \div 7 = 40$ (2) 42
    e (1) $2400 \div 8 = 300$ (2) 264
    f (1) $300 \div 6 = 50$ (2) 52
    g (1) $240 \div 6 = 40$ (2) 39
    h (1) $600 \div 12 = 50$ (2) 46
    i (1) $660 \div 11 = 60$ (2) 62
    j (1) $720 \div 12 = 60$ (2) 61
    k (1) $2000 \div 10 = 200$ (2) 194
    l (1) $910 \div 13 = 70$ (2) 67

12 **a** 14   **b** 10.56 kg

13 **a** 58   **b** £24 360   **c** £8.12

14 **a** 12 168   **b** 13

4 Order of operations

1 a 23
  b 4
  c 19
  d 53
  e 1
  f 13
  g 93
  h 25
  i 2
  j 3
  k 16
  l 6

2 No. Multiplication has to be completed first and so Neil should work out 5 multiplied by 6, which equals 30, and then add 4.

3 No. Multiplication has to be completed first $13 \times 3 = 39$ and $5 \times 4 = 20$ and then $39 - 20 = 19$. The calculator has not been programmed to use BODMAS

4 a $(\quad 7 \quad + \quad 4 \quad \div \quad 2 \quad) \quad \times \quad 8$
  b 72

5 a $(5 + 7) \div 3 + 7 = \boxed{11}$
  b $15 - 7 \times 2 = \boxed{1}$
  c $8 + (14 - 8) \div 3 = \boxed{10}$
  d $5 \times (16 - 11) - (6 + 4) \times 2 = \boxed{5}$
  e $24 \div 6 \div 2 = \boxed{2}$

6 a 4
  b 4
  c 16
  d 1

7 a 216
  b 1296
  c 50 625
  d 2187

8 a 24
  b 343
  c 9
  d 1

  e 1302
  f 487
  g 720
  h 135
  i 10
  j 7
  k 6
  l 14

9 a (1) $6 \times \boxed{8} + 6 = 54$
    (2) $\boxed{12} \div 3 - 2 = 2$
  b $6 \boxed{\times} 5 \boxed{-} 8 = 22$
  c $(4 \boxed{+} 6) \times \boxed{5} = 50$

10 1

11 a 77
  b $^-375$
  c $^-2.25$
  d $^-7$

12 a HOHO
  b SOS
  c ESSO OIL
  d BIBLE
  e SID
  f HEDGEHOG
  g GOSH
  h EGGS
  i LESLIE
  j SOLO
  k BOILED
  l HIGH
  m LEEDS
  n ISLE
  o HILL
  p BIG
  q BELL
  r SOLID
  s SLOB
  t HOBBIES

5 Measures

1 a m **e** mℓ
b km **f** mm
c cm² or mm² **g** m²
d sec **h** g

2 a 1.8 m < height of classroom door < 2.2 m
b 100 g < mass of cricket ball < 200 g
c 10 cm < length of a pencil < 20 cm
d 100 g < mass of an apple < 300 g
e 30 cm < width of a classroom chair < 60 cm
f 200 mℓ < capacity of a tankard < 1000 mℓ

3 a kg **c** km
b mℓ **d** ℓ

4 a 2000 m **e** 5.5 m **i** 3.245 m
b 5000 m **f** 4.72 m **j** 5.92 m
c 3600 m **g** 8 m **k** 6300 m
d 6 m **h** 6.5 m **l** 8.41 m

5 a 3000 g **d** 3650 g **g** 8.4 g
b 12 000 g **e** 3 g **h** 9.235 g
c 2500 g **f** 10 g

6 No. kg is a unit of weight and km is a unit of distance.

7 a 6000 mℓ **c** 250 mℓ
b 4750 mℓ **d** 3450 mℓ

8 a mm **c** min
b g **d** mℓ

9 a 1.35 m **b** 3.16 m

10 a 553 cm (5.53 m) **d** 2500 g (2.5 kg)
b 92 cm (0.92 m) **e** 8200 mg (8.2 g)
c 1635 mm (163.5 cm) **f** 8573 mℓ (8.573 ℓ)

11 a 300
b 3600
c 3300
d 2077 (or 2078 if you include one leap year and 2079 if you include two).

12 a 365 000 (or 365 250) **b** 8 760 000 (or 8 766 000)

13 22.5 min

14 40 min

15

weight (kg)	1	1.5	2	2.5	3
Cooking time in minutes (lamb)	60	90	120	150	180
Cooking time in minutes (turkey)	70	90	110	130	150

16 a 1 600 000 000 m² **b** 320 000

17 168 cm²

18 Yes. The stein would overflow as 2 pints is a larger volume than 1 litre.

19 9

20 24 km

21 a 16 km **b** 160 km

22 a £3.28 **b** 33.75 **c** 7.5

23 A = 60 B = 180

24 A = 6.5 B = 7.3 C = 8.9 D = 10.1 E = 10.7 F = 11.4

25 a 4.6 kg **b** 140 **c** 220 g

26 34°

27 124°

Unit Questions: **Number 3** — *Answers*

1 40 mℓ

2 a 260 cm
  b 300 cm
  c 258 cm
  d 2583 mm or 258.3 cm

3 An estimate would be $70 \times 8 = 560p = £5.60$. Beth's answer should be less than £5.60.

4 1036
  $8 \times 7 = 56$ therefore the answer must end in 6.

5

	a	b
Long jump	7 m	7.4 m
High jump	2 m	2.1 m
Shot putt	20 m	20.2 m
Javelin	78 m	78.0 m

6 7

7 a 144   g 108
  b 119   h 80
  c 132   i 33
  d 248   j 1287
  e 138   k 1568
  f 287   l £74.75

8 a (1) $300 \times 40 = 12\,000$ (2) 11 375
  b (1) $500 \times 40 = 20\,000$ (2) 16 724
  c (1) $200 \times 60 = 12\,000$ (2) 15 252
  d (1) $40 \times 400 = 16\,000$ (2) 15 124

9 a $20\,100 \div 75 = \mathbf{268}$
  b $20\,100 \div 268 = \mathbf{75}$

10 a (1) 14 r 1   (2) $14\frac{1}{2}$ (3) 14.5
  b (1) 8 r 2   (2) $8\frac{1}{2}$ (3) 8.5
  c (1) 6 r 1   (2) $6\frac{1}{5}$ (3) 6.2
  d (1) 7 r 2   (2) $7\frac{1}{4}$ (3) 7.25

11 e.g. $480 \div 8 = 60$

12 a 8   d 38   g 26
  b 1   e 1   h 56
  c 22   f 11   i 250

13 1

14 a 9 kg = **9000** g
  b 7 g = **7000** mg
  c 65 cm = **650** mm
  d 2 km = **2000** m
  e 23 m = **2300** cm
  f 2000 mℓ = **2** ℓ

15 a 394 cm (3.94 m)
  b 8675 mm (867.5 cm or 8.675 m)
  c 7292 g (7.292 kg)
  d 5.1 kg (5100 g or 5 100 000 mg)

16 a 40 km   b 15 miles

17 £3.33

Just Click Maths Interact

Pupil Book page 181

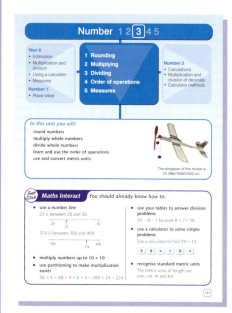

Pupils should already know how to:

- **use a number line**

  A random number is shown together with a number line. The number is to be dragged to its correct position on the scale.

- **multiply numbers up to 10 × 10**

  A matching game in which multiplication calculations and their values are shown on cards. Clicking a pair of matching cards causes them to disappear.

- **use partitioning to make multiplication easier**

  Missing values are entered to complete a multiplication by partitioning.

- **use tables to answer division problems**

  A matching game in which division calculations and their values are shown on cards. Clicking a pair of matching cards causes them to disappear.

- **use a calculator to solve simple problems**

  Single stage calculations are shown on screen, four at a time. A calculator is needed to find the answers.

- **recognise standard metric units**

  Six cards are displayed at a time showing a selection of units. The object is to identify the cards showing metric measurements of length.

Pupil Book page 208

Rounding and number problems

Maths Interact summary

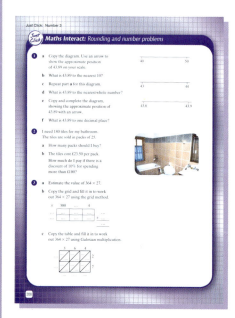

1. A number is represented to different levels of accuracy on a number line leading to statements about rounding.

2. Different types of rounding are required to solve problems associated with buying tiles for a bathroom.

3. Methods of multiplying a three figure number by a two figure number are illustrated using different grids. Estimation is encouraged as a check.

Pupil Book answers

1.
   a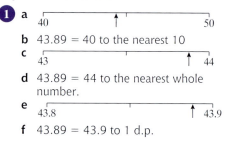

   b 43.89 = 40 to the nearest 10

   c

   d 43.89 = 44 to the nearest whole number.

   e

   f 43.89 = 43.9 to 1 d.p.

2. **a** 8   **b** £169.20

3. **a** Using rounding 400 × 30 = 12 000. Actual answer is 9828.

   b

	300	60	4	
20	6000	1200	80	7280
7	2100	420	28	2548
	8100	1620	108	9828

   c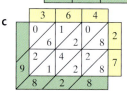

Algebra 1 2 **3** 4 5

Algebra 1
- Simple sequences
- Rules for sequences
- Writing rules in words
- Using letters to represent unknown values

1 **Multiples, factors and primes**

2 **Triangular and square numbers**

3 **Patterns and formulae**

4 **Graphs of simple functions**

Algebra 5
- Solving linear equations
- Plotting straight-line graphs
- Graphs from real-life situations

Framework teaching programme

52–59   Integers, powers and roots

108–109   Calculator methods

148–167   Sequences, functions and graphs

Overview

This unit is a mixture of number work dealing with patterns and types of number and algebra dealing with sequences and graphs. The first section looks at multiples, factors, common factors and primes. The second section looks at triangular and square numbers and square roots. The third section develops the work in **Algebra 2** on finding formulae for sequences. The final section looks at plotting straight-line graphs from simple equations.

1 Multiples, factors and primes

- ▶ Multiples and factors of integers
- ▶ Common factors
- ▶ Prime numbers
- ▶ Tests of divisibility

2 Triangular and square numbers

- ▶ Triangular numbers
- ▶ Square numbers
- ▶ Square roots

3 Patterns and formulae

- ▶ Rules to find terms in sequences and patterns
- ▶ Rules using algebra

4 Graphs of simple functions

- ▶ Generate coordinates that follow a rule
- ▶ Plot the graph of a simple function

 Maths Interact
See page 92
and Pupil Book 7^C pages 209 and 230.

New concepts

Triangular and square numbers

Prime numbers

Plotting graphs of functions

1 Multiples, factors and primes

Resources

Available on **Teacher Resource CD-ROM 7c:**

Worksheet A3-1-1 🔞 – 🔞
Extra Practice A3-1
Homework Sheet A3-1
Starter A3-1-1
Starter A3-1-2
Starter A3-1-3
Starter A3-1-4
Plenary A3-1-1

FRAMEWORK OBJECTIVES
Pages 52, 54, 56

▶ Multiples and factors of integers
▶ Common factors
▶ Prime numbers
▶ Tests of divisibility

Key Words

multiple

factor

prime

common factor

divisible

divisibility

integer

Starters

Project a 10 × 10, 1 to 100 number grid on the board. Carry out the activity explained in question 🔞 of the Pupil Book. Get pupils to come up to the board to do the shading in, and discuss the patterns that occur.

Using several copies of the number grid will allow you to draw all the patterns separately.

Teaching points

- Multiples of a number are found by multiplying it by an integer.
- Factors of a number are integers which divide into the number exactly.
- The common factors of two numbers are factors of *both* numbers.
- A prime number is a number which has exactly two factors, 1 and itself.
- One is not a prime number as it only has one factor.
- There are some simple tests you can do to see if one number is divisible by another.

Notes

With many of these concepts it is much easier to give examples than to try to write down a clear definition. Many pupils will understand the concept of multiples without being able to give a careful definition. Linking the idea to times tables is always useful.

Times tables can also be used to explain factors. Asking pupils to think of all the pairs of numbers that multiply together to give a number is a good way of finding factors. Pupils should understand that factors always come in pairs, apart from square numbers, where by definition one factor is the square root of the number (e.g. 6 × 6 = 36) and only occurs once.

Lower prime numbers are usually straightforward. It must be stressed that 1 is not a prime number, although this often seems strange to pupils. It is often difficult to tell which larger numbers are prime. For example, 111 may look as if it is prime but is in fact divisible by 3. Linking the prime number section with the divisibility section will allow pupils to use the divisibility tests to help them with this.

Homework

Unit Questions –

2 Sequences

FRAMEWORK OBJECTIVES

Pages 56, 108

▶ Triangular numbers
▶ Square numbers
▶ Square roots

Resources

Available on **Teacher Resource CD-ROM 7ᶜ:**

Extra Practice A3-2

Homework Sheet A3-2

Starter A3-2-1

Starter A3-2-2

Plenary A3-2-1

Starters

Pose the problem, 'If everyone in the classroom shakes hands with everyone else, how many handshakes will there be?' Discuss, and try if you dare! Approach the problem logically: Start with 2 pupils, get them to shake hands, and record the result. Repeat for 3 pupils and so on. The number of handshakes will be 1, 3, 6, 10, …; the triangular numbers (see note in the plenaries column).

Plenaries

After looking at Question ④ in the Pupil Book, you will be able to use the rule to work out the answer to the problem given in the starter (remember that with 30 in the class you would need the 29th triangular number).

Key Words

triangular number

square number

square root

Teaching points

- Triangular numbers are the sequence 1, 3, 6 10, 15, …
  These numbers can be used to make triangular patterns with dots.

- Square numbers are the sequence 1, 4, 9, 16, 25 …
  These numbers are found by squaring an integer and make square patterns with dots.

- The square root of a number. Square numbers have square roots which are integers but all positive numbers have square roots.

Notes

This section is fairly straightforward for most pupils. It is good for pupils to have something concrete to work with when they are learning about square and triangular numbers. Counters can be used or the shapes can be made using Multilink cubes or similar.

Pupils need to learn to use the square and square root keys on the calculator. Nearly all calculators work on the full algebraic logic now so the square key is pressed after the number is entered whereas the square root key is pressed before the number.

No mention is made in this book that all positive numbers actually have two square roots, a positive and a negative one. This is covered in the Extension pupil book and will be done in Core next year.

Homework

Unit Questions ❽ – ❿

3 Patterns and formulae

FRAMEWORK OBJECTIVES
Pages 148, 154, 156, 160

▶ Rules to find terms in sequences and patterns
▶ Rules using algebra

Resources

Available on **Teacher Resource CD-ROM 7ᶜ:**

Extra Practice A3-3
Homework Sheet A3-3
Starter A3-3-1
Starter A3-3-2
Starter A3-3-3
Plenary A3-3-1

Plenaries

- Check vocabulary: Compare 'formula' with 'equation' and 'expression'.
- Check misconceptions: The nth term for 4, 7, 10, 13, … is **not** $n + 3$.
- Check understanding: Position-to-term rule.

Key Words

sequence
term
rule
pattern
position-to-term rule
function machine
formula
nth term
generate

Teaching points

- Linear sequences go up (or down) by the same amount each time.
- This difference can be used to find the next term in a sequence.
- It is possible to find a formula for these sequences to work out any term in the sequence from the term number.
- This rule can be written in algebraic form.
- A formula is a rule written in algebra which includes an equals sign.
- The nth term of a sequence is a rule for finding any term in a sequence.

Homework

Questions ⑪ – ⑬

Notes

The first part of this section is relatively straightforward in that pupils can usually see patterns easily. The second part where pupils are shown how to find rules for sequences will be more difficult and pupils may need support. The problem is often that the fact that each term is, say, $+5$ from the previous one, produces a $\times 5$ in the formula. The fact that there are several stages to finding the position-to-term rule also makes it tricky. It is important that pupils follow the method logically.

To find a rule for the sequence 7,   11,   15,   19, …

$$7 \xrightarrow{4} 11 \xrightarrow{4} 15 \xrightarrow{4} 19$$

Step 1
Look at the gap between each term in the sequence. It is **4**. This means that the rule will start
number = **4** × term number.

Step 2
Write down the multiples of 4 and compare them with the terms of the sequence

Multiples of **4**: 4   8   12   16
Sequence   7   11   15   19

(each pair $+3$)

Step 3
To change the multiples of **4** into the sequence you need to add 3.

The rule is   **4** × term number **+ 3**
You can write this as   **4**n **+ 3**

This is known as the rule for the nth term or the nth term rule. Pupils often find it difficult when asked to find an nth term to realise that they are required to give an algebraic answer. They will often try to give a numerical answer.

4   Graphs of simple functions

FRAMEWORK OBJECTIVES
Page 164

▶ Generate coordinates that follow a rule
▶ Plot the graph of a simple function

Resources

Available on **Teacher Resource CD-ROM 7ᶜ:**

Extra Practice A3-4
Homework Sheet A3-4
Starter A3-4-1
Plenary A3-4-1

Starters

Have three formulae, such as $y = 3x - 2$, $y = x + 3$ and $y = 2x + 1$, written on the board ready. The whole class stand up. Give a pupil a number (for x) and ask them to substitute it into any one of the three formulae (tell them which one). If they give the correct answer for y, they get to sit down and pick the next pupil, number and formula. Stick to whole numbers between 1 and 12. Record results and use them to introduce the topic. If they get the answer wrong, they sit down but don't choose the next pupil which can be done again by the previous pupil.

Plenaries

Compare the steepness of lines with their equations. Can pupils spot any connections? (i.e. $y = \mathbf{2}x + 1$ would go along 1 and up **2**.) This serves as a useful checking tool when plotting algebraic graphs.

Maths Interact

Just Click

▶ The process of using a rule to calculate the y-coordinate of a point from the x-coordinate is demonstrated in an animation. The animation pauses automatically at key points to allow time for class discussion.

▶ This animation goes through the process of tabulating values for a rule, reading coordinates from the table and plotting the corresponding graph.

Teaching points

- Patterns of coordinates can be generated by applying a rule to an x-coordinate to generate a y-coordinate.
- Tables can be used to generate these patterns.
- Sequences of coordinates can be plotted on a graph.
- Formulae of the form $y = mx + c$ generate straight-line graphs.

Key Words

sequence
term
coordinate pair
x-axis
y-axis
pattern
coordinates
graph
rule
x-coordinate
y-coordinate

Notes

This section links coordinate patterns to the previous section as the idea of producing a coordinate sequence is essentially the same as producing a number sequence. The connection is that the x-coordinate is the term number and the y-coordinate is the term of the sequence.

Tables are often used to generate these sequences but pupils sometimes then lose the idea of the coordinate pair so this needs to be emphasised. If necessary, pupils can write out the coordinate pairs underneath their table.

Pupils should be able to plot the graphs, but the concept that all the points on the line obey the same rule may be slightly harder. Lines can be extended in either direction to show that this is true.

Homework

Unit Questions ⑭ – ⑮

Maths Interact

Pupil Book page 209

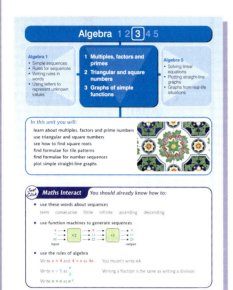

Pupils should already know how to:

- **use these words about sequences**

  term consecutive finite

  infinite ascending descending

  Choose one of the words from the list to complete a statement about sequences shown on the screen .

- **use function machines to generate sequences**

  Enter the missing numbers into a function machine to produce a sequence of output values.

- **use the rules of algebra**

  A matching game in which algebraic expressions and their simplified forms are shown on cards. Clicking a pair of matching cards causes them to disappear.

Pupil Book page 230

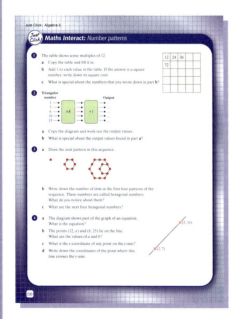

Number patterns

Maths Interact summary

1. A sequence of steps is carried out on a table of multiples of 12. The end result may be something of a surprise!

2. Triangular numbers are used as input values for a function machine. The output values demonstrate a relationship between triangular numbers and square numbers.

3. The first four hexagonal numbers are given, both as a pattern of dots and within a table. The next four hexagonal are to be found.

4. The equation of a line is to be determined from the coordinates of two points. The equation must then be used to complete the coordinates of some further points on the line.

Pupil Book answers

1. a

12	24	36	48	60
72	84	86	108	120
132	144	156	168	180
192	204	216	228	240
252	264	276	288	300

   b 25, 49, 121, 169, 289 are all square numbers.
   The square roots are: 5, 7, 11, 13, 17

   c The numbers produced are all prime numbers.

2. a The output is: 9, 25, 49, 81, 121
   b They are all square numbers.

3. a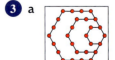

   b 1, 6, 15, 28. They are all triangular numbers.

   c 45, 66, 91, 120

4. a $y = 3x + 1$ c $x = 0$
   b $a = 37, b = 8$ d $(0, 1)$

Shape, Space and Measures 1 2 [3] 4 5

1 **Line symmetry**

2 **2-D representations of 3-D shapes**

3 **Constructions**

Framework teaching programme

Overview

This unit builds on the work in previous Shape, Space and Measures units on 2-D representations of 3-D objects and properties of 2-D shapes. The first section deals with simple line symmetry as preparation for **Shape, Space and Measures 4** in which line symmetry is covered again as well as transformations including reflection. Section 2 develops the work seen in **Shape, Space and Measures 1** and allows pupils to review their work on isometric drawings. Section 3 introduces constructions and this work is developed in **Shape, Space and Measures 5** where pupils go on to construct nets.

1 Line symmetry

▶ Drawing lines of symmetry on shapes
▶ Completing symmetrical patterns given the line symmetry

2 2-D representations of 3-D shapes

▶ Using isometric paper to draw 3-D objects

3 Constructions

▶ Drawing angles
▶ Constructing triangles

 Maths Interact

See page 110
and Pupil Book 7^C pages 231 and 248.

New concepts

Constructions

1 Line symmetry

FRAMEWORK OBJECTIVES

Page 188

Framework from Reception to Year 6 pages 106–107

▶ Drawing lines of symmetry on shapes
▶ Completing symmetrical patterns given the line symmetry

Resources

Available on **Teacher Resource CD-ROM 7ᶜ:**

Worksheet S3-1-1 ❶ – ❷
Worksheet S3-1-2 ❸
Worksheet S3-1-3 ❹ – ❺
Worksheet S3-1-4 ❶ – ❷
Extra Practice S3-1
Homework Sheet S3-1
Starter S3-1-1
Starter S3-1-2
Plenary S3-1-1
Squared paper

Starters

Have the word 'symmetry' ready-drawn in capital letters on the board. Ask which letters have no symmetry (R and Y). *Of the remaining letters, which is the odd-one-out?* (S has rotational symmetry, all the rest have one line of symmetry.)

Plenaries

Diagonal mirror lines often pose real problems for pupils (even just copying out the question from a book can be difficult). Show pupils how to rotate their page 45° to make the mirror line vertical in front of them. This makes questions much more straightforward.

Key Words

line of symmetry

mirror line

line symmetry

symmetrical

Teaching points

- If a shape is folded along a line of symmetry the two halves fit together with no overlap.
- The diagonals of a rectangle are not lines of symmetry.
- A parallelogram has no lines of symmetry.
- To complete a symmetrical pattern, work with each vertex of the given shape. Each vertex moves across the mirror line to the point which is the same distance away from the mirror line on the other side.

Notes

This section does not attempt to continue the work on classification of triangles and quadrilaterals from **Shape, Space and Measures 2**; this is left for **Shape, Space and Measures 5**.

In order that pupils are able to use symmetry to aid in the classification process and for reflections, this section provides the opportunity to revise line symmetry from previous years.

Homework

Unit Questions ❶ – ❷

2   2-D representations of 3-D shapes

Resources

Available on **Teacher Resource CD-ROM 7^c:**

Extra Practice S3-2
Homework Sheet S3-2
Starter S3-2-1
Plenary S3-2-1
Lined isometric paper
Dotty isometric paper

FRAMEWORK OBJECTIVES
Pages 198, 200

▶ Using isometric paper to draw 3-D objects

Starters

Ask questions such as: *I take two identical square-based pyramids and place them together so that their bases meet perfectly. How many edges/faces/vertices are there?* Number fans could be used to show the answers for this activity.

Key Words

2-D, 3-D

face, edge

vertex, vertices

cube, cuboid

prism, pyramid

cylinder

tetrahedron

sphere, hemisphere

Teaching points

- Definitions of face, edge and vertex.
- Mathematical names of common 3-D objects.
- How to draw a sketch of the common 3-D objects on ordinary paper.
- Isometric paper has a right way up.
- Drawing cuboids on isometric paper.

Notes

Much of this section is a recap of **Shape, Space and Measures 1** section 1. Nets are not covered again here as they are left for **Shape, Space and Measures 5** after pupils have covered constructions in the next section of this unit.

Drawing 2-D sketches of 3-D objects is a skill that is often taken for granted and the orange topic together with questions ❸ – ❻ aims to teach the skills required.

You may wish to use both isometric paper and dotty isometric paper for the yellow topic.

Homework

Unit Questions ❸ – ❺

3 Constructions

Resources

Available on **Teacher Resource CD-ROM 7ᶜ:**

Extra Practice S3-3
Homework Sheet S3-3
Starter S3-3-1
Plenary S3-3-1

FRAMEWORK OBJECTIVES
Pages 220, 222

▶ Drawing angles
▶ Constructing triangles

Other resources required

rulers   compasses
protractors or angle measurers

Starters

Have a shape, such as the one below, ready-drawn and labelled on the board.

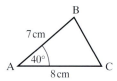

Give statements that may be true or false (focusing on the use of notation), such as AC = 8 cm (T), ∠ACB = 40° (F), $\hat{A}$ = 40° (T), ∠BAC = 40° (T). Pupils need to come to an agreement on their answer before you tell them whether or not they are correct.

Plenaries

Ensure that pupils realise that if they are asked to 'sketch' something in maths, it means a neat diagram that is labelled as necessary. It does not mean the same as it does in art lessons! 'Construct' implies that ruler/protractor/compasses should be used, and that the diagram should be accurate. (Pupils will be allowed some tolerance perhaps as much as ±2 mm and ±2°.)

Just Click Maths Interact

The toolbox pencil, ruler, compasses and protractor are all available to allow the teacher to demonstrate the basic construction techniques.

Key Words

construct

ruler

draw, sketch

protractor

measure

angle measurer

Teaching points

● Drawing an angle correct to the nearest degree.
● Constructing a triangle given two sides and the included angle.
● Constructing a triangle given two angles and the included side.

Notes

There is no need to do all of the parts in each of the questions as the drawing of angles and constructions will take most pupils quite a lot of time to do carefully and accurately.

When constructing a triangle given two sides and the included angle you can teach pupils to mark off the correct length on the second side drawn using compasses open to the required length. This gives a construction arc on the diagram produced but this additional complication has not been used here.

In questions **6** and **8** ensure that the pupils have the correct sketches before they go on to construct the triangles.

In Question **7** **f** pupils need to realise that they need to work out the missing angle before they can draw the construction.

Homework

Unit Questions **6** – **8**

1   Line symmetry   *Answers*

1 a   c   e

b   d   f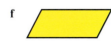

2 a   c

b   d

3 a   d

b   e

c   f

4 a   c

b   d

5 a   c

b   d

6 The two 90° angles are joined side by side to create an isosceles triangle. Because the two triangles are identical the sloping sides are equal and the line of contact is a line of symmetry.

2   2-D representations of 3-D shapes   *Answers*

1 a (1) Sphere   (2) 1 face, 0 edges, 0 vertices
  b (1) Triangular prism
    (2) 5 faces, 9 edges, 6 vertices
  c (1) Cuboid
    (2) 6 faces, 12 edges, 8 vertices
  d (1) Cylinder
    (2) 3 faces, 2 edges, 0 vertices

2 a Cuboid with 6 faces, 12 edges, 8 vertices.
    Dimensions 3 cm by 1 cm by 1 cm
  b L-shape with 8 faces, 18 edges, 12 vertices

3 a   b

4 Pupils following instructions to draw a square based pyramid.

5 **a** Tetrahedron **b** Triangular prism **c** Cylinder

6

7 **a**

or any orientation

b Pupil's drawings of five cuboids with dimensions correctly stated.

8 **a**

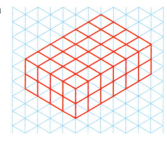

b 48 cubes

9 **a** Copy of diagram from pupil book.
b 11 **c** 24 **d** 16 **e** 28

---

3 Constructions   *Answers*

1 **a**
 10°

b
 20°

c
 30°

d
 60°

e
 70°

f
 80°

g
 55°

h
 35°

i
45°

j
75°

k
23°

l
36°

m
52°

n
69°

o
89°

p
3°

2 **a**
 100°

b
 120°

c
 130°

d
 160°

e
 170°

f
 110°

g
 115°

h
 135°

i
145°

j
155°

k
124°

l
98°

m
171°

n
148°

o
92°

p
179°

3 a 190° **i** 255°

b 240° **j** 315°

c 270° **k** 344°

d 300° **l** 232°

e 320° **m** 291°

f 350° **n** 357°

g 185° **o** 183°

h 225° **p** 268°

4 a
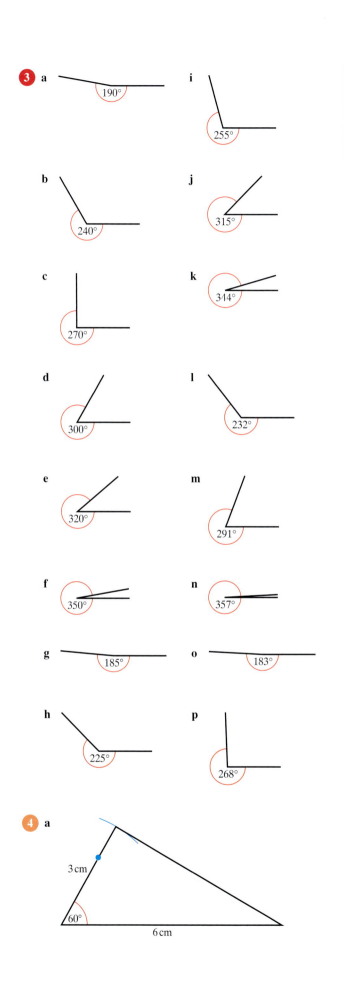

b
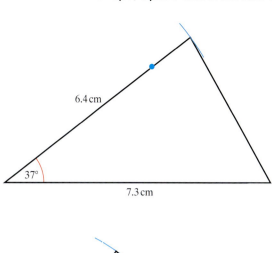

c
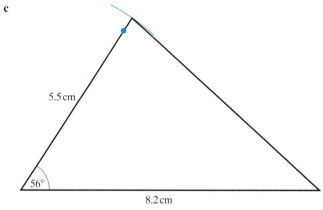

d
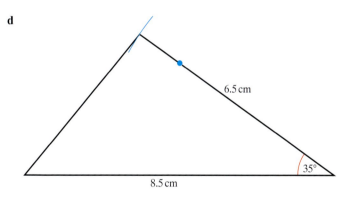

e
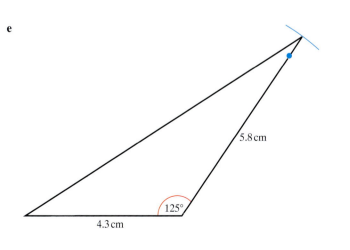

99

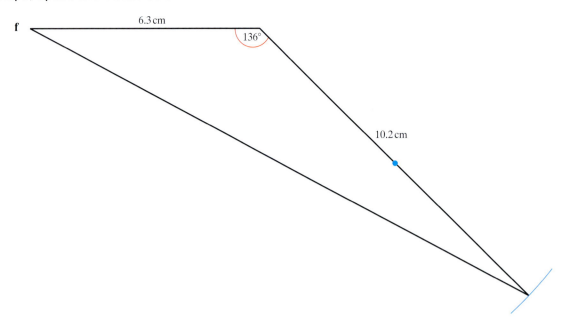

f

6.3 cm

136°

10.2 cm

5 a Sketch of the triangle in part **b** showing lengths and angles.

b

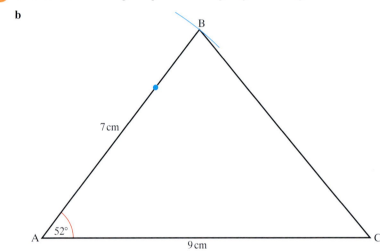

c BC = 7.2 cm, ∠ACB = 50°
(Allow ±2 mm and ±2°)

6 a (1)

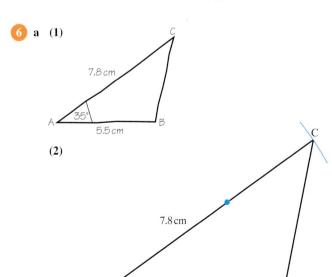

(2)

(3) BC = 4.5 cm (±2 mm)
∠ACB = 44° (±2°)
∠ABC = 101° (±2°)

b (1)

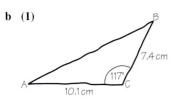

(3) AC = 15 cm (±2 mm)
∠BAC = 26° (±2°)
∠ABC = 37° (±2°)

(2)

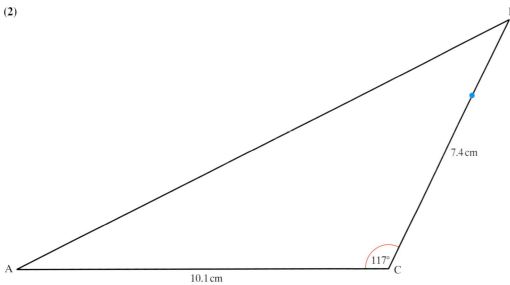

c (1)

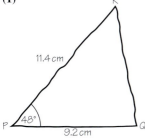

(3) QR = 8.7 cm (±2 mm)
∠PRQ = 53° (±2°)
∠PQR = 79° (±2°)

(2)

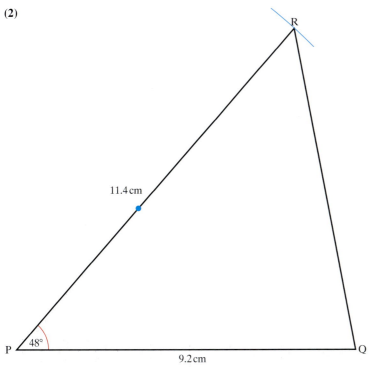

Shape, Space and Measures 3

d (1)

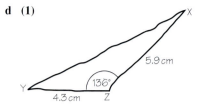

(2)

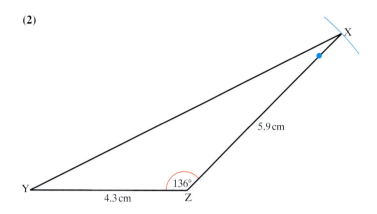

(3) XY = 9.5 cm (±2 mm)
∠XYZ = 26° (±2°)
∠YXZ = 18° (±2°)

7 a

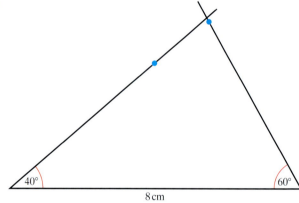

b

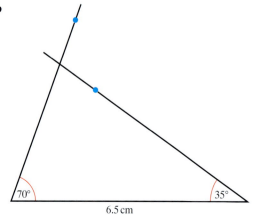

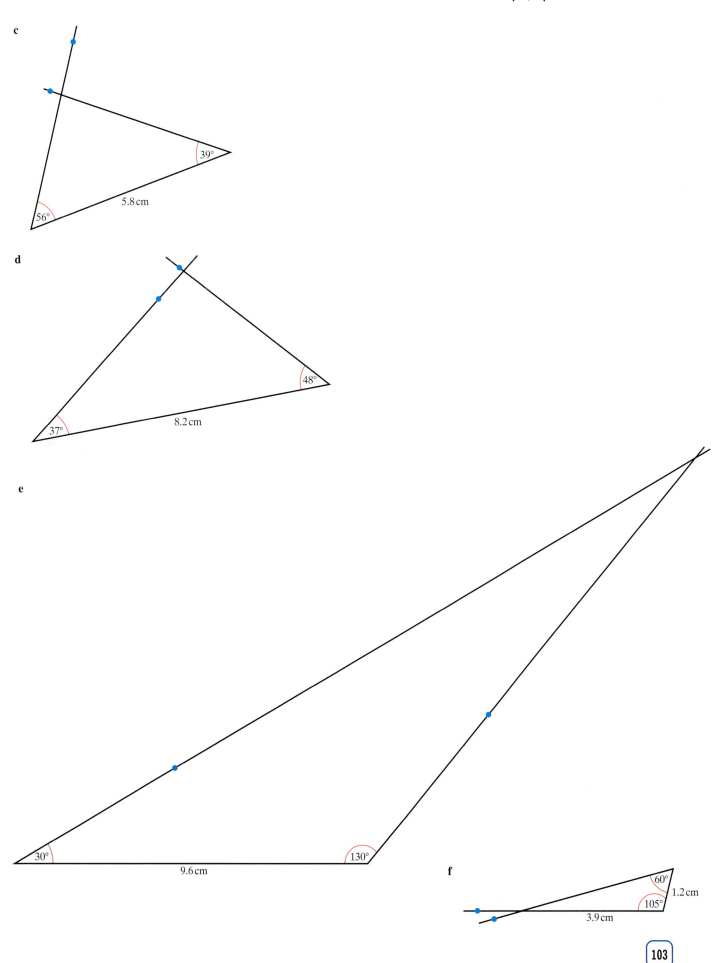

c

39°

5.8 cm

56°

d

48°

8.2 cm

37°

e

30°

9.6 cm

130°

f

60°

1.2 cm

105°

3.9 cm

8 a (1)

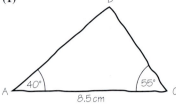

(3) ∠ABC = 85° (exact answer only)
AB = 7 cm (±2 mm)
BC = 5.5 cm (±2 mm)

(2)

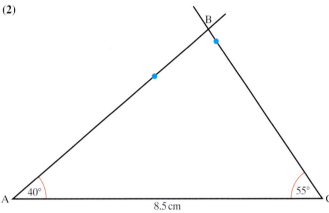

b (1)

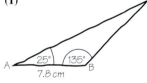

(3) ∠ACB = 20° (exact answer only)
AC = 16.1 cm (±2 mm)
BC = 9.6 cm (±2 mm)

(2)

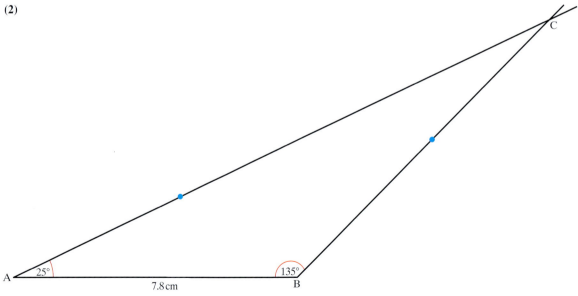

c (1)

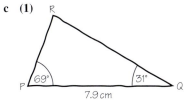

(2)

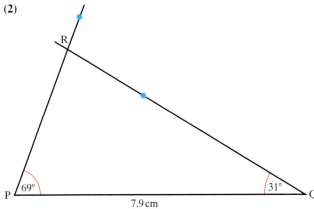

(3) ∠PRQ = 80° (exact answer only)
PR = 4.1 cm (±2 mm)
QR = 7.5 cm (±2 mm)

d (1)

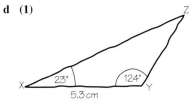

(3) ∠XZY = 33° (exact answer only)
XZ = 8.1 cm (±2 mm)
YZ = 3.8 cm (±2 mm)

(2)

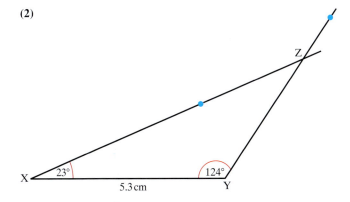

Unit Questions: **Shape, Space and Measures 3**   *Answers*

1   a   b

2   a   b   c   d

3   a   6 faces, 12 edges, 8 vertices   c   5 faces, 8 edges, 5 vertices   e   3 faces, 2 edges, 0 vertices
     b   4 faces, 6 edges, 4 vertices   d   5 faces, 9 edges, 6 vertices   f   1 face, 0 edges, 0 vertices

4

5   a   b   24

6   a

3.2 cm

55°

6.8 cm

b

8.7 cm

3.9 cm

39°

c

7.2 cm

132°

6.9 cm

7 a Sketch of the triangle in part **b**.

b

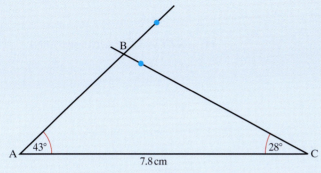

c AB = 3.9 cm, BC = 5.6 cm (±2 mm)

8 a (1)

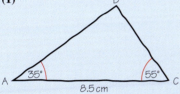

(3) AB = 7 cm (±2 mm)
BC = 4.9 cm (±2 mm)

(4) ∠ABC = 90° (exact answer only)

(2)

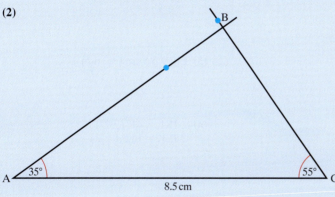

b (1)

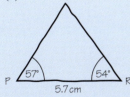

(3) PQ = 4.9 cm (±2 mm)
QR = 5.2 cm (±2 mm)

(4) ∠PQR = 69° (exact answer only)

(2)

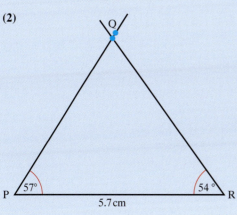

c **(1)**

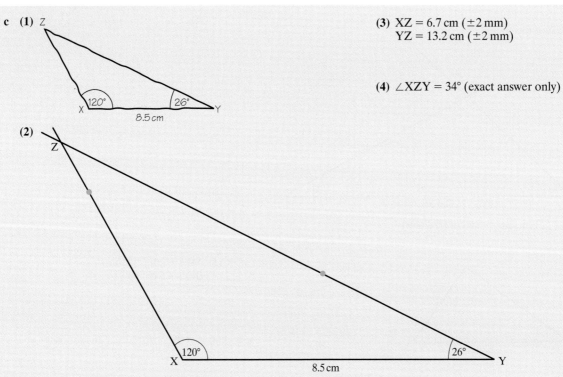

(3) XZ = 6.7 cm (±2 mm)
YZ = 13.2 cm (±2 mm)

(4) ∠XZY = 34° (exact answer only)

(2)

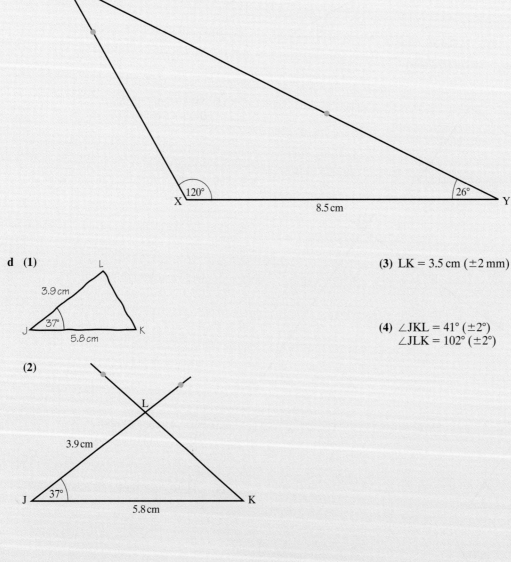

d **(1)**

(3) LK = 3.5 cm (±2 mm)

(4) ∠JKL = 41° (±2°)
∠JLK = 102° (±2°)

(2)

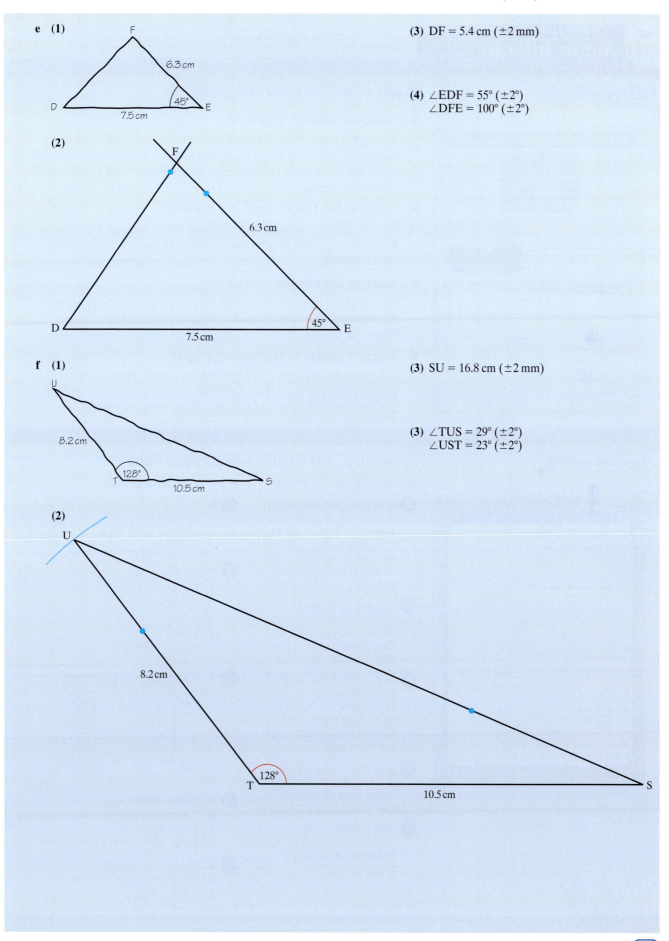

e **(1)**

F

6.3 cm

D   45°   E

7.5 cm

(3) DF = 5.4 cm (±2 mm)

(4) ∠EDF = 55° (±2°)
    ∠DFE = 100° (±2°)

(2)

F

6.3 cm

D   45°   E

7.5 cm

f **(1)**

U

8.2 cm

T 128°

10.5 cm   S

(3) SU = 16.8 cm (±2 mm)

(3) ∠TUS = 29° (±2°)
    ∠UST = 23° (±2°)

(2)

U

8.2 cm

T 128°

10.5 cm   S

Maths Interact

Pupil Book page 231

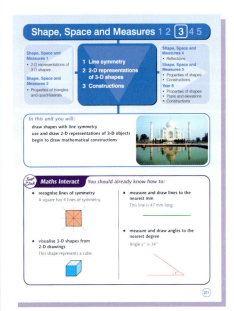

Pupils should already know how to:

- **recognise lines of symmetry**

  A shape is presented and pupils have to identify any lines of symmetry and draw them using the toolbox ruler and pencil. The Show button reveals another copy of the shape with any lines of symmetry in place.

- **visualise 3-D shapes from 2-D drawings**

  A 2-D drawing is shown together with a selection of 3-D images. Pupils have to decide which of the images may be represented by the drawing.

- **measure lines to the nearest mm**

  The program features a whiteboard ruler that may be dragged and rotated. The ruler is used to measure the length of a line drawn on screen.

- **measure angles to the nearest degree**

  The program features a whiteboard protractor that may be dragged and rotated. The protractor is used to measure an angle between 0° and 180° drawn at random on the screen.

Pupil Book page 248

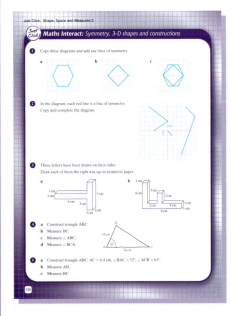

Symmetry, 3-D shapes and constructions

Maths Interact summary

1. A shape is presented and pupils have to identify its lines of symmetry. When the Show button is clicked the lines of symmetry are added to the diagram in red.

2. A partly completed diagram is shown and the object is to complete it so that the two red lines are both lines of symmetry.

3. A shape is shown and labelled with its measurements. Pupils have to re-draw the shape rotated through 90° on an isometric grid.

4. The ruler, compass and protractor tools are used to construct a triangle and to take measurements from it.

5. This is similar to question 4 but the information is presented without a diagram.

Pupil Book answers

1. a   b   c

2.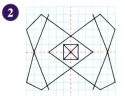

3. a   b

    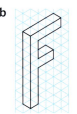

4. a   Pupils construction.
   b   7.3 cm − 7.9 cm
   c   70° − 72°
   d   36° − 38°

5. a   Pupils construction.
   b   6.0 cm − 6.6 cm
   c   5.3 − 5.9 cm

Number 1 2 3 **4** 5

Number 2
- Fractions
- Decimals
- Percentages

1 Percentages
2 Proportion
3 Ratio

Year 8
- Direct proportion
- Conversion graphs
- Three part ratios

Framework teaching programme

70–77	Fractions, decimals and percentages
78–79	Proportion
80–81	Understand and use ratios

Overview

This unit consists of three main teaching sections. The first recaps percentages, first seen in **Number 2**. It takes the topic on a little further covering more complicated calculations. The second section looks at proportion while the third covers the understanding and use of ratio.

1 Percentages

▶ Changing between percentages, decimals and fractions
▶ Finding a percentage of an amount
▶ Solving problems using percentages

2 Proportion

▶ Writing a proportion as a fraction
▶ Writing a proportion as a decimal or a percentage
▶ Using direct proportion

3 Ratio

▶ Comparing sizes using ratios
▶ Simplifing ratios
▶ Dividing something into a given ratio
▶ Linking ratio and proportion

 Maths Interact

See page 118
and Pupil Book 7^C pages 249 and 268.

New concepts

Proportion

Ratio

1 Percentages

Resources

Available on **Teacher Resource CD-ROM 7^C:**

Worksheet N4-1-1 **❶**, **❷** and **❹**

Extra Practice N4-1

Homework Sheet N4-1

Starter N4-1-1

Plenary N4-1-1

FRAMEWORK OBJECTIVES
Pages 70, 72, 74

▶ Changing between percentages, decimals and fractions

▶ Finding a percentage of an amount

▶ Solving problems using percentages

Key Words

fraction

percentage

decimal

equivalent

simplify

Starters

Use a counting stick to demonstrate equivalent fractions, decimals and percentages. Explain that the edge marked in centimetres can be interpreted as percentages, while the other edges show quarters, tenths (which can be used for 0.1, 0.2, 0.3, …) and fifths. Pupils can come to the front and point to requested distances along the stick. By turning the stick around you can reveal equivalences.

Plenaries

- Check that pupils are confident with the following facts: $0.3 = 30\%$, $0.4 \neq 4\%$, $0.6 = 60\%$, $0.02 = 2\%$, $0.015 = 1.5\%$

- Demonstrate the fact that an 8% increase, followed by a 12% increase is **not** the same as a 20% increase.

Teaching points

- How to change between percentages, decimals and fractions.
- How to find a percentage of an amount with and without a calculator.
- Solving real-life problems using percentages.

Notes

This section covers changing between fractions, decimals and percentages and asks pupils to cancel the resulting fractions to their simplest form. It then covers calculations using percentages. With a calculator this is done by expressing the percentage as a decimal and then multiplying. Without a calculator it uses the method of finding 10% by dividing by 10 and finding 1% by dividing by 100 and then using these as building blocks to calculate the required percentage. The finding method of 1% is slightly different from the method seen in **Number 2** where pupils found 10% then divided that by 10 to find 1%. It is important for pupils to see both ideas but they can clearly choose the one they prefer.

Homework

Unit Questions –

2 Proportion

FRAMEWORK OBJECTIVES
Page 78

▶ Writing a proportion as a fraction
▶ Writing a proportion as a decimal or a percentage
▶ Using direct proportion

Resources

Available on **Teacher Resource CD-ROM 7^c:**

Extra Practice N4-2
Homework Sheet N4-2
Starter N4-2-1
Plenary N4-2-1
Plenary N4-2-2

Key Words

proportion

fraction

compare

percentage

Starters

Use the recipe from question ⑭. The whole class stands up. The aim is to get everyone sitting down by answering a question correctly. Ask questions such as:
How many mushrooms would be needed to feed 6 shepherds?
How many shepherds could be fed with 750 g of mince?
I have 400 mℓ of stock. Is this enough to feed 17 shepherds?

Teaching points

- Finding a proportion as a fraction – using proportions to make simple comparisons.
- Finding a proportion as a decimal or a percentage.
- Using direct proportion – costs and simple currency changes.
- Very simple examples of the unitary method for proportion.

Notes

In many ways the idea of proportion is not new to pupils. It slightly formalises the idea of comparing two or more quantities. Pupils need to understand that proportion is a way of describing parts of a whole and this can be done using any of fractions, decimals or percentages. The section contains some very simple examples of the unitary method which is strictly part of the Year 8 syllabus.
For example, if 4 burgers cost £1.60 and you wish to find the cost of 22, it may be easier to divide the price by 4 to find the cost of 1 burger, then multiply by 22 to find the cost of 22.

Homework

Unit Questions ⑤ – ⑧

3 Ratio

FRAMEWORK OBJECTIVES

Page 80

▶ Comparing sizes using ratios
▶ Simplifying ratios
▶ Dividing something into a given ratio
▶ Linking ratio and proportion

Resources

Available on **Teacher Resource CD-ROM 7^C:**

Extra Practice N4-3

Homework Sheet N4-3

Starter N4-3-1

Plenary N4-3-1

Starters

See if you can get hold of any OS map extracts used by your geography department. Use them as a real-life example of ratio and discuss what the scale 1 : 50 000 actually means. Work out some real-life distances between points using the scale.

Plenaries

Ensure that pupils appreciate the fact that the order of the ratio is important. The answer to question a is 3 : 1, **not** 1 : 3.

Just Click Maths Interact

▶ The concept of a ratio and the notation used is presented as an animation using the animation player.

▶ This animation deals with the simplification of a ratio. Coloured counters are used to give a visual representation of the cancelling process.

Teaching points

● How to compare sizes using ratios.
● Cancelling ratios to their simplest form in the same way as fractions.
● Divide something into a given ratio. The ratios only have two parts.
● Linking ratio and proportion
  – changing between ratios and fractions and percentages.

Key Words

ratio

compare

cancel

percentage

proportion

divide

simplest form

fraction

decimal

Notes

Pupils need to contrast ratio with proportion. Ratio describes how to compare different parts of a whole, not two different wholes as in proportion. Cancelling ratio works in exactly the same way as cancelling fractions which was covered in **Number 2**. Pupils may wish to cancel ratios in stages. For example, 24 : 18 can be cancelled by 2 to give 12 : 9 and then by 3 to give 4 : 3. The pupil may spot that the original ratio can be cancelled by 6 to achieve this in one step. The main part of the section covers splitting an amount into a given ratio. This has several steps to it and pupils need to be encouraged to do it logically. Some of the later questions ask pupils to work back to the total amount given one of the parts. This can be quite demanding at this stage but is included as it helps the overall understanding of ratio.

Homework

Unit Questions **9** – **13**

1 Percentages

1

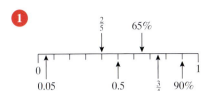

2

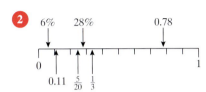

3 a $\frac{35}{100} = \frac{7}{20}$

b $\frac{15}{100} = \frac{3}{20}$

c $\frac{70}{100} = \frac{7}{10}$

d $\frac{16}{100} = \frac{4}{25}$

e $\frac{9}{100}$

f $\frac{38}{100} = \frac{19}{50}$

4

Fraction	$\frac{1}{2}$	$\frac{43}{50}$	$\frac{1}{8}$	$\frac{6}{25}$	$\frac{2}{25}$	$\frac{7}{20}$	$\frac{3}{10}$
Percentage	50%	86%	**12.5%**	24%	8%	**35%**	**30%**
Decimal	0.5	**0.86**	**0.125**	0.24	**0.08**	**0.35**	0.3

5 Spelling $\quad \frac{16}{20} = \frac{80}{100} = 80\%$

French $\quad \frac{28}{40} = \frac{70}{100} = 70\%$

Maths $\quad 58\%$

6 a £64.40

b £78.30

c £217.50

d 66.5 g

e 169 litres

f £2100

7 Pupils should show working.

a £58.80

b £45.50

c £292.50

d £1220

e 588 g

f 121.5 people

8 50% of 660 is 330.

So 58% must be more than 330 and cannot be 320

9

Level	3	4	5
Pupils	8	15	9

10 a 220

b 22, 220 − 22 = 198

c 10% of 220 is larger than 10% of 200 so the answer is smaller than 200.

11 26.4 g

13 **Cereal bar**

protein = 2.4 g

carbohydrate = 31.2 g

fat = 4 g

fibre = 2.4 g

Chocolate bar

protein = 2.8 g

carbohydrate = 25.6 g

fat = 11.6 g

fibre = 0 g

14 £290 304

15 Area = 90 cm^2

20% of area = 18 cm^2

∴ Each square is 9 cm^2 and the length of each side is 3 cm

2 Proportion — *Answers*

1
a 50% or $\frac{1}{2}$
b 33.3% or $\frac{1}{3}$
c 33.3% or $\frac{1}{3}$
d 0%

2 Answers should be around:
a 80% or $\frac{4}{5}$
b 25% or $\frac{1}{4}$
c 60% or $\frac{3}{5}$

3
a $\frac{17}{30}$
b $\frac{13}{30}$

4 $\frac{1}{4}$ or 25%

5 $\frac{3}{8}$ or 37.5%

6 $\frac{7}{48}$ or 14.6%

7 New luxury chocolate bar ($\frac{15}{40} = 37.5\%$ $\frac{9}{30} = 30\%$)

8 70%

9 Nathaniel's class
$\frac{23}{28} = 82.14\%$
$\frac{21}{27} = 77.77\%$

10 Red dice ($\frac{42}{257} = 16.3\%$ $\frac{56}{331} = 16.9\%$)

11
a Tax = £7360
Pension = £1920
NI = £3520
b 60%

12
a £3.60
b £6.00

13 163.20 euros

14 375 g mince
675 g potato
45 g mushrooms
150 mℓ stock

15
a £9.48
b £3.56

16 320 mℓ

17
a $198
b £200

18 390 mℓ

19 45 kg sharp sand
45 kg soft sand
15 kg cement

3 Ratio — *Answers*

1 12 : 5

2 2 : 1

3 a

B	B	B	G	G
B	B	B	G	G
B	B	B	G	G
B	B	B	G	G
B	B	B	G	G

b 3 : 2
c 2 : 3

4 a 11 : 6   b 6 : 11

5 17 : 3 or 680 : 120

6
a ÷3 (21 : 6) ÷3 **7 : 2**
b ÷5 (25 : 10) ÷5 **5 : 2**
c ÷4 (16 : 12) ÷4 **4 : 3**

7
a 3 : 1 d 2 : 1 g 3 : 2
b 3 : 1 e 5 : 2 h 21 : 11
c 3 : 1 f 3 : 2 i 7 : 5

8
a 1 : 2 d 15 : 7 g 2 : 1
b 2 : 3 e 8 : 11 h 1 : 3
c 2 : 1 f 17 : 13 i 1 : 4

9 1 : 6

10 a 120 cm   b 4 : 3

11 200 : 33

12 1 : 50

13 Sally £57   Jo £38

14 21

15 120 g and 160 g

16
a £20 : £30 f £100 : £20
b £28 : £42 g £90 : £80
c £35 : £49 h £150 : £210
d £36 : £30 i £5.80 : £8.70
e £18.75 : £31.25 j £450 : £270

17 30

18 45

19
a 1 : 3   b 2 : 3
c 1 carton of orange juice

20 33.75°, 56.25°

21 12 × 7.5

22 7 : 18 gives 25 shares of £24.
Paul £168, David £432.
15 : 38 gives 53 shares of £11.32.
Paul £169.80, David £430.16.
So Paul is better off with 15 : 38 arrangement.

23 a 3 : 1   b $\frac{1}{4}$ c 75%

24
a £62.50, £37.50
b £60, £40
c 11
d Andrew will always have more than half of the total proportions as he will always be older than Katy.

25 a 62.5% b 37.5% c 40% d 15%

26 a $\frac{65}{100}$ or $\frac{13}{20}$ b 13 : 7   c 220

27 Allstone has the best ratio (104 : 133). Degby has the worst ratio (2 : 21).

Unit Questions: **Number 4**   *Answers*

1

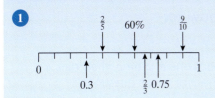

2

Fraction	$\frac{1}{4}$	$\frac{3}{5}$	$\frac{7}{10}$	$\frac{3}{8}$	$\frac{16}{25}$	$\frac{3}{50}$	$\frac{1}{20}$
Percentage	25%	**60%**	70%	**37.5%**	64%	**6%**	5%
Decimal	0.25	**0.6**	**0.7**	**0.375**	0.64	**0.06**	0.05

3
a £100.50
b £3680
c £49
d 122.4 g
e 313.5 mℓ
f £166.25

4 20

5 Class 7A (28.6%, 26.9%)

6 326.40 euros

7 342 mℓ

8

Item	Cost of 2	Cost of 5	Cost of 12
CD RW	£1.80	**£4.50**	**£10.80**
Printer paper	**£4.90**	£12.25	**£29.40**
Printer cartridge	**£31.20**	**£78.00**	£187.20

9
a 4 : 1   f 3 : 1
b 3 : 2   g 2 : 3
c 1 : 3   h 1 : 1
d 5 : 3   i 1 : 10
e 36 : 35   j 7 : 3

10 1 : 8

11 1 : 30

12
a £35 : £15
b £36 : £54
c £45 : £30
d £66.67 : £93.33
e £127.06 : £112.94
f £666.67 : £1333.33

13 3 : 2 equivalent to 60% : 40%
$\frac{2}{3} : \frac{1}{3}$ equivalent to $66\frac{2}{3}\% : 33\frac{1}{3}\%$
$\frac{2}{3} : \frac{1}{3}$ best for Maggie, 3 : 2 best for Claire.

Maths Interact

Pupil Book page 249

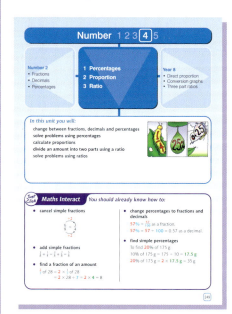

Pupils should already know how to:

- **cancel simple fractions**

  Select Examples to see the questions one at a time, then click Show to see the method. Select Practice to see questions displayed six at a time.

- **add simple fractions**

  Select Examples to see the questions one at a time, then click Show to see the method in separate stages. Select Practice to see questions displayed six at a time.

- **find a fraction of an amount**

  Select Examples to see the questions one at a time, then click Show to see the method in separate stages. Select Practice to see questions displayed six at a time.

- **change percentages to fractions and decimals**

  Select Examples to see one question of each type. Select Practice to see mixed type questions displayed four at a time.

- **find simple percentages**

  Select Examples to see the method applied to one question at a time. Select Practice to see questions displayed three at a time without the intermediate steps.

Pupil Book page 268

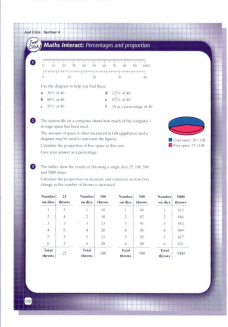

Percentages and proportion

Maths Interact summary

1 Percentage calculations are worked out using a pair of number lines, one showing a percentage scale.

2 Calculation of a proportion as a percentage within the context of free space in a computer memory system A calculator will be needed.

3 A simulation of dice throwing produces tables of results for 25, 100, 500 and 5000 throws. The frequency for each score is to be expressed as a proportion.

Pupil Book answers

1   a   12   c   22   e   35
     b   32   d   5   f   45%

2   64.9% (1 d.p.)

3   25:   0.2   0.16   0.12   0.24
             0.2   0.08 (to 2 d.p.)
   100:   0.18   0.18   0.13   0.2
             0.11   0.2   (to 2 d.p.)
   500:   0.14   0.16   0.18   0.17
             0.19   0.16 (to 2 d.p.)
  5000:   0.16   0.17   0.17   0.17
             0.16   0.16 (to 2 d.p.)

As the number of throws increases, the numbers are becoming more and more similar.

Algebra 1 2 3 **4** 5

Algebra 2
- Using letters for unknowns
- Using algebraic operations
- Collecting like terms
- Multiplying out a bracket
- Using simple formulae

1 Algebraic operations
2 Collecting like terms
3 Equations

Algebra 5
- Constructing and solving equations
- Using formulae

Framework teaching programme

112–125 Formulae, expressions and equations

Overview

This unit continues the work on algebra from **Algebra 2**. The unit spirals to revisit the correct order for algebraic operations including brackets, collecting like terms and multiplying out a bracket. The final section deals with the construction and solution of simple linear equations both mentally and using function machines. Formal algebra is used in **Algebra 5**.

1 Algebraic operations
- ▶ The correct order of algebraic operations
- ▶ Inverse operations

2 Collecting like terms
- ▶ Collecting like terms
- ▶ Multiplying out a bracket

3 Equations
- ▶ Solving simple equations mentally
- ▶ Solving equations using function machines

Just Click **Maths Interact**

See page 126
and Pupil Book 7^C pages 269 and 286.

New concepts

Constructing and solving linear equations

1 Algebraic operations

FRAMEWORK OBJECTIVES
Page 114

▶ The correct order of algebraic operations
▶ Inverse operations

Available on **Teacher Resource CD-ROM 7^C:**

Extra Practice A4-1
Homework Sheet A4-1
Starter A4-1-1
Plenary A4-1-1
Plenary A4-1-2

Plenaries

Write a mixture of equations ($2x + 4 = 6$, $3n - 3 = 2$, $2y = 8$, etc.), expressions ($2x + y$, $4q$, $p - 4d$, etc.) and formulae ($A = \frac{1}{2}bh$, $S = am$, $E = mc^2$, etc.) on the board. A pupil faces the board. You shout out either 'equation', 'expression' or 'formula' and the pupil has to 'swat' (hit) the correct ones on the board.

Key Words

order of operations

brackets

inverse

square

square root

Teaching points

- Multiplication and division have precedence over addition and subtraction.

- Using BODMAS to understand the order of algebraic operations.

- If $a + b = 8$ then $a = 8 - b$ and $b = 8 - a$.

- Addition and subtraction are inverse operations.

- If $a \times b = 12$ then $a = \dfrac{12}{b}$ and $b = \dfrac{12}{a}$.

- Multiplication and division are inverse operations.

- If $a^2 = 25$ then $a = \sqrt{25} = 5$.

- Squaring and square rooting are inverse operations.

Notes

This section is a revision of the work in **Algebra 2** section 1 although the basic work on notation is now assumed and the section covers the order of operations and inverse functions. Squares and square roots were not mentioned in **Algebra 2**.

BODMAS should now have been covered if you have done **Number 3** so it is used fully to explain the order of algebraic operations.

Question ❺ is based on the SATs question included in **Algebra 1**.

Two-stage inverses are covered using questions ❽ and ❾. Question ❽ does not require any algebraic explanation but the fact that the inverse of two operations is the inverse of each operation in the reverse order is required in question ❾, which will still be demanding for many pupils at this level even though they will have been exposed to the ideas here in **Algebra 2**.

Homework

Unit Questions ❶ – ❷

2 Collecting like terms

FRAMEWORK OBJECTIVES
Page 116

▶ Collecting like terms
▶ Multiplying out a bracket

Resources

Available on **Teacher Resource CD-ROM 7ᶜ:**

Worksheet A4-2-1 ❸
Extra Practice A4-2
Homework Sheet A4-2
Starter A4-2-1
Plenary A4-2-1
Plenary A4-2-2

Starters

Ask the pupils to pick a domino. Double the higher number (if they have picked a double then treat one number as high and the other low), multiply by 5, add 4 and add the lower number. Ask pupils to give their totals. 'Magically' tell the pupil their domino! Simply subtract 4 from their total, e.g. total is 47, subtract 4 = 43 so domino is 4, 3.

Plenaries

Do the trick with a domino m, n where m is the higher number. The various stages will produce $2m$ then $10m$ then $10m + 4$ then $10m + 4 + n$. As the magician, you subtract 4 so the expression becomes $10m + n$. The higher number is always in the tens column and the lower one in the units column.

Maths Interact

▶ This is a matching game in which the object is to identify pairs of like terms. Correctly matched terms disappear and play continues again until the screen is clear. A timer is available.

Teaching points

- Terms involving the same combination of letters are like terms.
- pq and qp terms are like terms.
- Adding and subtracting like terms to simplify expressions.
- Multiplying out a bracket by a single positive term.
- Multiplying out two separate bracketed expressions and collecting like terms for their sum.

Key Words

term

simplify

expression

brackets

Notes

Colour is used to highlight like terms in question ❶ but is removed in question ❷.

Remind pupils about perimeter before question ❻, which is based on the similar question in **Algebra 2**. Pupils have to draw a shape given its perimeter as an algebraic expression. Clearly there are many possible answers for this and you should discuss several different answers.

Multiplying a bracket by a half is covered in question ❾ and you could extend this work to include other fractions outside the bracket if you wish.

Powers are used in questions ❿–⓬. Question ⓫ is a Level 6 SAT question, which will be challenging for many pupils at this stage. You certainly need to ensure that pupils are familiar with area and perimeter.

Only the last part of question ⓬ includes an algebraic term outside a bracket. This was introduced during the exercise in **Algebra 2** as question ❾ in section 2 and you may wish to revise this before setting this question. Alternatively you can omit this part of the question of course and leave this for next year.

Worksheet A4-2-1 can be used to save pupils drawing the brick diagrams in question ❸ and allow them just to fill the diagrams in.

Homework

Unit Questions ❸ – ❻

3 Equations

FRAMEWORK OBJECTIVES
Pages 122, 124

▶ Solving simple equations mentally
▶ Solving equations using function machines

Resources

Available on **Teacher Resource CD-ROM 7ᶜ:**

Worksheet A4-3-1 **Function machines**
Extra Practice A4-3
Homework Sheet A4-3
Starter A4-3-1
Plenary A4-3-1

Starters

Pupils have number fans, wipeboards or use their fingers. The pupils have to solve the following balancing problems and show their answers. How much does a bag of sugar weigh each time? 2 bags of sugar and 2 kg balances with 8 kg, 1 bag of sugar and 2 kg balances with 6 kg, 4 bags of sugar and 3 kg balances with 11 kg, etc.

Plenaries

Pupils have wipeboards or use their exercise books. *The answer is 5, what's the equation?* Answers must involve two operations, e.g. $3x - 1 = 14$.

Key Words

equation

unknown

solution

solve

inverse

Teaching points

- An equation has an equals sign in it.
- There is only one solution for linear equations.
- Setting up equations from think of a number type problems and other situations.
- Solving equations mentally and intuitively.
- Solving equations formally using function machine diagrams.

Notes

The algebraic method for solving equations is not introduced at this stage and this is left for **Algebra 5**.

Don't be tempted to tell pupils that there is only one solution to every equation. While there is only one solution to a linear equation there are of course up to two solutions for a quadratic equation, up to three for a cubic and so on.

You can ask your pupils to solve all of the equations in the red topic using the function machines from the orange topic if you wish but the emphasis in the red topic is on the setting up of the equations and the actual solution is intended to be relatively simple.

You can use Worksheet A4-3-1 for all of the questions that require function machine diagrams if you don't want pupils to actually have to draw the machines. Questions **9** and **10** and Test Yourself **8** and **9** also require pupils to draw function machines so you could also use the sheet for these questions.

Homework

Unit Questions **7** – **10**

1 Algebraic operations   *Answers*

1   **a**   Multiply n by 6 and then add 3.

     b   Subtract 3 from n then multiply by 4.

     c   Divide n by 7 and then add 1.

     d   Divide n by 5 then subtract 9.

     e   Multiply n by 2 and then add 8.

     f   Subtract 2 from n and then multiply by 4.

     g   Multiply n by 6 and then subtract this from 8.

     h   Divide n by 2 and then subtract this from 10.

2   **a**   False. $a + b$ is the same as $b + a$.

     b   True

     c   False. $4n - 1$ means multiply n by 4 then subtract 1. $4(n - 1)$ means subtract 1 from n and then multiply by 4.

     d   True   **e**   True

3   **a** $4n - 3$ means multiply n by 4 and then subtract 3. $4(n - 3)$ means subtract 3 from n and then multiply by 4.

     b $\dfrac{n}{3} + 6$ means divide n by 3 and then add 6. $\dfrac{n + 6}{3}$ means add 6 to n and then divide by 3.

     c $2n$ means multiply n by 2. n^2 means multiply n by n.

     d $\dfrac{n}{7}$ means divide n by 7. $\dfrac{7}{n}$ means divide 7 by n.

     e $n - 10$ means subtract 10 from n. $10 - n$ means subtract n from 10.

     f $\dfrac{n}{5} + 3$ means divide n by 5 and then add 3. $n + \dfrac{3}{5}$ means divide 3 by 5 and then add n.

4   **a**

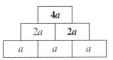

     b

     c

     d

5   **a** $a + 5, 4a$ **b** $b - 5, 4(b - 5)$ **c** $\dfrac{c}{4}, \dfrac{c}{4} + 5$

6   **a**   subtract 8   **e** $+3$ **i** $+20$

     b   add 3   **f** -10 **j**   square root

     c   multiply by 4   **g** $\div 3$ **k**   double

     d   divide by 8   **h** $\times 2$ **l**   square

7   **a**   If $a + b = 12$ then $a = 12 - \mathbf{b}$ and $b = \mathbf{12 - a}$

     b   If $c \times d = 10$ then $c = \dfrac{10}{\mathbf{d}}$ and $d = \dfrac{\mathbf{10}}{\mathbf{c}}$

     c   If $e = 16 - f$ then $f = 16 - \mathbf{e}$ and $e + f = \mathbf{16}$

     d   If $g = \dfrac{12}{h}$ then $h = \dfrac{12}{\mathbf{g}}$ and $g \times h = \mathbf{12}$

     e   If $p = q^2$ then $q = \sqrt{\mathbf{p}}$

     f   If $h = k^2$ then $k = \sqrt{\mathbf{h}}$

8   **a**   7   **b**   8   **c**   7   **d**   8   **e**   30   **f**   8

9   **a**   (1)   8

         (2)   Start with 35 then subtract 3 and then divide by 4. $(35 - 3) \div 4$

     b   (1)   7

         (2)   Start with 37 then add 5 and then divide by 6. $(37 + 5) \div 6$

2 Collecting like terms   *Answers*

1   **a** $12a$ **c** $3c$ **e** $10e + 6f$ **g** $-ij + 2kl$

     b $11b$ **d** d **f** $7g + 3h$ **h** $5mn + 6p$

2   **a** $7a$ **c** $8 + 8c$ **e** $5fg + 4h$ **g** $8lm + 7$

     b $4bc$ **d** $9de$ **f** $4i + 5jk$ **h** $5n + 8pq + rs$

3   **a**

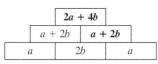

     b

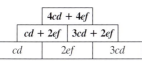

4   **a** $A = n + 2$

          $B = n + 11$

          $C = n + 12$

     b $3n + 11$

     c $3n + 25$

5   **a** $3a$ **b** $4bc$ **c** $5xy$ **d** mn

6   **a**   (1) $4a + 2b$

         (2) $2a + 4b$

         (3) $4a + 10$

     b   e.g.

         (rectangle with side $2a$ and base 6)

Algebra 4

7 a 4n + 5   b 3n + 4

8 a 3a + 3b   d 10g + 15h   g 24p + 8
   b 6c + 6d   e 12j + 8k   h 5qr + 10
   c 5e + 5f   f 12m + 6n   i 24 + 12s

9 a 11x + 22y   d 9x + 21y   g 7x + 20y
   b 16x + 18y   e 21x + 14y   h 5x + 16y
   c 10x + 18y   f 7x + 10y   i 8x + 11y
                                j 20x + 21y

10 a 3ab   c 10pq   e 20a²
    b 4cd   d 24st   f 6b²

11 a area = 15ab, perimeter = 6a + 10b
    b 3a by 4a

12 a 8a + 20b   c 8a + 11b   e 20a²
    b 8a + 4b   d 6ab   f 3ab + 2ac

3 Equations   *Answers*

1 a 12 b 21 c 13 d 15 e 6 f 6 g 21 h 24

2 a 4   b 7 c 7 d 6   e 10   f 12

3 1 a n + 7 = 19   n = 12   2 a 3n + 2 = 14 n = 4
   b n + 3 = 24   n = 21   b 2n + 5 = 19 n = 7
   c n − 5 = 8   n = 13   c 2n − 6 = 8   n = 7
   d n − 4 = 11   n = 15   d 4n − 3 = 21 n = 6
   e   3n = 18   n = 6   e n/2 + 3 = 8   n = 10
   f   5n = 30   n = 6   f n/3 − 2 = 2   n = 12
   g   n/7 = 3   n = 21
   h   n/2 = 12   n = 24

4 a 3a + 30
   b 3a + 30 = 180
   c a = 50 so angles are 50°, 60° and 70°

5 a n + 8   c 2n + 8 = 22
   b 2n + 8   n = 7
              7 and 15 biscuits

6 a List of any
     possible values of A, B, C and D.
   b (1) A + B = 8   (3) C + D = 12
     (2) A + C = 11   (4) A + B + C + D = 20
   c B + D = 9 All other additions will only be
     rearrangements of those seen so far.
     C − B = 3   B − C = ⁻3 (these are equivalent equations)
     D − A = 1   A − D = ⁻1 (these are equivalent equations)

7
n → ×2 → +7 → 35
14 ← ÷2 ← 28 ← −7 ← 35

8 a
n → ×3 → +8 → 44
12 ← ÷3 ← 36 ← −8 ← 44
   b
n → ×5 → −3 → 52
11 ← ÷5 ← 55 ← +3 ← 52

9 a (1)
n → ×4 → +7 → 39
8 ← ÷4 ← 32 ← −7 ← 39
   (2) n = 8
   b (1)
n → ×3 → +11 → 62
17 ← ÷3 ← 51 ← −11 ← 62
   (2) n = 17
   c (1)
n → ×5 → −3 → 62
13 ← ÷5 ← 65 ← +3 ← 62
   (2) n = 13
   d (1)
n → ×3 → −7 → 47
18 ← ÷3 ← 54 ← +7 ← 47
   (2) n = 18
   e (1)
n → ×8 → −11 → 85
12 ← ÷8 ← 96 ← +11 ← 85
   (2) n = 12
   f (1)
n → ÷4 → +8 → 19
44 ← ×4 ← 11 ← −8 ← 19
   (2) n = 44

10
y → ×2 → +11 → 17
3 ← ÷2 ← 6 ← −11 ← 17
y = 3

11 In each part pupils should have drawn a function machine
    and its inverse.
    a x = 7   c p = 14   e a = 8
    b y = 15   d q = 16   f b = 8

1 **a** Multiply n by 4 then add 1.
   b Subtract 2 from n and then multiply by 5.
   c Divide n by 5 and then add 7.
   d Divide n by 6 and then subtract 3.
   e Subtract 2 from n then multiply by 5 and then add 7.
   f Add 8 to n then multiply by 12 and then subtract 3.

2 **a** subtract 7   **g** $\div 4$
   b add 2   **h** $\times 7$
   c multiply by 5   **i** $+12$
   d divide by 9   **j** $+4$
   e $+1$ **k** halve
   f -5 **l** square root

3 **a** $12a$ **e** $9g + 6hi$
   b $3bc$ **f** $2jk + 7l$
   c $12 + 8d$ **g** $10mn + 2$
   d $2ef$ **h** $11pq + 3rs + 4t$

4 **a** $5a + 5b$ **f** $12m + 4n$
   b $7c + 7d$ **g** $24p + 6$
   c $4e + 4f$ **h** $3qr + 12$
   d $4g + 8h$ **i** $15 + 25s$
   e $12j + 18k$

5 **a** $6x + 10y$ **e** $7x + 16y$
   b $11x + 12y$ **f** $9x + 15y$
   c $13x + 22y$ **g** $5x + 18y$
   d $9x + 27y$ **h** $12x + 20y$

6 **a** $4a + 20b$ **c** $5a + 8b$ **e** $18ab$
   b $10a + 5b$ **d** $8ab$ **f** $2ab + 5ac$

7 **a** 11   **b** 24   **c** 9   **d** 3   **e** 6   **f** 8

8 **a** $4n + 3 = 23$
   b $n = 5$

9 **a**
$n = 8$

   b
$n = 9$

10 **a** (1)
   (2) $n = 9$

   b (1)
   (2) $n = 12$

   c (1)
   (2) $n = 8$

   d (1)
   (2) $n = 12$

   e (1)
   (2) $n = 11$

   f (1)
   (2) $n = 9$

   g (1)
   (2) $n = 6$

   h (1)
   (2) $n = 9$

   i (1)
   (2) $n = 6$

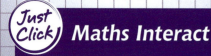

Maths Interact

Pupil Book page 269

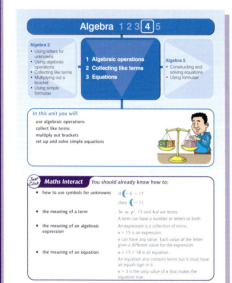

Pupils should already know how to:

- **use symbols for unknowns**

  Symbols representing unknown values are used to make very simple statements. The value of the symbol is to be found in each case.

- **recognise the meaning of a term**

  Six boxes are shown containing algebraic symbols. The object is to identify those boxes that contain a single term.

- **recognise the meaning of an algebraic expression**

  A very simple expression is defined in terms of a single variable. Choose a value for the variable and then enter the value of the expression.

- **recognise the meaning of an equation**

  Letters representing unknown values are used to make very simple equations. Pupils are asked to find the value of the letter that makes the equation true.

Pupil Book page 286

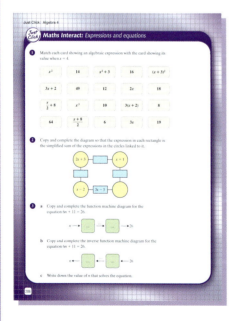

Expressions and equations

Maths Interact summary

1 A matching game in which algebraic expressions and their values are shown on cards. Clicking a pair of matching cards causes them to disappear.

2 Four algebraic expressions are to be dragged into place on a diagram so that conditions regarding the sums of the expressions are satisfied.

3 Complete a flow diagram by filling in the operations to match an equation. Then complete the inverse flow diagram and use it to solve the equation.

Pupil Book answers

1 $x^2 = 16$, $x^2 + 3 = 19$, $(x + 3)^2 = 49$, $3x + 2 = 14$, $2x = 8$, $\frac{x}{2} + 8 = 10$, $x^3 = 64$, $3(x + 2) = 18$, $3x = 12$, $\frac{x + 8}{2} = 6$

2

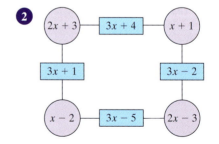

3 a

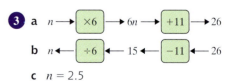

b $n \leftarrow \boxed{\div 6} \leftarrow 15 \leftarrow \boxed{-11} \leftarrow 26$

c $n = 2.5$

Shape, Space and Measures 1 2 3 4 5

Shape, Space and Measures 2
- Coordinates in all quadrants

Shape, Space and Measures 3
- Line symmetry

1 Reflections and translations

2 Rotations and rotation symmetry

Shape, Space and Measures 5
- Properties of shapes

Year 8
- Transformations

Framework teaching programme

202–212 Transformations and symmetry   14–17, 32–35 Solving problems

---

Overview

This unit builds on the work in previous Shape, Space and Measures units involving coordinates and symmetry. The main thrust of the unit is single transformations but the end of Section 2 also covers rotational symmetry.

There are only two sections in this unit but each could take about 3 hours as there are many questions that involve drawing diagrams and investigational work that could take quite some time. You can cover the work more quickly if you use the Worksheets.

1 Reflections and translations

▶ Transforming an object using a reflection
▶ Transforming an object using a translation

2 Rotations and rotation symmetry

▶ Transforming an object using a rotation
▶ Understanding and describing rotation symmetry

 Maths Interact

See page 134
and Pupil Book 7^c pages 289 and 310.

New concepts

Formal transformation notation   Rotation symmetry

1 Reflections and translations

FRAMEWORK OBJECTIVES
Pages 202, 204, 206, 212

▶ Transforming an object using a reflection
▶ Transforming an object using a translation

Resources

Available on **Teacher Resource CD-ROM 7ᶜ:**

Worksheet S4-1-1 **1** and **2**
Worksheet S4-1-2 **3** and **6**
Worksheet S4-1-3 **7** and **9** a
Worksheet S4-1-4 **11** and **13**
Extra Practice S4-1
Homework Sheet S4-1
Starter S4-1-1
Plenary S4-1-1
Plenary S4-1-2
Squared paper

Starters

Have a ready-drawn Cartesian grid on the board (axes from ⁻5 to 5) with letters of the alphabet placed at various points. Give the coordinates that will spell out a word or message. Ensure that all pupils are confident in the use of coordinates in all four quadrants – remember 'wise (*y*s) up! *x* is a cross (across)'.

Plenaries

Use the flashcards on Plenary S4-1-1 (preferably copied onto coloured paper and laminated) to discuss whether each shows a reflection, rotation, translation or enlargement. Some of them have more than one possibility.

Just Click — Maths Interact

▶ A triangle is shown with a mirror line. The line may be dragged and can be rotated. The image may be viewed as the mirror line is moved, or may be hidden and revealed.

Teaching points

- A transformation changes the position of an object.
- The object is the shape that you start with.
- The image is the shape that you get after performing a transformation on an object.
- The image of point A is labelled A′.
- In a reflection, each point on the object moves across the mirror line to the point which is the same distance away from the mirror line on the other side. You can use tracing paper to draw a reflection – see Notes below.
- Any point on the mirror line doesn't move in a reflection.
- The inverse of a reflection is the same reflection.
- A translation is a movement of a given length in a particular direction.
- Describe translations by saying how far right or left and how far up or down you have moved.
- Measure a translation by using corresponding points on the object and the image.
- The inverse of a translation is a translation in the opposite direction of the same distance.

Key Words

transformation	symmetrical
object	inverse
image	translation
reflection	mirror line
reflection symmetry	

Homework

Unit Questions **1** – **4**

Notes

While it is not mentioned in the text, you can encourage the use of tracing paper to help pupils draw a reflection. Trace the shape to be reflected together with the mirror line. Turn the tracing paper over and place the mirror line on the tracing paper over the actual mirror line and draw over the shape on the tracing paper to produce the reflection on the page. The use of tracing paper for rotations is covered in detail in Section 2.

A transformation can also change the size of an object. Such transformations are called enlargements (even if they make a shape smaller) and they are covered in Year 8 and in this unit of the Extension pupil book.

The dash notation allows you to match corresponding points on the image and the object. This allows you to consider the orientation of the image and decide upon the transformation that has been performed. For example,

without labelling, this diagram of an object and an image could be a translation or a reflection (or a rotation through 180°).

Once the object and image are labelled the orientation of the letters will be identical for a translation and different for a reflection (and a rotation).

Questions **8** and **9** require pupils to reflect without the assistance of squared paper. You should emphasise to pupils that the questions only require sketches of the images and not constructions!

Question **15** is an investigation that can be developed as a piece of Ma1 work.

2   Rotations and rotation symmetry

FRAMEWORK OBJECTIVES
Pages 208, 210

▶ Transforming an object using a rotation
▶ Understanding and describing rotation symmetry

Resources

Available on **Teacher Resource CD-ROM 7ᶜ:**

Worksheet S4-2-1 **6** and **7** a
Worksheet S4-2-2 **8**
Worksheet S4-2-3 **12** and **13**
Extra Practice S4-2
Homework Sheet S4-2
Starter S4-2-1
Starter S4-2-2
Plenary S4-2-1
Squared paper

Other resources required

tracing paper

Starters

- Take your class out to the staff car park and record the rotational symmetries of various hubcaps.

Plenaries

Challenge pupils to design a shape with certain properties such as 'order of rotational symmetry 6 and 6 lines of symmetry' or 'order of rotational symmetry 4 and no lines of symmetry'. Pupils can come to the board and draw their solutions.

Key Words

rotation, rotate

centre of rotation

congruent

rotation symmetry

symmetrical

order of rotation symmetry

Teaching points

- A rotation moves an object around a fixed point called the centre of rotation.
- Describe a rotation by giving the angle of the turn, the direction of the turn and the centre.
- The **inverse** of a rotation is a rotation through the **same angle** in the **opposite direction** around the **same centre**.
- Alternatively the inverse of a rotation is a rotation through the **angle 360° – the angle** of the original rotation in the **same direction** around the **same centre**.
- How to draw a rotation using tracing paper.
- Congruent means identical. An object and its image are congruent under a rotation, a reflection and a translation.
- A shape has rotation symmetry if it looks the same more than once as you rotate the shape around its centre through 360°.
- The order of rotation symmetry is the number of times the shape looks the same as it turns through 360°.
- Every shape therefore has rotation symmetry of at least 1 but a shape with rotation symmetry of order 1 is not symmetrical.

Homework

Unit Questions **5** – **7**

Notes

In a rotation an anticlockwise angle can be described using a positive angle and a clockwise one with a negative angle. So, strictly, you can describe a rotation using a centre and an angle. For example, a rotation of 90° anticlockwise about O would be a rotation of 90° about O whereas a rotation of 90° clockwise about O would be a rotation of ⁻90° about O. This has not been introduced in the section (it has been covered in the Extension pupil book) although the *Framework* does mention that 'a rotation is specified by a centre of rotation and an (anticlockwise) angle of rotation'. You can introduce this idea if you wish.

We would argue that rotation symmetry of order 1 means that there is no rotation symmetry but QCA insists on the use of rotation symmetry of order 1. You therefore need to ensure that pupils understand that a shape with no visible symmetry is still deemed to have order 1 rotation symmetry.

Question **12** requires pupils to describe all the symmetries of shapes which means that they need to give the number of lines of symmetry and the order of rotational symmetry for each shape.

1 Reflections and translations

Answers

1 a
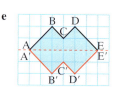

b

2 a
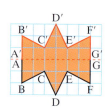

e

b
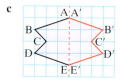

f
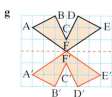

c
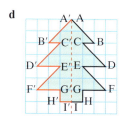

g
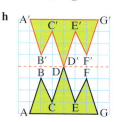

d
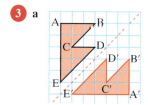

h
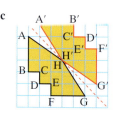

3 a
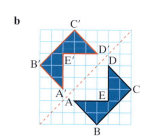

c
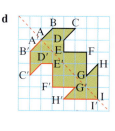

b

d

4 Use reflection in the same mirror line.

5 a (1)

(2) Yes

b (1) Any shape which when folded twice will form a rectangle.
e.g. It must have a rectangular "quarter".

(2) No

6 a (1), (3)
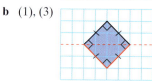
(2) Rectangle

b (1), (3)
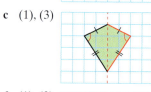
(2) Square

c (1), (3)
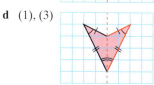
(2) Kite

d (1), (3)
(2) Arrowhead

7 a
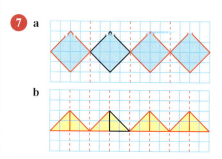

b

8 a AA BB CC DD EE FF GG HH II JJ

b A, H, I

c A B C D E F G H I J

d B, C, D, E, H, I

e H, I

f Must have a line of symmetry parallel to the mirror line.

9 a (1)
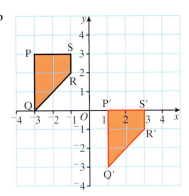

(2)
P E A R
ᑭ Ǝ∀ᴚ

(3)

b Pupil's own answers.

c Any word using the letters A, H, I, M, O, T, U, V, W, X
e.g. HIT

d Any word using the letters B, C, D, E, H, I, O, X
e.g. HIDE

10 For R to be reflected on to R′ the mirror line L would
have to be vertical.

11 a (1) 4 squares to the right
(2) 4 squares to the left

b (1) 4 squares up
(2) 4 squares down

c (1) 4 squares to the right and 2 squares up
(2) 4 squares to the left and 2 squares down

d (1) 3 squares to the right and 4 squares down
(2) 3 squares to the left and 4 squares up

e (1) 4 squares to the left and 3 squares down
(2) 4 squares to the right and 3 squares up

f (1) 4 squares to the left and 4 squares up
(2) 4 squares to the right and 4 squares down

12 Move the shape 2 right and 5 up

13 a, b
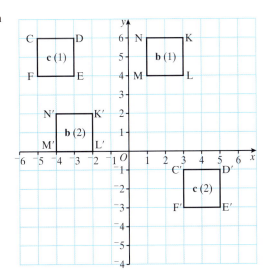

c P′(1, 0)   Q′(1, ⁻3)   R′(3, ⁻1)   S′(3, 0)

d Translation through 4 units to the left and 3 units up

14 a

15 a 1 unit to the right

b 1 unit to the right
2 units to the right
1 unit up
1 unit to the right and 1 unit up
2 units to the right and 1 unit up

c 5

d Investigation

2 Rotations and rotation symmetry
Answers

1 a 70° clockwise about A
  b 60° clockwise about O
  c 90° anticlockwise about A
  d 180° about O

2 a 290° clockwise about A or 70° anticlockwise about A
  b 300° clockwise about O or 60° anticlockwise
  c 270° anticlockwise about A or 90° clockwise
  d 180° about O

3 Pupils following instructions to rotate triangle ABC onto A'B'C'.

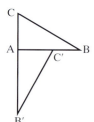

4 a 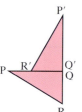   **c**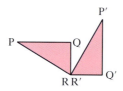

  b   **d**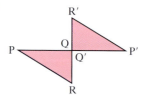

5 a The shape would go to the same image.
  b If you rotate an image through 180° it doesn't matter which way you turn, clockwise or anticlockwise.

6 a–d

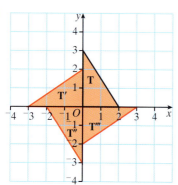

  e Rotate triangle T‴ through 180° about O.

7 a 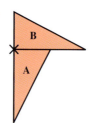   **b** 90°

8 a *The shape is a quadrilateral.*
   The shape is a kite.
  b (5, 7)
  c (7, 5)
  d (7, 1)

9 a 8   **d** 6
  b 5   **e** 4
  c 1 (or no rotational symmetry)   **f** 2

10 a 5   **c** 10   **e** 5
  b 6   **d** 7   **f** 8

11 a 6   **d** 5
  b 4   **e** 4
  c 3   **f** 1 (because of pattern on coin)

12 a Rotation symmetry order 2.
  b Rotation symmetry order 3, 3 lines of symmetry.
  c Rotation symmetry order 5, 5 lines of symmetry.
  d Rotation symmetry order 6, 6 lines of symmetry.
  e Rotation symmetry order 2, 2 lines of symmetry.
  f Rotation symmetry order 8, 8 lines of symmetry.

13

		Number of lines of symmetry			
		0	1	2	3
Order of rotational symmetry	1	E	F		
	2	B		C	
	3	D			A

14 34° (360° ÷ 6 = 60°, 60° − 26° = 34°)

1 a 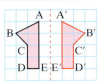   b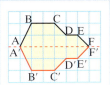

2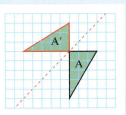

3 a–b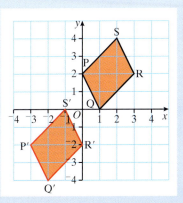

c   P′(⁻3, ⁻2)
   Q′(⁻2, ⁻4)
   R′(0, ⁻2)
   S′(⁻1, 0)

d   Translation through 3 units to the right and 4 units up

4 a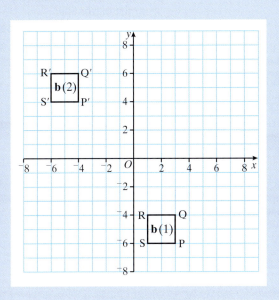

5 a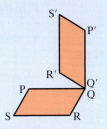

b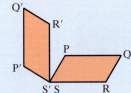

c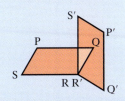

d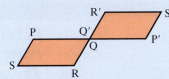

6 a–e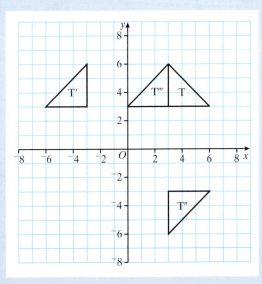

f   Rotation 180° about (3, 0)

7 a 6   d 6   g 6 (flower head only) or 1
   b 1   e 3   h 4 (blades only) or 1
   c 4   f 15   i 1 (because of pattern on the coin)

Just Click Maths Interact

Pupil Book page 289

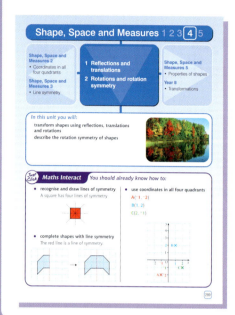

Pupils should already know how to:

- **recognise and draw lines of symmetry**

  A shape is presented and pupils have to identify any lines of symmetry and draw them using the toolbox ruler and pencil. The Show button reveals another copy of the shape with any lines of symmetry in place.

- **complete shapes with line symmetry**

  A partly completed shape is shown on a grid and a line of symmetry is given. The object is to correctly complete the shape.

- **use coordinates in all four quadrants**

  Coordinates of three points A, B and C are given. Clicking on a grid marks the positions of these points. Once all three have been placed their positions may be adjusted.

Pupil Book page 310

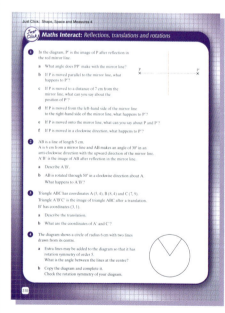

Reflections, translations and rotations

Maths Interact summary

1. A point P and its image P' after reflection in a mirror line are shown on screen. P may be dragged to different positions and P' moves in response. The emphasis is on allowing pupils to explore properties of reflection. A toolbox ruler is available so that measurements may be taken.

2. This activity is similar to the one above but, this time, it is a line AB that is reflected.

3. An animation shows a translation applied to a triangle on a grid of squares. The object is to complete a statement describing the translation.

4. The pencil, ruler, compass and protractor tools are available to adapt a given diagram so that it has rotation symmetry of order 5.

Pupil Book answers

1. **a** 90°
   b P' also moves parallel to the mirror line.
   c P' is also 7 cm from the mirror line on the opposite side to P.
   d P' moves from the right hand side to the left hand side of the mirror line.
   e P and P' are in the same position on the mirror line.
   f P' moves in an anti-clockwise direction to P on the opposite side of the mirror line.

2. **a** A'B' is a line of length 5 cm. A' is 6 cm from the mirror line, on the opposite side to A, and A'B' makes an angle of 30° clockwise from the downwards vertical.
   b A'B' is rotated through 50° anti-clockwise about A'.

3. **a** 5 to the left and 3 down.
   b A' = (0, 1) C' = (2, 6)

4. **a** 72°
   b Pupil's diagram.

Handling Data 1 2 3

Handling Data 1
- Averages
- Interpreting diagrams
- Calculating probabilities

Handling Data 2
- Questionnaires
- Drawing diagrams

1 Probability: theory and practical

2 Statistics: diagrams and averages

3 Statistics project

Year 8
- Drawing scatter graphs
- Drawing frequency diagrams
- Comparing data

Framework teaching programme

248–255 Collect and organise data

262–265 Construct graphs and diagrams

268–271 Interpret graphs and diagrams

276–284 Probability

24–25   Solving problems

Overview

This unit is rather different from all the others in the book. It consists of two revision sections and a practical statistics project. The first section revises the probability first seen in **Handling Data 1**. The section also includes a practical probability simulation using dice and pieces of card.

The second section revises statistical diagrams and calculations also first seen in **Handling Data 1**. The two sets of questions provide data for pupils to draw diagrams and calculate averages. Pupils are asked to decide which diagrams are best and which averages best represent the data. There is an extra page of teaching focusing on comparing two sets of data using range and an average as this wasn't covered explicitly in **Handling Data 1**.

The final section is a statistical project based on a data set which is provided on the CD ROM and also in paper form. The data is a large survey of adults in the UK and centres on their consumption of fruit and vegetables. There are no Unit Questions. This is because the project is designed to take most of the time allocated to this unit. This project can also be

used for homework. There is a *Test yourself* should you wish to use it.

1   Probability: theory and practical
- ▶ Probability scales
- ▶ Calculating probabilities
- ▶ Probability experiment

2   Statistics
- ▶ Drawing diagrams
- ▶ Calculating averages
- ▶ Calculating the range
- ▶ Comparing two sets of data using range and an average

3   Statistics project
- ▶ Full project

 Maths Interact

See page 142
and Pupil Book 7^C pages 311 and 326.

New concepts

Probability simulation

Comparing two sets of data using the range and an average

Planning a statistics project

1 Probability: theory and practical

FRAMEWORK OBJECTIVES
Pages 22, 276, 278, 280, 282, 284

▶ Probability scales
▶ Calculating probabilities
▶ Probability experiment

Resources

Available on **Teacher Resource CD-ROM 7c:**

Extra Practice D3-1
Homework Sheet D3-1
Starter D3-1-1
Plenary D3-1-1

Starters

Draw the probability line on the board as well as a dice, coin and a four section spinner (two sections being the same colour). Two pupils stand up and you point to somewhere on the line – say even chance. The pupils have to come up with a correct event – such as getting a head on the coin – before the other one. The faster one stays standing to play someone else.

Plenaries

Encourage pupils to only use fractions, decimals or percentages to express probabilities. Make sure no pupil tries to describe their answers using words such as 1 in 4, etc.

Maths Interact

Just Click

▶ Simple random events are described in random order and the object, in each case, is to calculate the probability as a fraction in its lowest terms. Check and Show buttons are available to test or display answers.

Key Words

probability	scale
equally likely	tally
impossible	likely
certain	unlikely
event	

Teaching points

- This section revises the work covered in **Handling Data 1** Section 3. The new element is the simulation.
- Points to revise:
  - Probabilities can be marked on a scale using words or numbers.
  - Some probabilities cannot be calculated.
  - Probability experiments can be used to model real life.

Homework

Continue with questions from the exercise.

Notes

The aim of this section is to revise the work first covered in **Handling Data 1** Section 3. As this is likely to have been covered much earlier in the year, this is a good chance to emphasise some of the main points.

Question ⑨ is a probability simulation.

There are two things that can go wrong on the chocolate production line. There is a $\frac{1}{20}$ chance that the bar does not come out of the mould properly and a $\frac{1}{6}$ chance that the wrapper is in the wrong place.

Pupils should design a simple simulation for each of these. The easiest way to do the $\frac{1}{20}$ chance is to cut out 20 pieces of card and write 'OK' on 19 of them. They write 'stuck in mould' on the 20th and then put all of the cards into an envelope. Each time a card is pulled out this simulates a chocolate bar coming out of the mould.

A dice can easily be used to simulate the wrapper problem. Simply choose a number to represent the fact that the wrapper is in the wrong place and then all the other numbers mean that it is OK.

Next, pupils need to design a recording system. Working in threes will probably work best. One pupil is the mould simulation, one the wrapper simulation and the third records the results. They record how many bars they produce before something goes wrong.

They should perform the experiment at least 20 times and then find an average.

More reliable results can be gained by collecting the whole class's results.

You can ask pupils to write-up this project if you wish.

2 Statistics: diagrams and averages

FRAMEWORK OBJECTIVES
Pages 256, 258, 260, 262, 264, 272

▶ Drawing diagrams
▶ Calculating averages
▶ Calculating the range
▶ Comparing two sets of data using rang and an average

Available on **Teacher Resource CD-ROM 7^C:**

Extra Practice D3-2
Homework Sheet D3-2
Starter D3-2-1
Plenary D3-2-1

Starters

Draw five squares on the board. Ask the pupils to give as many combinations of five numbers with an average of 10. Possible answers could be 10, 10, 10, 10, 10; 6, 8, 10, 12, 14 etc. Most pupils will use the mean. Use 10, 10, 10, 10, 50 to introduce the need for the mode and 8, 9, 10, 11, 50 to introduce the need for the median.

Plenaries

Help pupils to remember which average is which by using:

```
                          M
             M            I
MEAN        MODE        MEDIAN
 D           S            D
DIVIDE       T            L
                          E
```

If the pupils use a calculator for the mean, remember BODMAS. Pupils must put brackets around the sum:
$(12 + 14 + 16) \div 3 = 14$ **not**
$12 + 14 + 16 \div 3 = 31.333333$.

Key Words

bar chart
median
pie chart
mode
line graph
range
mean
modal class/group

Teaching points

● This section revises the work covered in **Handling Data 1** Sections 1 and 2. It is designed to be preparation for the project in Section 3.

● Points to revise:
 – Drawing bar charts, frequency diagrams and line graphs.
 – Calculating mean, median and mode.
 – Calculating the range.
 – Two distributions can be compared using an average and the range.

Notes

For details of how to draw each diagram, pupils should refer back to **Handling Data 1** and **Handling Data 2**. Questions ❶ to ❼ ask pupils to draw diagrams of different types of data. However, each question does not tell pupils which type of diagram to draw and leaves them to decide this for themselves. Questions ❽ to ⓫ ask pupils to calculate averages and range and then ask them to identify the best average to use in each situation. Questions ⓮ to ⓰ look at the comparison of two sets of data using averages and range. A higher average is often preferable, but if averages are quite similar then a smaller range may indicate greater consistency. This may be the decisive factor in the selection of someone for a team etc. A class discussion at the end of this exercise would be useful. If pupils have used ICT to produce their diagrams then it might be possible for the whole class to see them and engage in constructive criticism.

Homework

Continue with questions from the exercise.

3 Statistics project

Resources

Available on **Teacher Resource CD-ROM 7ᶜ:**

Homework Sheet D3-3

Starter D3-3-1

FRAMEWORK OBJECTIVES
Pages 24, 248–270

▶ Produce a complete statistics project

Teaching points

- There are five stages to completing a statistics project.
  - **Stage 1:** Decide on the question you want to answer.
  - **Stage 2:** Decide what data you need to collect and collect it.
  - **Stage 3:** Present and analyse your data.
  - **Stage 4:** Write about your analysis of the data.
  - **Stage 5:** Decide on the answer to your original question.

Homework

Continue with project

Notes

This is an unusual section and is not in the format of the rest of the book.

It is in the form of a statistics project.

The data comes from the Office of National Statistics and consists of the results of a large survey into the eating of fruit and vegetables. The data is available from the website at www.ons.gov.uk and is also supplied on the teacher resource CD.

The data in the survey is:

Gender	Male or Female
Age	Given in years
Marital	Marital Status of respondant
Level of Education	Highest Level of Education Achieved
Nationality	Nationality of respondant
Ethnic Group	Ethnic Group of respondant
Gross Income	Gross Income of respondant
Region	Region where respondant lives
Question 1	Do you think you eat enough fruit and veg each day?
Question 2	Why do you not eat enough fruit and veg?
Question 3	What do you think is a 'portion' of satsumas?
Question 4	What do you think is a 'portion' of frozen veg?
Question 5	How many portions of fruit and veg did you eat yesterday?
Question 6	How did this amount compare to your usual intake?
Question 7	How many portions of fruit and veg do you think experts recommend that you eat a day?
Question 8	Would you like to eat more fruit and veg?

There are 1819 records in the spreadsheet and this is too many for pupils to work with, unless they are using ICT. The idea of sampling is not covered formally at this level, but pupils can cut down the data by removing columns that they do not need or by taking a sample.

One way to produce a sample of 100 for example is to highlight every 18th line in colour and then to delete all the lines that remain in white.

Pupils should be encouraged to decide on what question they are interested in answering before starting anything else. These can range from the simple analysis of one column (e.g. how many people gave each answer to one question) to linking eating habits to age and income bracket. The word hypothesis has not been used at this stage, but could be introduced.

Once pupils have decided on their question and which data they are going to use they should produce diagrams and calculations to help answer the question. Pupils should be discouraged from producing lots of diagrams just for the sake of it. If they are using ICT (e.g. Excel) it is easy to present the same data in a variety of ways and then select the best. This can be a valuable learning experience.

Finally, pupils need to write about what they have found out and try to answer their original question.

This project uses secondary data. To use primary data, pupils would have to design and use a questionnaire or a data collection sheet. We have not included this in the text so Year 7 pupils are not required to undertake a survey. You could of course do this if you wish.

There is no exercise of questions in this section, as pupils will be doing their project.

1 Probability: theory and practical *Answers*

1 $\frac{3}{250}$

2 a $\frac{1}{9}$

    b $\frac{3}{9} = \frac{1}{3}$

    c $\frac{2}{9}$

    d 0

3 a $\frac{3}{10}$

    b $\frac{1}{10}$

    c 0

    d $\frac{9}{10}$

    e $\frac{7}{10}$

    f $\frac{3}{10}$

4 a There are 5 sections on the spinner and 2 sections are red.

    b Red $\frac{2}{5}$

       Blue $\frac{2}{5}$

       Yellow $\frac{1}{5}$

5 Katherine may prefer one sort of sandwich.

6 a Ten times. The dice is fair and each number has an equal chance of being thrown.

    b Probably not. Experiments do not usually give the theoretical results.

7 a In this small sample just because the spinner has not landed on other colours does not mean they do not exist.

    b Any spinner with at least one red, one blue and one green section.

8 He could keep a record of his class's attendance over a period of time. He could look in the register and work out his class's attendance percentage.

9 Simulation.

2 Statistics *Answers*

1
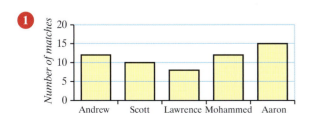

2
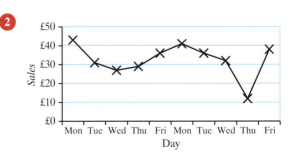

3

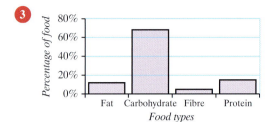

4

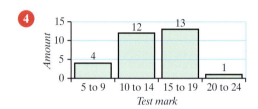

5

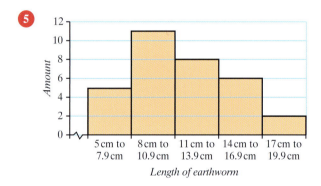

6

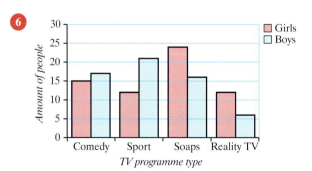

7

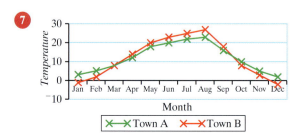

8 a   mode: 132, 164, 165

  b   median: 164

  c   mean: 161.067 or 161.06̇

  d   range: 53

Mean. No extreme values and the mean uses all the data values.

9 a   mode: £270, £290

  b   median: £280

  c   mean: £253

  d   range: £230

Median. Three of the values are much smaller than the others.

10 a   mode: 0

  b   median: 0.5

  c   mean: 1.2

  d   range: 4

Mode. Most likely outcome. Gives a real data value.

11 a   mode: 15, 16, 17

  b   median: 16

  c   mean: 17

  d   range: 9

Mean. No extreme values and the mean uses all the data values.

12 £0.50–£0.99

13 a   Mean = 49.8

  b   No, the average is below 50 so the machine is not working properly.

14 a   Joanna = 14.2 min
        = 14 min 12 sec
     Toni = 13.4 min
        = 13 min 24 sec

  b   Joanna = 11 min
     Toni = 4 min

  c   By car because Toni has the lower average and range.

15 **a** James: Mean = 16.2

               Range = 8

       Andy: Mean = 16

               Range = 2

     Belinda: Mean = 15.8

               Range = 6

b James has the highest mean but also has the highest range, so he is less consistent.

Andy has a lower mean than James, but has a small range so he is the most consistent.

Belinda has the lowest mean but has the best second and third scores.

c Andy, as he is most likely to consistently score well.

 16 **a** Brendan was better at catching with his writing hand.

b Writing hand times had one or two large values increasing the mean and range but not affecting the median.

---

3 Statistics project   *Answers*

Pupils produce a full statistics project.

Maths Interact

Pupil Book page 311

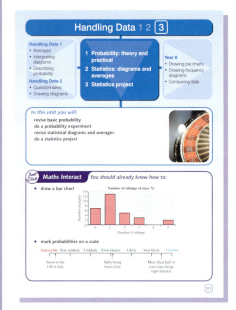

Pupils should already know how to:

- **draw a bar chart**

  Information about the number of siblings that pupils have may be entered in order to produce a bar chart.

- **mark probabilities on a scale**

  The screen shows a probability scale labelled in words to describe the likelihood of an event. An event, selected at random, is also displayed and may be dragged to the appropriate position on the scale. No answers are given. The object is to generate discussion rather than to finalise an answer. It may be possible to use the activity to introduce the idea of a continuous scale since some events will have a probability that lies between the labelled points.

Pupil Book page 326

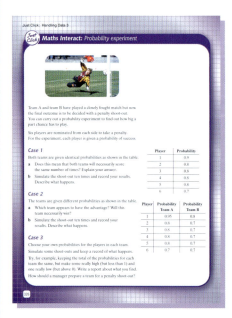

Probability experiment
Maths Interact summary

1 There are three probability experiments, each simulating a penalty shoot-out between two football teams. In the first, the players in both teams have matching probabilities of success. In the second, the players in one team have higher probabilities of success than the other and, in the third, pupils may assign their own probabilities to each player. In each experiment, pupils can see how the probabilities affect the outcomes over 10 games.

Pupil Book answers

1 Case 1:

a This does not mean that both teams will necessarily score the same number of times in the short term. For example; player one will only score 9 out of ten times, this does not mean that player one on both teams will score or miss in the same shoot-out.

b Pupil's results.

Case 2:

a Team A appear to have the advantage. Whilst they are more likely to win, they are not guaranteed to get a goal with every shot.

b Pupil's results.

Case 3:

Pupil's results.

Number 1 2 3 4 ⑤

1 **Multiples, factors and primes**

2 **Number skills**

3 **Multiplying and dividing with decimals**

4 **Using a calculator**

Framework teaching programme

Overview

This unit is predominantly a revision of much of the work from this year including multiples, factors and prime numbers, tests for divisibility, mental skills, using fractions, decimals and percentages and the use of a calculator. The work is extended to include LCMs and HCFs and multiplication and division of decimals, which were not covered in **Number 3**.

1 Multiples, factors and primes

▶ Multiples, factors, prime numbers and tests for divisibility
▶ Lowest Common Multiple (LCM) and Highest Common Factor (HCF)

2 Number skills

▶ Mental multiplication and division

▶ Mental calculations with fractions, decimals and percentages
▶ Finding a fraction of an amount

3 Multiplying and dividing with decimals

▶ Multiplying involving decimals
▶ Dividing involving decimals

4 Using a calculator

▶ Brackets, memory, square root and sign change keys
▶ Interpreting and checking a calculator answer

 Maths Interact

See page 152
and Pupil Book 7^C pages 327 and 348.

New concepts

Lowest Common Multiple (LCM)
Highest Common Factor (HCF)

Multiplying and dividing decimals by integers

1   Multiples, factors and primes

Resources

Available on **Teacher Resource CD-ROM 7^C:**

FRAMEWORK OBJECTIVES
Pages 52, 54

▶ Multiples, factors, prime numbers and tests for divisibility

▶ Lowest Common Multiple (LCM) and Highest Common Factor (HCF)

Extra Practice N5-1
Homework Sheet N5-1
Starter N5-1-1
Plenary N5-1-1
Plenary N5-1-2

Starters

Explain that 6 is a perfect number because the factors of 6 are 1, 2, 3 and 6, and $1 + 2 + 3 = 6$.

Similarly, 12 is an abundant number because $1 + 2 + 3 + 4 + 6 > 12$. 9 is a deficient number since $1 + 3 < 9$. Challenge the class to find another abundant and deficient number.

Plenaries

Check misconceptions:

- The best definition of a prime number is 'a number with exactly 2 factors'. This gets around the common misconception that 1 is a prime number.

- A list of the first five multiples of a number should include the number itself. Hence the first five multiples of 6 are 6, 12, 18, 24, 30, and **not** 12, 18, 24, 30, 36.

Just Click   Maths Interact

▶ Information about factors, primes and tests for divisibility is broken down and presented as an animation. Playback may be controlled with the animation player to allow time for class discussion before moving on.

▶ This animation demonstrates how to find the LCM and the HCF of a pair of numbers.

Teaching points

- The multiples of a number are the answers in the number's times table.
- The factors of a number are the integers that divide exactly into the number.
- To factorise a number you write it as a product of two integers. There are different factorisations possible for all numbers except primes.
- Prime numbers have exactly two factors.
- 1 is not a prime number.
- 2 is the only even prime number.
- The tests for divisibility by 2, 3, 4, 5, 6, 8, 9 and 10.
- Common multiples of numbers are multiples shared by the numbers.
- The lowest common multiple (LCM) is the smallest of the common multiples.
- To find the lowest common multiple, write out the lists of the multiples of the numbers until you find the first number that appears in all the lists.
- Common factors of numbers are factors of each of the numbers.
- The highest common factor (HCF) is the largest of the common factors.
- To find the highest common factor, write out the lists of all the factors of the numbers and look for the last number that appears in all the lists.

Key Words

multiple	divisor
factor	divisible,
prime	divisibility
integer	common factor
factorise	

lowest common multiple (LCM)

highest common factor (HCF)

Homework

Unit Questions ❶ – ❹

Notes

The red topic is revision of **Algebra 3** section 1 and you may choose to omit much of the work here. However, the orange topic includes the new material of LCM and HCF.

Encourage pupils to list all the factors of each number when looking for the HCF and to be systematic with the lists of multiples when searching for the LCM. The LCM of two numbers is the product of those numbers if the two numbers have no common factors. Any common factors can be used to divide the product of the two numbers to

give the LCM. So the LCM of 4 and 9 is 36 but the LCM of 4 and 10 is 20 because of the common factor of 2. Much more work on this is covered over the next two years and pupils will learn to use the prime factor decompositions of numbers to find the LCM and the HCF.

Questions ⓮ and ⓱ encourage pupils to understand the use of the LCM when adding and subtracting fractions and the HCF when cancelling fractions to lowest terms.

2 Number skills

FRAMEWORK OBJECTIVES
Pages 52, 66, 68, 70, 72, 88, 98, 100

▶ Mental multiplication and division
▶ Mental calculations with fractions, decimals and percentages
▶ Finding a fraction of an amount

Resources

Available on **Teacher Resource CD-ROM 7**^C:

Worksheet N5-2-1 **3 in a row**
Extra Practice N5-2
Homework Sheet N5-2
Starter N5-2-1
Plenary N5-2-1
Plenary N5-2-2

Starters

Pupils fill a 3 by 3 grid with a selection of numbers between 5 and 32. Read out mixed numbers such that the corresponding improper fraction has a numerator between 5 and 32. Pupils have to work this out in their heads and cross off a number if they have got it. First to get 3 in a row wins.

Teaching points

- How to perform mental calculations (using suitable jottings but not formal written methods).
  Specifically:
    doubling and halving
    multiplying and dividing by 10, 100, 1000, …
    partitioning
    use of factors
    simple percentages of amounts
    simple fractions of amounts.
- The equivalence of percentages, fractions and decimals.

Key Words

double

halve

multiply

divide

partitioning

factor

fraction

decimal

percentage (%)

amount

mixed number

improper fraction

Notes

This section is spiralled revision of **Number 1** sections 1 and 3 and most of **Number 2**. Pupils should therefore be familiar with most of the content.

To practise the skills in the red topic you could ask pupils to make up their own game based on the **3 in a row** game and blank game boards that are provided on Worksheet N5-2-1. They need to think of 6 numbers to multiply and 6 to multiply by. They then need to work out the answers to all 36 pairings and randomly fill in the grid. They could also do a division game but they need to be careful not to make problems that are messy at this stage with long decimal answers. You could also ask pupils to make up a mental test for each other.

While the yellow topic is essentially a brief revision of **Number 2** section 2, improper fractions are now included.

Homework

Unit Questions ❺ – ❼

3 Multiplying and dividing with decimals

FRAMEWORK OBJECTIVES
Pages 102, 104, 106

▶ Multiplying involving decimals
▶ Dividing involving decimals

Resources

Available on **Teacher Resource CD-ROM 7^C:**

Extra Practice N5-3
Homework Sheet N5-3
Starter N5-3-1
Plenary N5-3-1

Plenaries

Ensure that pupils understand that all valid methods of multiplication and division are equally acceptable. Give a question for to the class, for each pupil to complete individually. Get pupils to explain their method to their neighbour.

Key Words

multiply, multiplication

digit

decimal number

estimate

round

approximately

calculate, calculation

divide, division

Teaching points

- Multiplying a whole number by a single digit.
- Multiplying a decimal with one or two decimal places by a single digit.
- Estimating the answer to a multiplication of a decimal by rounding the decimal number to a simple integer.
- Dividing a decimal with one or two decimal places by a single digit.
- Estimating the answer to a division of a decimal by rounding the decimal number to an integer multiple of the divisor and by rounding both numbers in the quotient to make the division easy to do.

Notes

Pupils have seen integer multiplication and division in **Number 3** but this is the first time that they have been asked to use written methods other than jottings to do multiplication and division involving a decimal number.

The traditional method of multiplication is used with integers first as revision. Any of the multiplication methods used in **Number 3** can of course still be used here. Pupils are encouraged to use estimation to check all answers.

The method for division is the same method as that used for whole numbers but pupils need to be able to think about the product of a single digit with decimals of the form 0.a and 0.0b. This is introduced in the orange topic but questions ❼ and ❽ introduce multiples of 0.0b and you will need to emphasise this in your teaching.

Money is used to provide some meaningful context to some questions in this section.

Question ⓭ requires pupils to calculate a mean from a given total.

Homework

Unit Questions ❽ – ⓫

4   Using a calculator

FRAMEWORK OBJECTIVES
Pages 28, 108, 110

▶ Brackets, memory, square root and sign change keys
▶ Interpreting and checking a calculator answer

Resources

Available on **Teacher Resource CD-ROM 7ᶜ:**

Extra Practice N5-4
Homework Sheet N5-4
Starter N5-4-1
Plenary N5-4-1

Plenaries

- Discuss differences between calculators, especially the **+/−** or **(−)** keys and the fact that some (older) calculators require the square root key to be pressed after the number.
- Check misconceptions: £28.6 is meaningless and incorrect.
  $1 \div 6 \neq 0.166666667$ (some calculators show this rounded answer)

Key Words

negative

square

square root

brackets

calculator: clear, display, enter, key

Teaching points

- How to use a calculator properly. In particular how to:
  – clear a calculator display   – enter a negative number using the **(−)** key
  – use the **x^2** key   – use the **√** key
  – use brackets both when explicitly used in questions and when required within calculations involving square roots and fractions
  – enter time using decimal equivalents of hours and minutes and minutes and seconds
  – work out a remainder when doing a division
  – understand the recurring calculator display for thirds and including a string of 9s arising when the calculator fails to round this to the equivalent whole number.
- How to interpret a calculator display in terms of the units of the answer.
- Checking an answer to a problem by performing an inverse calculation.

Homework

Unit Questions ⑫ – ⑭

Notes

This section is written for the Casio fx-83 MS.

Many calculators have a reset button on the back of the calculator and pressing this can be useful if pupils have any problems with strange displays. It is obviously important that you ensure that pupils are fully aware of their own machines in this section and understand which keys they need to use.

The use of the memory has not been emphasised in this section as the correct key sequences can all be done using brackets but you can allow pupils to store parts of the calculation in the memories and then combine the parts later if you wish.

This section deals with the skills necessary to use a calculator efficiently. You can allow pupils to make up any question and swap with a friend to see who can produce the most difficult!

The use of the **° ′ ″** (or **DMS**) key has not been covered in this section for entering time but you can introduce its use if you wish.

There is plenty of scope to allow pupils to make up their own word problems in question ⑦ for extra practice. You will need to emphasise the letters that they can use and the corresponding numbers, namely:

⓪ –O/D, ① –I, ③ –E, ④ –H, ⑤ –S,
⑥ –G, ⑦ –L, ⑧ –B

You may wish to point out to pupils that 0.9 recurring is exactly the same as 1. They will need some convincing but if they accept that 0.3 recurring is one third then multiplying this statement by 3 will help. As soon as you terminate the chain of 9s then the answer is not exactly 1; you need an infinite string of 9s for the result to hold.

1 Multiples, factors and primes

1 a 3, 6, 9, 12, 15, 18, 21, 24, 27, 30
   b 7, 14, 21, 28, 35, 42, 49, 56, 63, 70
   c 20, 40, 60, 80, 100, 120, 140, 160, 180, 200
   d 50, 100, 150, 200, 250, 300, 350, 400, 450, 500

2 a 6, 12, 18, 24, 30
   b 16, 32, 48, 64, 80
   c 20, 40, 60, 80, 100
   d 60, 120, 180, 240, 300

3 a $1 \times 72 = 72$
     $2 \times 36 = 72$
     $3 \times 24 = 72$
     $4 \times 18 = 72$
     $6 \times 12 = 72$
     $8 \times 9 = 72$
   b 1, 2, 3, 4, 6, 8, 9, 12, 18, 24, 36, 72

4 a 1, 2, 4, 8
   b 1, 2, 3, 4, 6, 12
   c 1, 2, 11, 22
   d 1, 2, 3, 5, 6, 10, 15, 30
   e 1, 2, 3, 4, 5, 6, 10, 12, 15, 20, 30, 60
   f 1, 2, 4, 5, 10, 20, 25, 50, 100
   g 1, 2, 4, 5, 8, 10, 20, 25, 40, 50, 100, 200
   h 1, 2, 5, 10, 25, 50, 125, 250

5 a 1, 2, 4
   b 1, 3, 9
   c 1, 2, 4, 8, 16
   d 1, 5, 25
   e 1, 2, 3, 4, 6, 9, 12, 18, 36
   f 1, 7, 49
   g 1, 2, 4, 8, 16, 32, 64
   h 1, 3, 9, 27, 81

6 a (1) 4, 6, 4, 8, 12, 9, 12, 8
     (2) 3, 3, 5, 3, 9, 3, 7, 5
   b All numbers have an even number of factors except for **square** numbers which have an odd number of factors.

7 2

8 a 4 (1, 2, 4), 9 (1, 3, 9), 25 (1, 5, 25), 49 (1, 7, 49)
   b 60, 72, 84, 90 and 96 all have 12 factors.

9 a 11, 13, 17, 31, 37, 71, 73, 79, 97
   b Yes. 2 (1 + 1) or 8 (4 + 4)
   c $1 + 16 = 17$ $9 + 64 = 73$
     $1 + 36 = 37$ $16 + 25 = 41$
     $4 + 9 = 13$ $16 + 81 = 97$
     $4 + 25 = 29$ $25 + 36 = 61$
     $4 + 49 = 53$ $25 + 64 = 89$
   d 2 (1 + 1) and 7 (1 + 6)

10 a 16, 84, 158, 432, 746, 1800, 8712
    b 84, 432, 525, 549, 897, 1800, 8712
    c 16, 84, 432, 1800, 8712
    d 525, 1800
    e 84, 432, 1800, 8712
    f 16, 432, 1800, 8712
    g 432, 549, 1800, 8712
    h 1800

11 a No (3, 41)   e No (13, 19)   i No (31, 41)
    b No (7, 23)   f Yes   j No (37, 67)
    c Yes   g Yes   k No (59)
    d No (11, 13)   h No (29, 37)   l Yes

12 a 4, 8, 12, 16, 20, 24, 28, 32, 36, 40
    b 6, 12, 18, 24, 30, 36, 42, 48, 54, 60
    c 12, 24, 36
    d 12

13 a 6   c 60   e 48   g 42
    b 24   d 16   f 36   h 143

14 When you add or subtract fractions they must have the same denominator. The number that you use for the common denominator is the **Lowest Common Multiple (LCM)** of the denominators that you have in the original fractions.

15 a (1) 1, 2, 3, 4, 6, 12
      (2) 1, 2, 3, 5, 6, 10, 15, 30
    b 1, 2, 6
    c 6

16 a 3   c 5   e 8   g 1
    b 4   d 8   f 6   h 1

17 When you cancel fractions to their lowest terms you need to divide the numerator and the denominator by their **Highest Common Factor (HCF)**.

2 Number skills — *Answers*

1
a 12 400 i 53.9
b 13.8   j $29\frac{1}{6}$
c 41.5   k 420
d 4.7   l 6
e 5600   m 315
f 0.866   n £29.85
g 108   o 1900
h 27   p 120

2
a (1) 20 mm
 (2) 47 mm
 (3) 3000 mm
 (4) 2540 mm
b (1) 2 m
 (2) 4.71 m
 (3) 0.85 m
 (4) 2.354 m

3 60 cm or 0.6 m

4 23 ($8 \times 2.5 + 3$)

5 3 ($a + b + c = 18, 18 - 8 - 7 = 3$)

6 Game

7

	Fraction	Decimal	Percentage
a	$\frac{3}{4}$	0.75	75%
b	$\frac{7}{100}$	0.07	7%
c	$\frac{3}{5}$	0.6	60%
d	$\frac{1}{8}$	0.125	12.5%
e	$\frac{4}{5}$	0.8	80%

8
a $\frac{5}{10}, \frac{6}{12}, \frac{8}{16}, \frac{9}{18}, (\frac{7}{14}$ given)
b $\frac{12}{8}$
c (1) $\frac{10}{4}, \frac{20}{8}$
 (2) $\frac{14}{4}, \frac{21}{6}, \frac{28}{8}$
 (3) $\frac{18}{4}, \frac{27}{6}, \frac{36}{8}$

9
a 11 g
b 4.5 g

10
a 10% of £600 = 600 ÷ **10** = **£60**
 1% of £600 = **60 ÷ 10** = **£6**
  (or 600 ÷ 100)
 $\frac{1}{2}$% of £600 = **600 ÷ 200 = £3**
 or $\frac{1}{2}$% of £600 = **£6 ÷ 2** = **£3**
b (1) £180 (4) £222
 (2) £30 (5) £384
 (3) £12 (6) £105

11
a 147 kg
b 474.5 lb

12 18 Explanation needed e.g.
25% of 24 = $\frac{24}{4}$ = 6
75% of 24 = 6 × 3 = 18

13
a 8 min e 64
b 9   f 60 km
c 24   g 60 min
d 24   h 88

14
a 36 lb
b 252 lb
c $1\frac{2}{5} = \frac{7}{5}$
 so $1 \times 1\frac{2}{5}$ is the same as ÷5 and ×7 which is what has been done in **a** and **b**.

3 Multiplying and dividing with decimals — *Answers*

1
a

Th	H	T	U
	3	4	7
×			8
2	7	7	6
	2	3	5

b (1) 277.6
 (2) 27.76

2
a 1526
b 200 × 7 = 1400
 (and 20 × 7 = 140
 so 220 × 7 = 1540)
c (1) 152.6
 (2) 15.26

3 Pupils may use different estimates in **3** and **4**.
a (1) 118.5 (2) 20 × 5 = 100
b (1) 372 (2) 50 × 8 = 400
c (1) 403.2 (2) 70 × 6 = 420
d (1) 436.8 (2) 70 × 6 = 420
e (1) 424.9 (2) 60 × 7 = 420
f (1) 451.8 (2) 50 × 9 = 450
g (1) 49.36 (2) 6 × 8 = 48
h (1) 17.22 (2) 2 × 7 = 14
i (1) 42.78 (2) 7 × 6 = 42
j (1) 29.96 (2) 4 × 7 = 28
k (1) 9.63 (2) 1 × 9 = 9
l (1) 24.64 (2) 3 × 8 = 24

4
a (1) 7 × 4 = 28 (2) £24.92
b (1) 6 × 15 = 90 (2) £88.08
c (1) 8 × 2 = 16 (2) £14.32

5
a (1) £19.92
 (2) £13.44
 (3) £13.58
 (4) £11.61
b £75.45

6
a
```
   211.2
 - 160      8 × 20
   51.2
 -  48      8 ×  6
    3.2
 -   3.2    8 × 0.4
    0.0
 Answer:     26.4
```
211.2 ÷ 8 = **26.4**

b
```
   128.1
 -  70      7 × 10
   58.1
 -  56      7 ×  8
    2.1
 -   2.1    7 × 0.3
    0.0
 Answer:     18.3
```
128.1 ÷ 7 = **18.3**

7 **a** (1) 48
(2) 4.8
(3) 0.48

b 0.32

c
```
    257.12
 −   240        8 × 30
    17.12
 −    16        8 × 2
     1.12
 −    0.8       8 × 0.1
     0.32
 −    0.32      8 × 0.04
     0.00
```
Answer: **32.14**

257.12 ÷ 8 = 32.14

8
```
    367.15
 −   350        7 × 50
    17.15
 −    14        7 × 2
     3.15
 −    2.8       7 × 0.4
     0.35
 −    0.35      7 × 0.05
     0.00
```
Answer: **52.45**

367.15 ÷ 7 = 52.45

9 **a** (1) 18.7   (2) 90 ÷ 5 = 18
b (1) 17.9   (2) 160 ÷ 8 = 20
c (1) 18.4   (2) 120 ÷ 6 = 20
d (1) 25.7   (2) 150 ÷ 6 = 25

e (1) 34.9   (2) 210 ÷ 7 = 30
f (1) 34.8   (2) 270 ÷ 9 = 30
g (1) 1.49   (2) 8 ÷ 8 = 1
h (1) 2.79   (2) 21 ÷ 7 = 3
i (1) 14.59 (2) 90 ÷ 6 = 15
j (1) 27.46 (2) 210 ÷ 7 = 30
k (1) 27.12 (2) 270 ÷ 9 = 30
l (1) 34.86 (2) 240 ÷ 8 = 30

Pupils may use a different estimate in each part (2).

10 £7.68

11 **a** 24p   **b** 16p

12 £17.89

13 75.6

---

4 Using a calculator

Answers

1 **a** 640   **j** 10 100.25
b 3991   **k** 41 290.24
c ⁻920   **l** 29
d ⁻9984   **m** ⁻1972
e 1792   **n** 19 410
f ⁻100 048   **o** ⁻174
g 13   **p** 16
h ⁻168   **q** 822
i 4.25   **r** ⁻4554

2 **a** (1) 43.863 424 4   (2) 43.9
b (1) 31.144 823   (2) 31.1
c (1) 9.695 359 715 (2) 9.7
d (1) 44.665 422 87 (2) 44.7
e (1) 67.141 641 33 (2) 67.1
f (1) 1.462 873 884 (2) 1.5
g (1) 8.124 038 405 (2) 8.1
h (1) 64.179 435 96 (2) 64.2
i (1) 1802.76   (2) 1802.8

3 **a** 2.0   **d** 3.8
b 3.3   **e** 13.1
c 1.8   **f** 0.3

4 **a** 4.5   **d** 8.4
b 2.25   **e** 4.1
c 5.2   **f** 12.7

5 **a** 2   **d** 25   **g** 24
b 2   **e** 21   **h** 2
c 7   **f** 50   **i** 34

6 **a** 8 mins 20 secs
b 33 mins 20 secs
c 206 hours 40 mins
d 39 hours 10 mins
e 35 days 10 hours
f 55 days 20 hours

7 **a** LOOSE
b BILGE
c BLEEDS
d GILLS
e SHOES
f SHE'S

8
a £312.20

b 312 m 20 cm

c 312 hours 12 mins

9
a $\frac{2}{3}$

b The calculator shows nine sixes. (Some calculators will give the last digit as a 7, rounding it up.)

c 6.666 666 667

$400 \div 60 = 6\frac{2}{3}$

d (1) $6\frac{2}{3}$

(2) $33\frac{1}{3}$

(3) $666\frac{2}{3}$

10
a 4384.44 ÷ 68.4 = 64.1 or 4384.44 ÷ 64.1 = 68.4

b 6413.48 ÷ 71.9 = 89.2 or 6413.48 ÷ 89.2 = 71.9

c 36.3 × 7.7 = 279.51

d 74.9 × 1187.9 = 88 973.71

Unit Questions: **Number 5**   *Answers*

1
a 4, 8, 12, 16, 20

b 5, 10, 15, 20, 25

c 12, 24, 36, 48, 60

d 25, 50, 75, 100, 125

2
a 1 × **24** = 24   3 × **8** = 24
2 × **12** = 24   4 × **6** = 24

b 1, 2, 3, 4, 6, 8, 12, 24

c (1) 1, 2, 3, 4, 6, 12
(2) 1, 2, 4, 5, 10, 20
(3) 1, 5, 25
(4) 1, 2, 4, 5, 10, 20, 25, 50, 100

3 2, 3, 4, 5, 6, 8, 9, 10 All of the given numbers are divisors of 360.

4
a (1) 8   (2) 4

b (1) 12   (2) 6

c (1) 40   (2) 4

d (1) 60   (2) 4

e (1) 80   (2) 8

f (1) 100   (2) 10

g (1) 60   (2) 2

h (1) 40   (2) 1

5
a 240   e 91.3

b 3.8   f 5

c 4900   g £69.65

d 35   h 255

6
a 10% of £800 = 800 ÷ **10** = **£80**
1% of £800 = **800** ÷ **100** = **£8**
                (**or 80 ÷ 10**)
$\frac{1}{2}$% of £800 = **8** ÷ **2** = **£4**

b (1) £240
(2) £16
(3) £140

7
a 12 min   e 60

b 12 kg   f 66 m

c 27   g 49 min

d 24   h 42

8
a (1) 136.5   (2) 30 × 5 = 150

b (1) 370.2   (2) 60 × 6 = 360

c (1) 66.16   (2) 8 × 8 = 64

d (1) 21.91   (2) 3 × 7 = 21

9
```
    365.92
  −  320        8 × 40
    ─────
     45.92
  −   40        8 × 5
    ─────
      5.92
  −   5.6       8 × 0.7
    ─────
      0.32
  −   0.32      8 × 0.04
    ─────
      0.00
```
Answer: **45.74**

365.92 ÷ 8 = 45.74

10
a (1) 16.7   (2) 80 ÷ 5 = 16

b (1) 26.4   (2) 180 ÷ 6 = 30

c (1) 2.35   (2) 14 ÷ 7 = 2

d (1) 31.72   (2) 240 ÷ 8 = 30

Pupils may use a different estimate in each part (2).

11 1.2 kg ((5 − 2.6) ÷ 2)

12
a 1296   d 12

b 102   e 180

c 19   f 72

13
a 37

b 139 hours 3 min

14 38 429.3 ÷ 533 = 72.1 or
38 429.3 ÷ 72.1 = 533

Number 5

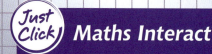
Maths Interact

Pupil Book page 327

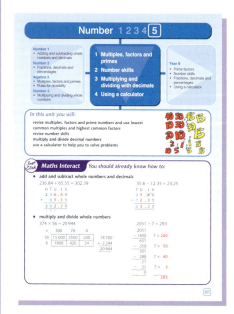

Pupils should already know how to:

- **add and subtract whole numbers and decimals**

  Select Examples to see the questions one at a time, then click Show to see the method. Select Practice to see questions displayed eight at a time.

- **multiply and divide whole numbers**

  Select Examples to see the questions one at a time, then click Show to see the method. Select Practice to see questions displayed eight at a time.

Pupil Book page 348

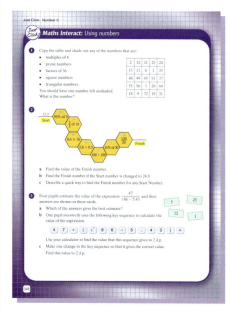

Using numbers

Maths Interact summary

1 Numbers are presented in a 5 × 5 grid along with a list of number types. The object is to click all of the numbers in the grid that belong to the types listed until only one number remains visible.

2 A diagram shows a Start number and a sequence of steps leading to a Finish number. In addition to completing the missing steps, pupils are asked to look for a simple connection between the Start and Finish numbers.

3 The activity involves estimating the value of an expression and then calculating its value to 2 d.p. using a calculator.

Pupil Book answers

1 35

2 a 12.8
   b 25.1
   c Add 0.3

3 a 5
   b 12.23
   c Swap the order of the first bracket and the square root, giving 5.24

Algebra 2
- Using simple formulae

Algebra 3
- Generating sequences using coordinates

Algebra 4
- Recognising like terms solving equations

1 **Equations**
2 **Formulae**
3 **Functions and mappings**
4 **Straight lines**
5 **Real-life graphs**

Year 8
- Solving equations
- Using formulae
- Functions and mappings
- nth terms of sequences
- The equation of a straight line in the form $y = mx + c$

Framework teaching programme

122–143 Equations, formulae and identities
154–177 Sequences, functions and graphs

32–35 Solving problems

Overview

This unit revises and extends the work on equations, substitution, functions and straight lines. Construction of equations is covered first and the algebraic solution of equations is then introduced. Substitution and deriving formulae, including sequence rules, are revised in Section 2. Functions and mappings from **Algebra 1** are revised in Section 3 and algebraic notation is introduced to describe them. The meanings of m in equations of the form $y = mx$ and c in equations of the form $y = x + c$ and $y = c - x$ are introduced although the general algebraic form of the equation of a straight line is not. Finally pupils begin to look at linear graphs from real-life situations.

1 Equations
- ▶ Constructing equations and solving them
- ▶ Solving equations using algebra

2 Formulae
- ▶ Substituting into simple formulae
- ▶ Deriving and using simple formulae

3 Functions and mappings
- ▶ Writing functions using algebra
- ▶ Showing functions using mapping diagrams

4 Straight lines
- ▶ Plotting points that follow a rule
- ▶ Drawing straight-line graphs
- ▶ Recognising straight-line equations
- ▶ Recognising straight-line graphs parallel to the axes

5 Real-life graphs
- ▶ Drawing and interpreting linear graphs
- ▶ Interpreting and explaining linear real-life graphs

 Maths Interact

See page 164
and Pupil Book 7^C pages 349 and 378.

New concepts

Solving equations with the unknown on either side algebraically

Deriving formulae

Plotting and interpreting linear graphs from real-life situations

Algebra 5

1 Equations

FRAMEWORK OBJECTIVES
Pages 122, 124

▶ Constructing equations and solving them
▶ Solving equations using algebra

Resources

Available on **Teacher Resource CD-ROM 7^C:**

Extra Practice A5-1
Homework Sheet A5-1
Starter A5-1-1
Plenary A5-1-1
Plenary A5-1-2

Starters

Pick a card from a full pack. Look at it yourself, but don't show the class. Make up 'Guess my number' problems such as: *If you multiply my number by 3 and take away 2, you get 28. What is the number?* Reveal your card when ready. Once the class understand the idea, get them to make up problems for each other. Use 10 as the value for each picture card and 1 or 11 for an Ace.

Plenaries

Most pupils prefer the 'function machine' approach to solving equations. Emphasise why this method is essentially the same as the algebraic method. They will need this approach for harder equations here, for which the 'function machine' method breaks down (e.g. unknowns on both sides).

Key Words

unknown

equation

solve

solution

inverse

therefore (∴)

substitute

Teaching points

- Setting up and solving linear equations using function machine diagrams.
- Solving linear equations using formal algebra.
- If the unknown appears on the right-hand side of an equation, rewrite the equation with the sides swapped over so that the unknown is on the left-hand side.
- Solve an equation by seeing what is being done to the unknown. Use the inverse operations in the opposite order.
- Show the inverse operations being done on both sides of the equation.
- Check that the solution to an equation is correct by substituting into the original equation and checking that it works.

Notes

The algebraic method for solving equations was not introduced in **Algebra 4** but pupils did solve equations using function machines and so this is covered relatively quickly here. Questions **7** and **8** introduce the algebraic solution of equations starting with one-step equations and then with structured two-step problems. Questions **9** and **12** aim to show the importance of using the inverse operations of the ones in the equation.

The use of therefore (∴) in the algebraic solution of an equation should only be encouraged with the best pupils at this level. This has not been emphasised in the questions as it is better at this stage to ensure that pupils concentrate on showing the operation being used on both sides of the equation and you should certainly only use the shorthand shown once pupils have fully practised writing out full solutions. Pupils can also be tempted to overuse the therefore symbol.

Homework

Unit Questions –

2 Formulae

Resources

Available on **Teacher Resource CD-ROM 7^C:**

Extra Practice A5-2
Homework Sheet A5-2
Starter A5-2-1
Starter A5-2-2
Plenary A5-2-1
Plenary A5-2-2

FRAMEWORK OBJECTIVES
Pages 140, 142

▶ Substituting into simple formulae
▶ Deriving and using simple formulae

Key Words

formula, formulae

substitute

derive

variable

Starters

Have three expressions, such as $3x - 2$, $x + 3$ and $2x + 1$ written on the board ready. The whole class stands up. Give a pupil a number (for x) and ask them to substitute it into any one of the three expressions (tell them which one). If they give the correct answer, they get to sit down and pick the next pupil, number and expression. Encourage pupils to stick to whole numbers between 1 and 15, or simple decimals. If they get the answer wrong, they sit down but don't get to choose the next person. This can be done again by the previous pupil.

Teaching points

- Substituting into a formula written in words.
- Substituting into a formula written in algebra.
- Substitution means **replace** the variable with the value given.
- Deriving a simple formula by looking at patterns from considering simple cases.
- Using a derived formula to solve for a particular case.

Notes

Many pupils will still find substitution difficult as they frequently fail to replace the variable with the numerical value. Pupils often have the letter and the number in the expression they derive.

You need to emphasise in question ⑧ that pupils can only draw edges of a trapezium using the 3 directions used on isometric paper.

So they can't draw this trapezium for example.

Question ⑨ looks at the derivation of the rule for a sequence as a revision of sequences from **Algebra 3**.

Homework

Unit Questions ❸ – ❹

3 Functions and mappings

FRAMEWORK OBJECTIVES

Pages 160, 162

▶ Writing functions using algebra
▶ Showing functions using mapping diagrams

Resources

Available on **Teacher Resource CD-ROM 7ᶜ:**

Extra Practice A5-3
Homework Sheet A5-3
Starter A5-3-1
Starter A5-3-2
Plenary A5-3-1

Starters

Two pupils stand at the front of the class with a whiteboard each. These pupils are a function machine and a two-stage rule, such as '×2' and '+4', is on their boards. Other pupils 'pass through' the function machine, calling out their input and output values. You could get some pupils to go through backwards and discuss inverses.

Plenaries

Based on question **8**. Pupils have to give a **two**-stage function that maps the red numbers onto the blue numbers.

Maths Interact

▶ A mapping is defined and the corresponding function machine may be shown after some class discussion. Input values of 3, 5 and 10 are used and the corresponding output values are calculated. Clicking New generates a different mapping of the same form.

Teaching points

- Using function machines.
- Writing a function using algebraic notation moving from writing functions in words, e.g. input × 3 + 1 = output being written as $y = 3x + 1$.
- Writing a function using mapping notation, e.g. $y = 3x + 1$ being written as $x \mapsto 3x + 1$.
- Substituting into functions to find connected values of the variables.
- Using values found by substitution to draw a mapping diagram for a function.
- Only draw mapping diagram lines for integer input values that map to within the range of values shown on the output scale.

Key Words

function machine

input

output

function

mapping

Notes

This section develops the work seen in section 3 of **Algebra 1**. There the emphasis was on the use of function machine diagrams without the use of the algebraic notation for functions and mappings. Pupils now use their experience of algebra to write functions and mappings using the correct notation.

In the orange topic there is an emphasis on drawing a table of values. This will help pupils to deal with the drawing of graphs of functions in the next section so it should be encouraged.

When drawing mapping diagrams, pupils need to think about the lines that can be drawn so that they stay within the diagram drawn. So, for example, in the teaching example you cannot show the line from an input value of $x = 4$ because it would need to map to 13 on the output line which is off the scale of the diagram. You should ensure that pupils understand the requirement to only show the mapping lines from integers on the input line that stay within the range of the output line in questions **9** and **10** although of course the mappings do still exist for other values.

Homework

Unit Questions **5** – **6**

4 Straight lines

Available on **Teacher Resource CD-ROM 7^C:**

Extra Practice A5-4
Homework Sheet A5-4
Starter A5-4-1
Plenary A5-4-1

FRAMEWORK OBJECTIVES
Pages 164, 166

▶ Plotting points that follow a rule
▶ Drawing straight-line graphs
▶ Recognising straight-line equations
▶ Recognising straight-line graphs parallel to the axes

Starters

Pupils stand in 3 rows of 10 (based on a class of 30). The pupil at the bottom left-hand corner is the origin. The pupil standing next to that one is $(1, 0)$, the pupil behind is $(0, 1)$, etc. Call out coordinates such as $(4, 2)$ and that pupil must sit down. If they sit down correctly, that person can pick the co-ordinate of the next person to sit down and so on. If they sit down incorrectly, they stand up again.

Plenaries

Pupils stand in 3 rows of 10 (based on a class of 30). The pupil at the bottom left-hand corner is the origin. The pupil standing next to that one is $(1, 0)$, the pupil behind is $(0, 1)$, etc. Call out equations such as $x = 2$ and all the pupils on that line must sit down. If they sit down correctly, each person gets a point. Pick new lines such as $y = 2, y = x$, etc.

Key Words

point	table
coordinates	origin
x-coordinate	axis, axes
y-coordinate	x-axis, y-axis
line	horizontal
graph	vertical

Teaching points

- Finding the relationship between the y and x coordinates of points on lines.
- Plotting a straight line using a table of values.
- Recognising equations of the form $y = mx$, $y = x + c$ and $y = c - x$ as being of straight lines.
- The meaning of m in equations of the form $y = mx$.
- The meaning of c in equations of the form $y = x + c$ and $y = c - x$.
- Equations of horizontal lines (parallel to the x-axis) are of the form $y = c$.
- Equations of vertical lines (parallel to the y-axis) are of the form $x = a$.

Homework

Unit Questions **7**

Notes

All pupils should be confident with coordinates but the use of algebra to describe straight lines can often be difficult and you will need to be careful to ensure that pupils grasp the concepts before beginning the exercise. The meaning of m in equations of the form $y = mx$ and c in equations of the form $y = x + c$ and $y = c - x$ are the main purposes of the section. The strict meaning of gradient is not covered here and you may wish to extend the concept of gradient and introduce the definition that

$$\text{gradient} = \frac{\text{vertical change}}{\text{horizontal change}}.$$

Hence for a line with gradient m, $\dfrac{\text{up}}{\text{across}} = m$ for any triangle drawn to the line.

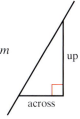

Questions **3** and **4** are likely to cause problems for less able pupils at this level but for more able pupils insist that the answers they give include negative and fractional coordinates.

Questions **9** and **13** are adapted from SAT papers and both are at level 6 and therefore could be difficult for less able pupils.

Question **11 c** is very challenging as it requires the pupils to write down the equation of lines that are the reflection of given lines in the y-axis. The key is to realise that e.g. the reflection of $y = x + 1$ in the y-axis must still pass through $(0, 1)$ so the equation will still have a $+1$ term. The question then requires pupils to understand that the reflected line will have a negative x term that matches the previously positive term. This is seriously challenging and should only be attempted by the most able pupils at this level.

5 Real-life graphs

FRAMEWORK OBJECTIVES

Pages 172, 174, 176

▶ Drawing and interpreting linear graphs
▶ Interpreting and explaining linear real-life graphs

Resources

Available on **Teacher Resource CD-ROM 7ᶜ:**

Extra Practice A5-5
Homework Sheet A5-5
Starter A5-5-1
Plenary A5-5-1

Starters

Pupils draw a set of axes, vertical is labelled 'Distance' and the horizontal is labelled 'Time'. Describe a 400 m hurdle race between three athletes – *Sam, Hannah and Josh. Hannah starts off the slowest but maintains a steady pace for the whole race. Josh starts off the fastest but slows down as the race progresses. Sam falls over a hurdle after 100 m, thinks about crying but doesn't and continues getting faster and faster. Hannah wins the race in 50 seconds with Josh coming last after 60 seconds.* Pupils draw the graphs of the three athletes during the race. (See Starter A5-5-1 for a solution.)

Plenaries

In plotting graphs, ensure pupils appreciate the significance of:

● labelling the axes correctly with titles and units

● scales are usually marked with multiples of a number at equal spaces along the axis.

Scales might not always start at zero.

Key Words

graph	sketch graph
conversion graph	interpret
straight-line graph	
axis, axes	

Homework

Unit Questions **8**

Teaching points

● When drawing a graph label both axes in equal steps.

● The same scale does not have to be used on both axes.

● If an axis doesn't start at zero, use the symbol  to show that part of it is missing.

● A conversion graph allows one quantity to be converted into another. The graph must be given or drawn from a given formula after producing a table of values.

● How to read up and across or across and down to convert units using a conversion graph.

● The meaning of straight lines on a sketch graph:

 The two quantities are increasing together. The rate of increase is constant.

 One quantity is decreasing as the other increases. The rate of decrease is constant.

One quantity is unchanged as the other changes.

● Points on a graph may not always have a meaning and so a straight line should not strictly be drawn and the graph should merely consist of a series of points.

Notes

When given a formula there is no need to have a conversion graph as you can substitute values into the formula as required to convert values but a graph provides a pictorial view of the relationship and using the graph can be much quicker than repeatedly solving a substitution question.

Questions **4** and **5** show pupils how to draw a conversion graph. The relationship between the quantities has to be given as a formula and some points need to be plotted by substituting values of one of the quantities into the formula. For linear relationships only two points are

strictly needed although pupils should be encouraged to use three points to provide an automatic check as all three points should be in a straight line.

Ensure that pupils understand how to draw the scales on graph axes. It is not uncommon for pupils to label a scale using equal spaces between whatever values they calculate from the formula. Knowing how to omit parts of the axes is a subtle skill and you may prefer to avoid this at this stage.

Interpreting graphs is a difficult concept. The contexts used in questions **6** – **8** are designed to allow pupils to achieve at least some success.

1 Equations — *Answers*

1 a $n \longrightarrow \boxed{\times 2} \longrightarrow \boxed{+3} \longrightarrow 11$

b $4 \longleftarrow \boxed{\div 2} \xleftarrow{\ 8\ } \boxed{-3} \longleftarrow 11$

c $n = 4$

2 a $n \longrightarrow \boxed{\times 5} \longrightarrow \boxed{-2} \longrightarrow 13$

b $3 \longleftarrow \boxed{\div 5} \xleftarrow{\ 15\ } \boxed{+2} \longleftarrow 13$

c $n = 3$

3 a $n \longrightarrow \boxed{\times 3} \longrightarrow \boxed{+2} \longrightarrow 20$
$6 \longleftarrow \boxed{\div 3} \xleftarrow{\ 18\ } \boxed{-2} \longleftarrow 20$
$n = 6$

b $n \longrightarrow \boxed{\times 5} \longrightarrow \boxed{+5} \longrightarrow 105$
$20 \longleftarrow \boxed{\div 5} \xleftarrow{\ 100\ } \boxed{-5} \longleftarrow 105$
$n = 20$

c $n \longrightarrow \boxed{\times 8} \longrightarrow \boxed{+30} \longrightarrow 110$
$10 \longleftarrow \boxed{\div 8} \xleftarrow{\ 80\ } \boxed{-30} \longleftarrow 110$
$n = 10$

d $n \longrightarrow \boxed{\times 2} \longrightarrow \boxed{-6} \longrightarrow 14$
$10 \longleftarrow \boxed{\div 2} \xleftarrow{\ 20\ } \boxed{+6} \longleftarrow 14$
$n = 10$

e $n \longrightarrow \boxed{\times 4} \longrightarrow \boxed{-37} \longrightarrow 363$
$100 \longleftarrow \boxed{\div 4} \xleftarrow{\ 400\ } \boxed{+37} \longleftarrow 363$
$n = 100$

f $n \longrightarrow \boxed{\times 7} \longrightarrow \boxed{-70} \longrightarrow 140$
$10 \longleftarrow \boxed{\div 7} \xleftarrow{\ 210\ } \boxed{+70} \longleftarrow 140$
$n = 30$

4 a $6n + 1 = 37$

b $n \longrightarrow \boxed{\times 6} \longrightarrow \boxed{+1} \longrightarrow 37$
$6 \longleftarrow \boxed{\div 6} \xleftarrow{\ 36\ } \boxed{-1} \longleftarrow 37$

c $n = 6$

5 Pupils should have drawn the function machine and inverse function machine in each part (2).
a (1) $3n + 1 = 16$ (2) $n = 5$
b (1) $4n + 2 = 26$ (2) $n = 6$
c (1) $3n - 2 = 25$ (2) $n = 9$

d (1) $8n - 2 = 38$ (2) $n = 5$
e (1) $\dfrac{n}{2} - 10 = 52$ (2) $n = 124$
f (1) $\dfrac{n}{3} - 7 = 11$ (2) $n = 54$
g (1) $\dfrac{n}{4} + 1 = 25$ (2) $n = 96$

6 Emma did the inverse functions in the wrong order. She had to add 6 to 24 before dividing by 3.

7 a (1) $x = 60$ (2) $x = 27$ (3) $x = 10$
b (1) $x = 8$ (2) $n = 20$ (3) $n = 55$

8 a
$5n + 3 = 23$
$5n + 3 - 3 = 23 - 3$
$5n = 20$
$\dfrac{5n}{5} = \dfrac{20}{5}$
$n = 4$

b
$2n - 9 = 11$
$2n - 9 + 9 = 11 + 9$
$2n = 20$
$\dfrac{2n}{2} = \dfrac{20}{2}$
$n = 10$

9 a Subtract 2 from both sides.
b Subtract 2 from both sides, then divide both sides by 7.
c 2

10 a (1) $2n + 7 = 41$ (2) $n = 17$
b (1) $3n + 18 = 45$ (2) $n = 9$
c (1) $4n + 19 = 119$ (2) $n = 25$

11 5

12 a Jordan should divide both sides by 4.
b 5

13 a False **d** True **g** False
b True **e** False **h** False
c True **f** False **i** True

14 a

6	3	3
9	6	
15		

c

4	6	10
10	16	
26		

b

8	4	7
12	11	
23		

d

15	8	3
23	11	
34		

15 a g
$g - 3$
$g + 2$
$2(g - 3)$
b $g + g - 3 + g + 2 + 2g - 6 = 23,\ 5g - 7 = 23$
c 6 ($g = 6$ is the solution of the equation)

2 Formulae *Answers*

1　**a**　£11　　　**c**　£21
　　b　£11.50　　**d**　£30.50

2　**a**　600　　　**c**　990
　　b　900　　　**d**　3600

3　**a**　2.4　　　**c**　11
　　b　5.25　　　**d**　1500

4　**a**　120 km/h　　**c**　622 km/h
　　b　150 km/h　　**d**　31700 km/h

5　**a**　(1) $p = 22$　　(2) $p = 22$
　　　　(3) $p = 22$
　　b　They are all different ways of
　　　　writing the same formula.

6　46.5 °C

7　**a**　18 cm^2　　　**b**　78 cm^2

8　**a–c** Pupils' own trapezia
　　d　$a = c$
　　e　$a + b = d$
　　f　$b = 5, c = 4$

9　**a**
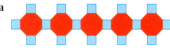
　　b　16
　　c　61
　　　　There will be 1 more than 3×20.
　　d　To work out the number of
　　　　squares, s, you **multiply** the
　　　　number of octagons, n, by **3** and
　　　　add **1**
　　e　$s = 3n + 1$

10　**a**　If $a = b$ and $c = b$ then $a = c$
　　b　If $ab = 0$ then $a = 0$ or $b = 0$

3 Functions and mappings *Answers*

1　**a**
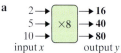

input $\times$ 8 = output
$x \times 8 = y$
$y = 8x$

　　b
$x \times 5 + 2 = y$
$y = 5x + 2$

　　c
$x \times 2 - 4 = y$
$y = 2x - 4$

2　**c**
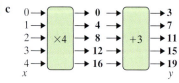

$x \times 4 + 3 = y$
$y = 4x + 3$

　　b

x	0	1	2	3	4
y	3	7	11	15	19

3　**a**　$y = 3x + 1$　　　**c**　$y = 5x + 2$
　　b　$y = 2x + 5$　　　**d**　$y = 3x - 5$

4　**a**　10　　　　**d**　4
　　b　11　　　　**e**　5
　　c　17　　　　**f**　0

5　**a**　$x \leftarrow \boxed{\div 4} \leftarrow \boxed{+1} \leftarrow y$
　　b　(1) 3　　(2) 5　　(3) 18

6　**a**　x is mapped to $x + 6$.　　**d**　x is mapped to $2x + 3$.
　　b　x is mapped to $x - 1$.　　**e**　x is mapped to $3x - 5$.
　　c　x is mapped to $2x$.　　　**f**　x is mapped to $4x + 1$.

7　**a**　$x \mapsto 3x + 1$　　　**d**　$x \mapsto 3x - 5$
　　b　$x \mapsto 2x + 5$　　　**e**　$x \mapsto 5x - 10$
　　c　$x \mapsto 5x + 2$　　　**f**　$x \mapsto 4x - 12$

8　**a**　$x \mapsto x + 1$　　　**d**　$x \mapsto 2x + 1$
　　b　$x \mapsto 2x$　　　　**e**　$x \mapsto 5x - 2$
　　c　$x \mapsto x - 2$　　　**f**　$x \mapsto 3x + 2$

9　**a**　When $x = 0$　$x \mapsto 2 \times 0 + 4 = 4$　$0 \mapsto 4$
　　　　　　　　$x = 1$　$x \mapsto 2 \times 1 + 4 = 6$　$1 \mapsto 6$
　　　　　　　　$x = 2$　$x \mapsto 2 \times 2 + 4 = 8$　$2 \mapsto 8$
　　　　　　　　$x = 3$　$x \mapsto 2 \times 3 + 4 = 10$　$3 \mapsto 10$

　　b

x	0	1	2	3
$2x + 4$	4	6	8	10

　　c

10
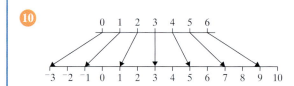

4 Straight lines

1 a B (3, 4)   c A (3, 2)   e C (⁻1, 3)
  b D (⁻2, ⁻2)   d E (⁻4, ⁻2)

2 a The *y*-coordinate is always **2** more than the *x*-coordinate. The equation of the blue line is *y* = *x* + 2.
  b The *y*-coordinate is always **1** less than the *x*-coordinate. The equation of the red line is *y* = *x* − 1.

3 Any 4 points such that the *y*-coordinate is 5 more than the *x*-coordinate e.g.: (0, 5) (1, 6) (3, 8) (⁻1, 4) (0.5, 5.5)

4 Any 4 points such that the *x*-coordinate and the *y*-coordinate sum to 10 e.g.: (0, 10) (2, 8) (3, 7) (⁻1, 11) (0.5, 9.5)

5 b

x	⁻1	0	1	2
y	0	1	2	3

a, c–d

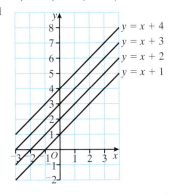

  e The line *y* = *x* + 5 will cross the *y*-axis at (0, **5**)

6 a, b

x	0	1	2	3	4	5	6	7	8
y	⁻2	⁻1	0	1	2	3	4	5	6

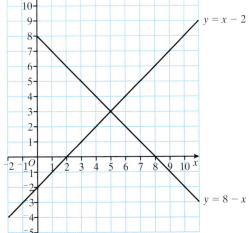

c

x	0	1	2	3	4	5	6	7	8
y	8	7	6	5	4	3	2	1	0

  See part **b** for graph.

  d (5, 3)

7
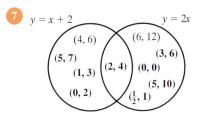

8
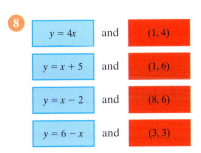

9 Yes, 3 × 25 = 75.

10 A *y* = 4*x*
   B *y* = 2*x*
   C *y* = *x* + 3
   D *y* = *x* − 2
   E *y* = *x* + 1

11 a (1) *y* = *x* + 3   (2) *y* = *x* + 5
  b
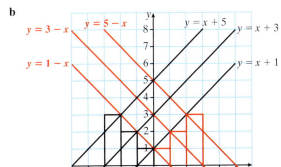

  c (1) *y* = ⁻*x* + 1 or *y* = 1 − *x*
   (2) *y* = ⁻*x* + 3 or *y* = 3 − *x*
   (3) *y* = ⁻*x* + 5 or *y* = 5 − *x*

12 a (4, 1)

b

$x = 2$,	$y = 4$ and	(2, 4)
$x = 1$,	$y = 3$ and	(1, 3)
$x = 5$,	$y = 2$ and	(5, 2)
$x = 3$,	$y = 1$ and	(3, 1)

c

$x = 1$	$x = 2$	$x = 3$	$x = 4$

The equations of vertical lines start with $x =$.

d

$y = 1$	$y = 2$	$y = 3$	$y = 4$

The equations of horizontal lines start with $y =$.

13 Line **D** has equation $x = 4$
Line **A** has equation $y = 4$
Line **B** has equation $y = x$
Line **C** has equation $y = \frac{3}{2}x - 2$

5   Real-life graphs   *Answers*

1 a 30 feet
   b 7 m
   c Cameron, as 4 metres is approximately 13 feet.

2 a 60 g (Allow 55 g – 65 g)
   b 7 ounces
   c 70 ounces: if 200 grams = 7 ounces
          then 2000 grams = 70 ounces

3 a 400 mm
   b 275 mm (Allow 275 mm to 280 mm)
   c The spring stretches proportionally to the mass added.
          So points in between those plotted still have a meaning.
   d If there is no weight added to the spring it will not stretch.
   e The relationship is linear. Mass and stretch are related
          by a straight-line formula.

4 a 95 minutes

   b

Weight of meat (lb)	1	2	3	4	5	6	7	8
Cooking time (minutes)	65	95	125	155	185	215	245	275

   c, d

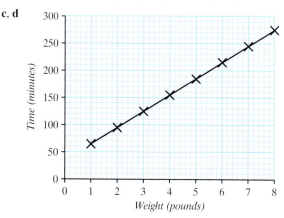

   Weight (pounds)

   e 110 minutes (Allow a tolerance of ±5 mins, the pupils
          are using the graph)

5 a 3 litres

   b

0	5	10	15	20	25	30	35
3.8	3.4	3	2.6	2.2	1.8	1.4	1

   c, d

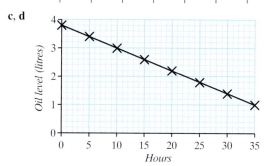

   Hours

   e 3.2 litres
   f 22.5 hours (Allow 22 to 23)

6 a Yes the graph is not a horizontal line.
   b The population decreased for a while but has started to
          increase again.

7 a The number of full-time female teachers has remained
          constant.
   b The total number of full-time teachers is decreasing.

8 a Usually the longer spent on the Internet the more
          expensive it becomes,. This is the opposite to what is
          shown.

   b

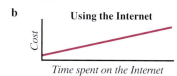

   Using the Internet

   Cost

   Time spent on the Internet

   The pupils may consider a monthly scheme in which
   surfing is 'free'. It is not free but the graph would be
   horizontal.

Unit Questions: **Algebra 5**   *Answers*

1 a $3n + 1 = 34$

b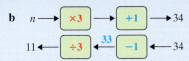

c $n = 11$

2 a Subtract 3 from both sides.

b 12

3 a $X = 27$ **c** $X = 3$ **e** $X = 38$
b $X = 16$ **d** $X = 4$ **f** $X = 5$

4 a 20

b 40   Each shape has 4 triangles for every hexagon, therefore 10 hexagons have 10×4 triangles.

c $t = 4h$

5 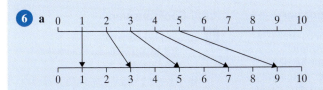 $y = 3x - 4$

6 a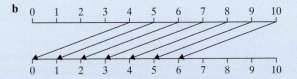

b

7 a-d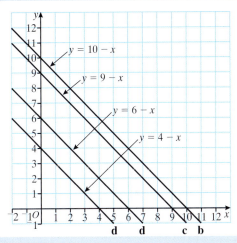

b-d Pupil's own tables of values for each of the lines above.

e The line $y = 7 - x$ will cross the x-axis at **(7, 0)** and the y-axis at **(0, 7)**. The equation of the line that crosses the x-axis at (3, 0) and the y-axis at (0, 3) is **$y = 3 - x$**.

8 a, b, d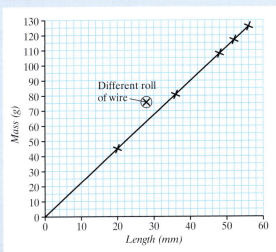

c The wire is thicker as it is heavier than the same length of wire from the original roll.

e 123 g ($\pm$2 g)

f 400 mm (90 g → 40 mm so 900 g → 400 mm)

Algebra 5

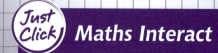

Maths Interact

Pupil Book page 349

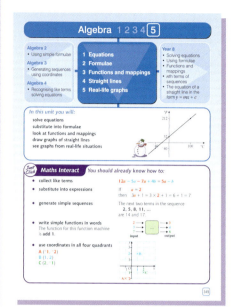

Pupils should already know how to:

- **collect like terms**

  A matching game in which algebraic expressions and their simplified forms are shown on cards. Clicking a pair of matching cards causes them to disappear.

- **substitute into expressions**

  Expressions of the form $y = ax + b$ and $y = a + bx$ are presented. The object in each case is to find the value of y for a given value of x.

- **generate simple sequences**

  Four partly completed arithmetic sequences are shown with missing values to be determined.

- **write simple functions in words**

  A single stage function machine is shown including three pairs of input and output values. The object is to describe the rule for the function in words.

- **use coordinates in all four quadrants**

  Coordinates of three points A, B and C are given. Clicking on a grid marks the positions of these points. Once all three have been placed their positions may be adjusted.

Pupil Book page 378

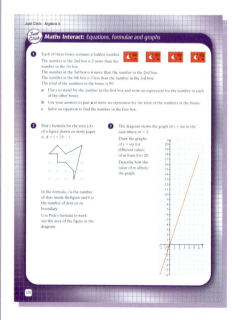

Equations, formulae and graphs

Maths Interact summary

1. Simple expressions are selected to represent statements about hidden values. A further statement leads to the formation of an equation which is to be solved.

2. Pick's formula is used to calculate the area of a figure presented on dotty paper.

3. The graph of $y = mx$ is shown where, initially, $m = 3$. The value of m may be adjusted up or down between 0 and 20 to see the corresponding effect on the graph.

Pupil Book answers

1. a 2nd box: $x + 2$,
      3rd box: $x + 6$
      4th box: $x + 3$

   b $4x + 11 = 91$

   c $x = 22$

2. 5.5 cm^2

3. Pupils graphs. m affects how steep the graph is, or the graph's gradient.

Shape, Space and Measures 1 2 3 4 [5]

Shape, Space and Measures 2
- Properties of triangles and quadrilaterals

Shape, Space and Measures 3
- Line symmetry
- Constructions

Shape, Space and Measures 3
- Rotation symmetry

1 Solving geometrical problems

2 Constructions

Year 8
- Using properties of shapes to explain results
- 2-D representations of 3-D shapes
- Constructions

Framework teaching programme

184–189 Geometrical properties of 2-D shapes

220–223 Constructions

Overview

This unit develops the use of properties of 2-D shapes from **Shape, Space and Measures 2** to enable pupils to explain the solution to geometrical problems. Line symmetry from **Shape, Space and Measures 3** and rotation symmetry from **Shape, Space and Measures 4** are also used. The first section gives an introduction to the concept of proof, albeit at a very informal level at this stage.

There is also a revision of constructions from **Shape, Space and Measures 3** before the work is extended to the introduction of the accurate construction of nets of simple 3-D solids.

There are only two sections in this unit but each could take up to 3 hours because of the number of drawings involved.

1 Solving geometrical problems
- ▶ Identifying side, angle and symmetry properties of 2-D shapes
- ▶ Using properties of shapes to solve problems

2 Constructions
- ▶ Constructing triangles using ruler and protractor
- ▶ Constructing nets of solids

Just Click Maths Interact

See page 178
and Pupil Book 7^C pages 379 and 396.

New concepts

Use of properties of shapes to explain results

Construction of nets

165

1   Solving geometrical problems

FRAMEWORK OBJECTIVES
Pages 184, 186, 188

▶ Identifying side, angle and symmetry properties of 2-D shapes
▶ Using properties of shapes to solve problems

Resources

Available on **Teacher Resource CD-ROM 7^C:**

Worksheet S5-1-1
Worksheet S5-1-2
Extra Practice S5-1
Homework Sheet S5-1
Starter S5-1-1
Plenary S5-1-1

Starters

Does anyone in the class know why October is the 10th month (when *oct* relates to 8: octopus, octave) and December is the 12th (when *dec* relates to 10: decimal, decibel)? Discuss the fact that the two Roman rulers, Julius Caesar and Augustus Caesar, had months named after them, hence shifting the last four months of the year two places along. (*Oct-* and *dec-* are Greek in origin by the way.)

Plenaries

A square is a rectangle. The special name for a rectangle that is not a square is 'oblong' (and this is from the Latin *oblongus* which means 'more long than wide, oblong').

Key Words

parallel

perpendicular

polygon

quadrilateral

pentagon

hexagon

octagon

decagon

regular

irregular

convex

concave

Teaching points

- The names of the different triangles: isosceles, equilateral, scalene and right-angled.
- The names of the different quadrilaterals: square, rectangle, parallelogram, rhombus, trapezium, kite, arrowhead, delta.
- Describe a 2-D shape by referring to the sides, the angles and the symmetries.
- Talk about pairs of equal sides, equal angles, right angles, parallel and perpendicular sides, the number of lines of symmetry and the order of rotation symmetry as appropriate.
- A polygon is a 2-D shape with straight sides.
- All triangles and quadrilaterals are polygons.
- Other polygons have special names: pentagon (5 sides), hexagon (6 sides), octagon (8 sides) and decagon (10 sides).
- A regular polygon is one in which all the sides and the angles inside the shape (interior angles) are equal. Otherwise the polygon is irregular.
- A concave polygon contains at least one reflex angle.
- A convex polygon has no reflex angles inside the shape.
- Angle properties and symmetry can be used to explain general results about shapes.

Notes

You may wish to revise the properties of triangles and the quadrilaterals that are given at the start of the red topic in detail before starting this section. The pupils last saw these in **Shape, Space and Measures 2**.

Other polygons have special names, which you may care to mention:

7 sides – heptagon	11 sides – hendecagon
9 sides – nonagon	12 sides – dodecagon.

While question **6** is a SAT question in which pupils had to imagine the shapes, you may wish to allow pupils to cut out the shapes using Worksheet S5-1-1 to help them see how to arrange them to make the required combined shapes.

Homework

Unit Questions **1** – **3**

2 Constructions

FRAMEWORK OBJECTIVES
Pages 220, 222

▶ Constructing triangles using ruler and protractor
▶ Constructing nets of solids

Resources

Available on **Teacher Resource CD-ROM 7^c:**

Worksheet S5-2-1
Worksheet S5-2-2
Extra Practice S5-2
Resource sheet S5-2-1
Resource sheet S5-2-2
Homework Sheet S5-2
Starter S5-2-1
Plenary S5-2-1
Plenary S5-2-2
Plenary S5-2-3

Starters

Draw an array of squares on the board such as the one below. Challenge the class: *How many different ways are there to add one square such that the resulting 'hexomino' is the net of a cube?*

Plenaries

Use Resource sheet S5-2-1 and Resource sheet S5-2-2 to show the class some nets of various shapes. Using whiteboards, pupils sketch what they think the corresponding 3-D shape is, and name it if possible. Ensure that pupils realise that if they are asked to 'sketch' something in maths, it means a neat diagram that is labelled as necessary. It does not mean the same as it does in art lessons! 'Construct' implies that ruler/protractor/compasses should be used, and that the diagram should be accurate. (They will be allowed tolerances up to ± 2 mm and ± 2°.)

Maths Interact

The toolbox pencil, ruler, compasses and protractor are all available to allow you to demonstrate the required construction techniques.

Teaching points

- Using a ruler and protractor to construct a triangle given:
  – two sides and the included angle
  – two angles and the side in between them.
- Leave all the construction lines on the diagram.
- Missing sides and angles can be measured on a construction.
- How to construct the net of:
  – a cube
  – a cuboid
  – a regular tetrahedron
  – a triangular prism
  – a square-based pyramid.

Key Words

construct
draw, sketch
measure
ruler
protractor
angle measurer
net
perpendicular
vertex, vertices

Notes

When constructing a triangle given two sides and the included angle you can teach pupils to mark off the correct length on the second side drawn using compasses open to the required length. This gives a construction arc on the diagram produced but this additional complication has not been used, as the constructions required this year do not include the need for compasses.

The constructions for the nets of all the solids required, except the cuboid, are covered in question ⑭ and you should ensure that pupils are confident doing these as well as the cuboid. You can obviously ask pupils to construct these other shapes in different sizes to give them extra practice.

Homework

Unit Questions ❹ – ❽

1 Solving geometrical problems

Answers

1 a (1)

(2) Isosceles triangle

b (1)

(2) Square

c (1)

(2) Parallelogram

2

	All sides equal	One line of symmetry
Triangle	Equilateral	Isosceles triangle
Quadrilateral	Rhombus	Kite

3 a A parallelogram has no lines of symmetry. A trapezium only has one vertical one through the centre. The rest are correct.

b They are the same.

c Rhombus: order 2
Parallelogram: order 2
Rectangle: order 2
Trapezium: order 1

d No, triangles can be equilateral (with 3 lines of symmetry), isosceles (with 1 line) or scalene (with 0 lines).

4 Imagine the grid numbered like this

•1   •2   •3   •4

•5   •6   •7

•8   •9

•10

a
9	+	3	+	1	=	13
1, 2, 5	5, 6, 8	1, 3, 8		1, 4, 10		
2, 5, 6	6, 8, 9	2, 4, 9				
2, 3, 6	6, 7, 9	5, 7, 10				
3, 6, 7	8, 9, 10					
3, 4, 7						

b
3	+	3	+	18			=	24
1, 4, 6	1, 7, 9	1, 6, 2	5, 3, 2	2, 7, 3				
4, 10, 6	4, 8, 5	1, 6, 5	5, 3, 6	2, 7, 6				
1, 10, 6	10, 2, 3	4, 6, 3	3, 9, 7	7, 8, 9				
		4, 6, 7	3, 9, 6	7, 8, 6				
		10, 6, 8	9, 5, 8	8, 2, 5				
		10, 6, 9	9, 5, 6	8, 2, 6				

c   18
1, 6, 3	4, 6, 2	10, 6, 7
1, 6, 8	4, 6, 9	10, 6, 5
3, 5, 1	2, 7, 4	7, 8, 10
3, 5, 8	2, 7, 9	7, 8, 5
8, 2, 3	9, 3, 2	5, 9, 7
8, 2, 1	9, 3, 4	5, 9, 10

5 a Anywhere on the line $x = 6$ except $(6, 1)$

b $(4, 5)$ or $(8, 5)$ or $(6, 3)$ or $(6, \bar{}1)$

6 a, b   **c, d**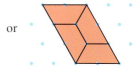

e, f    or

7 a, b

A   E

B   F

C   G

D   H

c A (1) 2
(2) 2
(3) 1
(4) Right-angled isosceles triangle

B (1) 2
(2) 2
(3) 1
(4) Right-angled isosceles triangle

C (1) 0
(2) 0
(3) 0
(4) Scalene triangle

D (1) 2
(2) 2
(3) 1
(4) Isosceles triangle

E (1) 2
(2) 2
(3) 1
(4) Right-angled isosceles triangle

F (1) 2
(2) 2
(3) 1
(4) Isosceles triangle

G (1) 0
(2) 0
(3) 0
(4) Right-angled scalene triangle

H (1) 0
(2) 0
(3) 0
(4) Scalene triangle

8 a Irregular pentagon

b Concave

c 1

9 a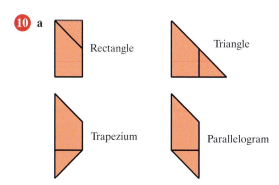

b Various

10 a

Rectangle

Triangle

Trapezium

Parallelogram

b Rectangle. 2 pairs of equal sides, 4 right-angles

Triangle (isosceles, right angled). 2 sides equal, angles 90°, 45°, 45°

Trapezium. 1 pair of parallel sides

Parallelogram. 2 pairs of equal sides, 2 pairs of equal angles.

11 a Kite

b Two pairs of equal sides adjacent to each other. The diagonals bisect at right angles. One line of symmetry.

c (1)

(2)

(3)

(4)

d You can create a maximum of 6 sides with one small and one large square as shown in part (4). Seven or eight sides can only be created if the squares overlap on all sides like this: . An octagon needs 8.

12 a Obtuse angles are greater than 90° and all angles in a triangle sum to 180°. So if one angle is greater than 90°, the other angles must be less than 180° − 90° = 90°, i.e. not obtuse.

b A triangle can be isosceles with one line of symmetry. If it has two lines of symmetry it will have a third and be equilateral.

13 She folded the paper in half vertically, then in half horizontally.

Then she made a cut across the folded corner at 45°.

14 Yes. As the square moves around the part which moves out always equals the part that moves in, shown in green.

15 a

b

c The two identical right-angled triangles can be placed as shown.

Because they are identical the two sloping sides are equal so the overall shape is an isosceles triangle.

2 Constructions   *Answers*

 a

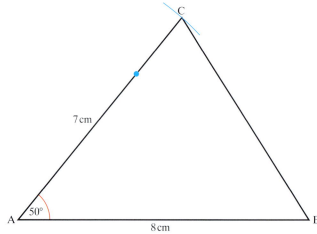

b

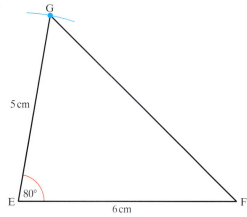

c

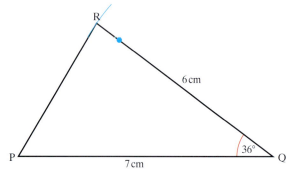

2 a

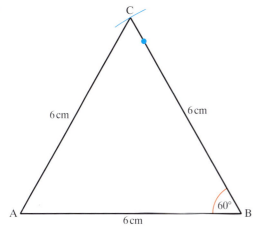

b (1) 60°   (2) 60°

c 180°

d Yes, because the angles in a triangle always add up to 180° and all three angles in an equilateral triangle are equal.

3

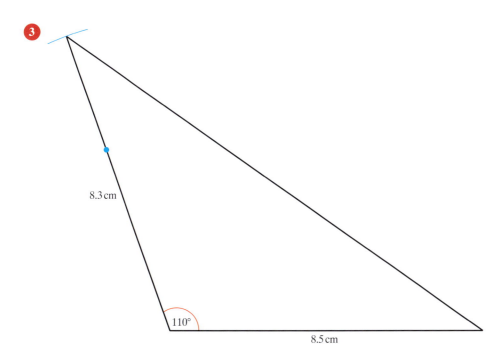

4

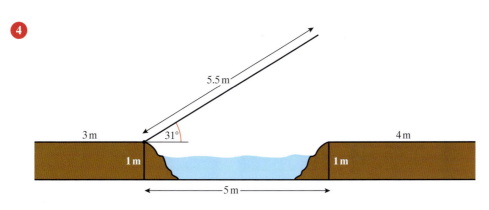

5 **a** (1)

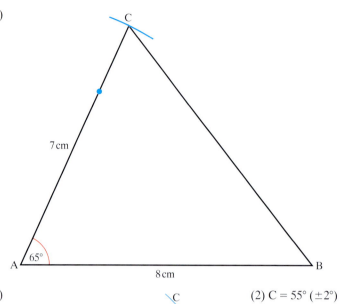

7 cm

65°

A

8 cm

B

C

(2) C = 63° (±2°)

b (1)

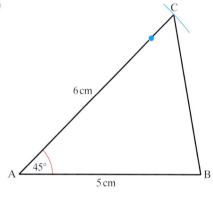

C

6 cm

45°

A

5 cm

B

(2) C = 55° (±2°)

c (1)

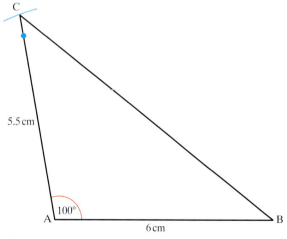

C

5.5 cm

100°

A

6 cm

B

(2) C = 44° (±2°)

d (1)

C

5.1 cm

123°

A

5.4 cm

B

(2) C = 29° (±2°)

6 a

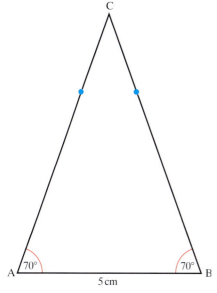

b

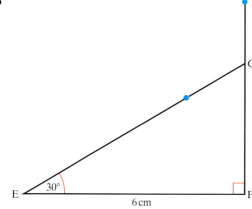

c

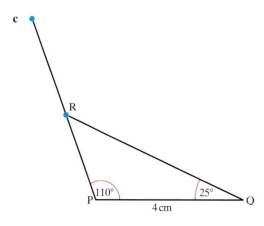

7 **a** (1) 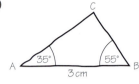 (2) 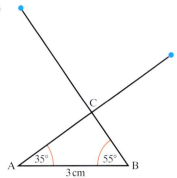 (3) C = 90°

b (1)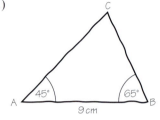

(2) 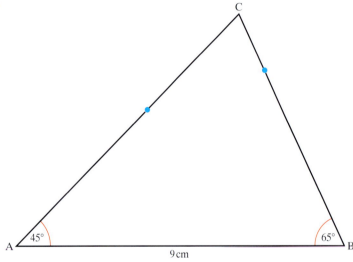 (3) C = 70°

c (1)

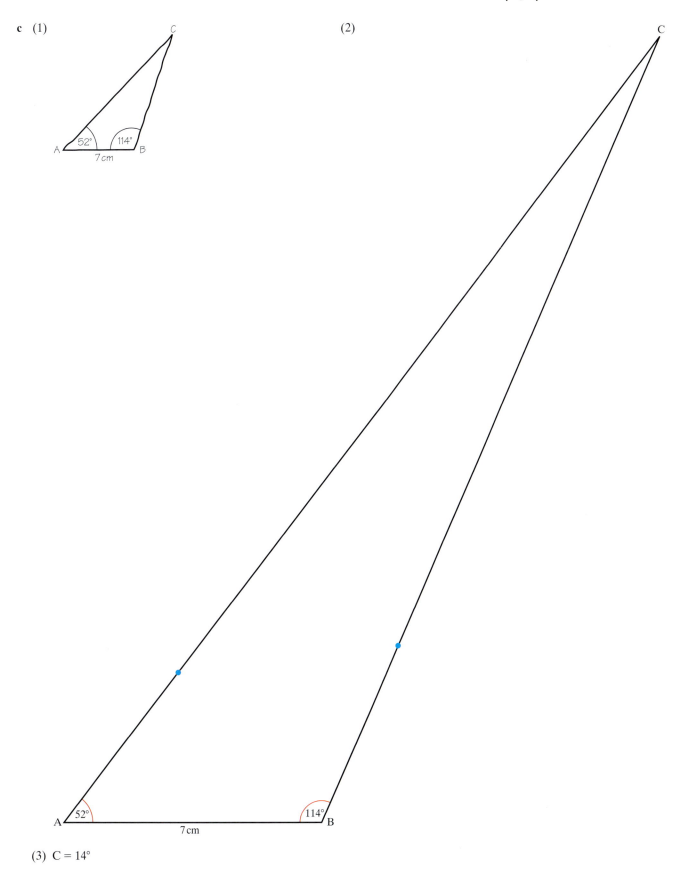

C

A 52° 114° B
7 cm

(2)

C

A 52° 114° B
7 cm

(3) C = 14°

8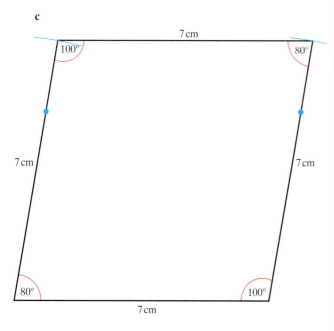

Ferry port — 200 m — Office
35° 80°
Ferrry port

9 **a** Pupils following instructions to draw rhombus shown.

b

4 cm
130° 50°
4 cm
4 cm
50° 130°
4 cm

c

7 cm
100° 80°
7 cm 7 cm
80° 100°
7 cm

10 **a** A, C and G

b FG

11 **a** and **b** The blue and green rectangles should alternate.
The green one on the left should be on the right.

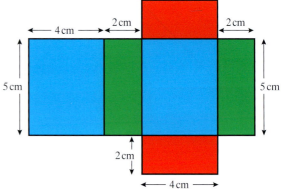

4 cm   2 cm   2 cm
5 cm   5 cm
2 cm
4 cm

12

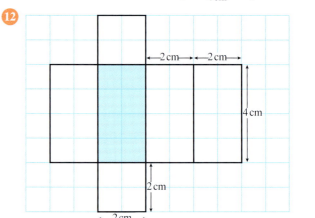

2 cm 2 cm
4 cm
2 cm
2 cm

13 These diagrams show the nets drawn on 1 cm squared paper.

a (1) Sketch of net below.
(2)

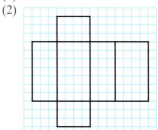

b (1) Sketch of net opposite. (2)

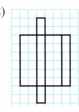

c (1) Sketch of net below.
(2)

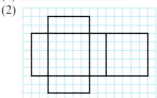

14 Pupil's constructions of 2-D shapes and nets following instructions in pupil book.

Unit Questions: **Shape, Space and Measures 5** — *Answers*

1 a Irregular as it is a hexagon with unequal sides.

  b Concave because it has 3 reflex angles.

  c This shape is an **irregular**, **concave hexagon**.

  d Irregular concave quadrilateral.

2 For example:

  a

  b

  c

3 a (1) It is only possible to make a rhombus that is a square.

  (2)

  (3)

  b All quadrilaterals made by overlapping two squares will have at least one angle of 90°. An isosceles trapezium does not have a 90° angle, so it will be impossible to make.

4 a

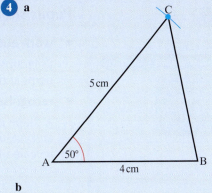

  b

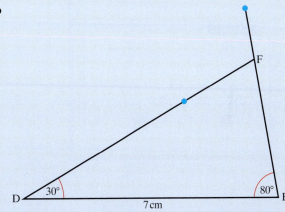

5

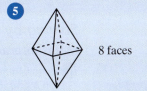 8 faces

6 a BD   **b** AB   **c** B and F

7 a (7, 6)   **b** (4, 8) and (10, ⁻2)

8 Construction of net, adding flaps, cutting out and making triangular prism.

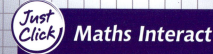

Maths Interact

Pupil Book page 379

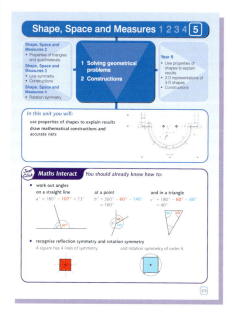

Pupils should already know how to:

- **work out angles on a line, at a point and in a triangle**

  Diagrams are presented including unknown angles on a line, at a point and in a triangle at random.

- **recognise reflection symmetry and rotation symmetry**

  A shape is presented and the object is to describe its reflection and rotation symmetry. Copies of the shape may then be revealed that illustrate these properties.

Pupil Book page 396

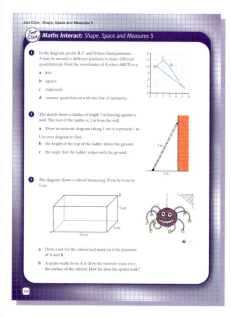

Solving by drawing

Maths Interact summary

1. A quadrilateral ABCD is shown on a grid. B, C and D have fixed positions but A may be moved to produce different types of quadrilateral.

2. The pencil, ruler, compass and protractor tools are available to produce a scale drawing on screen. Measurements are then taken from the drawing to answer the questions.

3. The drawing and measuring tools are available again here in a problem solving activity involving the net of a cuboid.

Pupil Book answers

1. a (2, 2), (2, 1), (2, 0)
   b (2, 3)
   c (3, 2), (4, 1), (5, 0), (1, 2), (0, 1)
   d (2, 6)

2. a 6.7 m
   b 73°

3. a Pupil's net drawing.
   b 13.5 cm (1 d.p.)